Epictetus' *Handbook* and the *Tablet of Cebes*

D1596410

Life is full of misfortune and disappointment, so how can we be happy and flourish?

Nearly 2000 years ago, musing on this problem of human flourishing and how it may be secured, the Stoic teacher Epictetus instructed his students in the Stoic art of living. This new translation of Epictetus' *Handbook* brings his ancient teachings to those who wish to live the philosophic life by finding a way to live happily in the world without being overwhelmed by it. In this book, readers will learn how to sustain emotional harmony and a 'good flow of life' whatever fortune may hold in store for them. This modern English translation of the complete *Handbook* is supported by the first thorough commentary since that of Simplicius, 1500 years ago, along with a detailed introduction, extensive glossary, index of key terms, and helpful tables that clarify Stoic ethical doctrines at a glance.

Accompanying the *Handbook* is the *Tablet of Cebes*, a curious and engaging text from an unknown author. In complete contrast to the *Handbook*'s more conventional philosophical presentation, the *Tablet* is an allegory that shows progress to philosophical wisdom as a journey through a landscape inhabited by personifications of Happiness, Fortune, the Virtues and Vices. It is apparent that there are Stoic influences on this work, making it a fitting companion text to the *Handbook* of Epictetus.

Keith Seddon is a freelance academic, author, and practising Stoic. He is Professor of Philosophy at Warnborough University.

Epictetus' *Handbook* and the *Tablet of Cebes*
Guides to Stoic Living

Keith Seddon

Routledge
Taylor & Francis Group

LONDON AND NEW YORK

First published 2005
by Routledge
2 Park Square, Milton Park, Abingdon, Oxon OX14 4RN

Simultaneously published in the USA and Canada
by Routledge
270 Madison Ave, New York, NY 10016

Routledge is an imprint of the Taylor & Francis Group

© 2005 Keith Seddon

Typeset in Garamond by
HWA Text and Data Management, Tunbridge Wells
Printed and bound in Great Britain by
TJ International Ltd, Padstow, Cornwall

British Library Cataloguing in Publication Data
A catalogue record for this book is available from the British Library

Library of Congress Cataloging-in-Publication Data
Seddon, Keith, 1956–
    Epictetus' Handbook and the Tablet of Cebes: guides to Stoic living
    / Keith Seddon. – 1st ed.
        p.   cm.
    Includes bibliographical references and index.
    1. Epictetus. Manual.   2. Kabâetos Thâebaiou pinax.   3. Conduct of life.
    4. Stoics   I. Epictetus. Manual. English.   II. Kebâetos Thâebaiou pinax. English.
    III. Title.
    B561.M53S44 2005
    188-dc22   2005008169

ISBN 0–415–32451–3 (hbk)
ISBN 0–415–32452–1 (pbk)

Wherever I go it will be well with me.

Epictetus, Discourses 4.7.14

This is what constitutes the virtue of the person who flourishes well and who enjoys a smooth flow of life – to do everything in harmony with both the spirit that dwells within each person and the will of the One who orders the universe.

Diogenes Laertius, Life of Zeno
in Lives of Eminent Philosophers 7.88

Contents

Preface

Stoic ethics aims at supplying to those who would live the philosophic life what they need to live well and what they need to avoid living badly. It is the latter enterprise of removing those things that make life go badly that will be the most easily understood, and probably the most welcomed. What makes our lives go badly is feeling that things are wrong, living from day to day with negative emotions that taint what satisfaction and enjoyment may come our way. We can feel oppressed by people who put unwelcome demands upon us, and we can feel dissatisfaction that our efforts have produced such feeble results. And perhaps worst of all, we are aware that any effort that we may make to do well in life (however we conceive of this enterprise prior to exposure to the Stoic perspective) is set against the background of our inevitable deaths, and for some, against the background of illness or some other substantial source of unremitting suffering.

From within the Stoic tradition that was founded by Zeno of Citium in about 300 BC, Epictetus teaches his students how to adopt a new Stoic perspective on their lives, in which our distress and suffering take on a different significance. As Epictetus will show us in the course of this book, the Stoic practitioner finds a way to eliminate distress and dissatisfaction, and if successful, they will be able to make progress towards the ideal of flourishing fully.

We should have no qualms in seeing this enterprise as progress towards a spiritual enlightenment, in which the world and one's place in it are seen in a radically new light. It is this realisation of what human beings really are and how we should engage in life that Epictetus sought to convey to his students in his school nearly 2,000 years ago.

The Cynics who foreshadowed the Stoic movement (one of Zeno's teachers was Crates the Cynic) conceived of the philosopher as a messenger sent by Zeus to save human beings from their folly and show them how to flourish in a way that befits their true nature (see *Discourses*

3.22.23–8). It is in this spirit that I have myself tried to embrace and practise Stoic philosophy, and it is in this spirit that I am presenting my translation and commentary of Epictetus' *Handbook*.

In attempting a distillation of Epictetan Stoic ethics, the short *Handbook* inevitably makes omissions which the following Introduction to Epictetus aims to fill, not with the purpose of correcting an error, but with the intention of providing the reader with what they need to understand Epictetus and take up Stoic living if they so desire. The most important of these omissions is probably Epictetus' programme of the 'three topics' (see Introduction, 'The three *topoi*') which is not referred to directly in the *Handbook*; and neither is the Stoic doctrine of the preferred and dispreferred things which a student of Stoicism is obliged to know, and so this is treated in the section 'What is really good' in the Introduction to Epictetus.

It is hoped that the reader will find useful the 'Key Terms' listed at the beginning of each commentary to the chapters of the *Handbook*. Within the commentaries, the key terms appear in **bold type** with the intention of helping readers to locate and return to the places where the terms are introduced and to the places where significant discussions occur. An *Index of Key Terms in the Handbook of Epictetus* will be found at the end of the book. The terms I have listed are by no means intended to be exhaustive, and I am sure some readers will want to add to these lists with further terms I have chosen not to emphasise, and equally I am sure I have included some terms that some readers will think are not really merited by the insight afforded in the discussions that follow them.

I thought at first as I translated the *Handbook* that the text was essentially disorganised, presenting its ideas in haphazard fashion. But I have changed my mind on this, and I am suspicious that the progression of ideas I think I found is a genuine feature of the text, and not merely a reflection of my own thoughts clarifying as I pursued my studies. And thus I recommend to the reader that they acquaint themselves with Epictetus by reading the *Handbook* from the beginning to the end. My commentaries were written in the order they appear, and I hope that my presentation has at least some merit in developing an exposition of Epictetus that proceeds in an orderly and meaningful fashion that the reader can follow if, again, they read the book in the order in which the pages are fastened together.

Very different in character is the *Tablet of Cebes*, probably dating from the late first or early second centuries AD, from the hand of an unknown author who offers a graphic allegory of the journey to Happiness through a strange, bewildering and somewhat disturbing landscape portrayed in a fictional tablet (*pinax*) found by the narrator in a temple. This text speaks largely for itself, I feel, especially to the reader who has an acquaintance with Stoic ethics, so my attempt to elucidate it is in consequence deliberately muted. The reader will find some basic facts and suppositions outlined in the Introduction to the *Tablet of Cebes*, and in Glossary B I have endeavoured to identify the functions of the personified figures.

For the reader in a hurry, I would direct them to the Glossaries which they can explore by following the cross references. For Epictetus, terms to be followed up in the *Handbook* can be located via the *Index of Key Terms in the Handbook of Epictetus*; and for Cebes, similarly, the locations in the text where the figures appear are indicated in the entries of Glossary B.

For the translation of the *Handbook*, I have used the Greek text of Oldfather's 1928 edition, supplemented by Boter's 1999 edition; and for the translation of the *Tablet of Cebes*, I have used the Greek text of Praechter's 1885 edition, which faces the 1983 translation of Fitzgerald and White.

Acknowledgements

An earlier version of the Introduction to Epictetus was first published in 2001 in the Internet Encyclopedia of Philosophy (as the article on Epictetus) hosted by The University of Tennessee at Martin [http://www.utm.edu/research/iep], and Glossary A (now substantially expanded) also started life as an appendix to the article. I am grateful to the publishers for permission to reproduce my revised versions of these texts in this current edition.

I would like to thank all those participants in the International Stoic Forum at Yahoo Groups [http://groups.yahoo.com/group/stoics] for the interesting and illuminating discussions we have had over the past few years on all matters Stoic. My understanding of Stoic ethics, both theoretical and practical, has been much enhanced by these discussions, and special mention should be made of the Forum's Moderator, Jan Garrett, for his patience, erudition, and commitment to elucidating Stoic philosophy. I would also like to extend my appreciation to five other forum participants for their helpful comments and suggestions on an earlier draft of the book: Steven Paul Hamilton, Paul Lanagan, Steve Marquis, Paul Ryan, and Grant Sterling. And I would like to thank Francis McGee and Joseph Murray for reading the proofs.

Throughout the time I have been studying Epictetus and Cebes, I have enjoyed and benefited from the thoughtful input of my wife, Jocelyn Almond, and I am pleased to include her drawing of the Path to True Education in Appendix 2.

Keith H. Seddon
Hertfordshire, England
February 2005

Abbreviations

DL   Diogenes Laertius, *Lives of Eminent Philosophers*, available in
       the Loeb edition (1931) with facing Greek text. Volume 2
       contains the chapter on Zeno of Citium, the founder of the
       Stoic school, which is a major source for Stoic philosophy.
       This volume also contains Diogenes' chapters on Antisthenes,
       Diogenes of Sinope and other Cynics, and chapters on
       Cleanthes, Chrysippus and other Stoics.
Ep.   Seneca, *Ad Lucilium Epistulae Morales* (Moral Letters to
       Lucilius).
Fin.   Cicero, *De Finibus Bonorum et Malorum* (On Moral Ends).
FW   John T. Fitzgerald and L. Michael White, *The Tabula of
       Cebes*, (1983). Chico, CA: Society of Biblical Literature.
LS   A. A. Long and D. N. Sedley, *The Hellenistic Philosophers*, vol.
       1 (1987). References are to sections or selections within
       sections (LS 65, LS 60F1).
MA   Marcus Aurelius, *Meditations*.
ND   Cicero, *On the Nature of the Gods*.
NQ   Seneca, *Natural Questions*.
Simpl. Simplicius, *On Epictetus' Handbook*. References are to the
       Dübner page numbers (which are given in Brittain and
       Brennan's two-volume edition).
Stob. Arius Didymus, *Epitome of Stoic Ethics*, in John Stobaeus,
       Anthology 2, 7.5–12, available in two translations from
       Inwood and Gerson (1997), and Pomeroy (1999); the latter
       features facing Greek text, extensive notes, and a Greek–
       English glossary.
TD   Cicero, *Tusculan Disputations*.

Part I

The *Handbook* of Epictetus

Stoic transformation of the soul

Introduction to Epictetus

Overview

Epictetus (pronounced Epic-TEE-tus) was an exponent of Stoicism who flourished in the early second century AD about 400 years after the Stoic school of Zeno of Citium was established in Athens. (He was probably born sometime around AD 55, and died about AD 135.) He lived and worked, first as a student and teacher in Rome, and then as a teacher with his own school in Nicopolis in Greece. Our knowledge of his philosophy and his method as a teacher comes to us via two works composed by his student Arrian, the *Discourses* and the *Handbook*. Although Epictetus based his teaching on the works of the early Stoics (none of which survives) which dealt with the three branches of Stoic thought, logic, physics and ethics, the *Discourses* and the *Handbook* concentrate almost exclusively on ethics.

The role of the Stoic teacher was to encourage his students to live the philosophic life, whose end was *eudaimonia* ('happiness' or 'flourishing'), to be secured by living the life of reason, which – for Stoics – meant living virtuously and living 'in accordance with nature'. The *eudaimonia* ('happiness') of those who attain this ideal consists of *ataraxia* (imperturbability), *apatheia* (freedom from passion), *eupatheiai* ('good feelings'), and an awareness of, and capacity to attain, what counts as living as a rational being should.

The key to transforming oneself into the Stoic *sophos* (wise person) is to learn what is 'in one's power', and this is 'the correct use of impressions' (*phantasiai*), which in outline involves not judging as good or bad anything that appears to one. For the only thing that is good is acting virtuously (that is, motivated by virtue), and the only thing that is bad is the opposite, acting viciously (that is, motivated by vice). The person who seeks to make progress as a Stoic (*ho prokoptôn*) understands that their power of rationality is a fragment of God whose material body

– a sort of rarefied fiery air – blends with the whole of creation, intelligently forming and directing undifferentiated matter to make the world as we experience it. The task of the *prokoptôn*, therefore, is to 'live according to nature', which means (a) pursuing a course through life intelligently responding to one's own needs and duties as a sociable human being, but also (b) wholly accepting one's fate and the fate of the world as coming directly from the divine intelligence which makes the world the best that is possible.

Life

It is possible to draw only a basic sketch of Epictetus' life. Resources at our disposal include just a handful of references in the ancient texts, to which we can add the few allusions that Epictetus makes to his own life in the *Discourses* – see for instance 1.18.15 (his lamp is stolen), 2.24.18 (liked to join the play of children), 4.1.151 (mentions his own infirmities).

Epictetus was born in about AD 55 in Hierapolis in Phrygia (modern-day Pamukkale, in south-western Turkey). '*Epiktêtos*' means 'acquired', and we may reasonably suppose that this name originated in consequence of his somehow coming to Rome, probably when still a boy, to be the slave of Epaphroditus who was a rich and powerful freedman, having himself been a slave of the Emperor Nero. (Epaphroditus had been Nero's secretary until the latter's forced suicide in AD 68, and in AD 81 he resumed his secretarial role under the Emperor Domitian at whose orders he was put to death in AD 95 for the offence of assisting Nero's suicide.) Whilst still a slave, Epictetus studied with the Stoic teacher Musonius Rufus, a proportion of whose teachings survive as extracts in the anthologies of Stobaeus, and as fragments in the writings of Aulus Gellius and others (see Lutz 1947, 6–9; for references to Musonius in the *Discourses* see 1.1.26–7, 1.7.32, 1.9.29–31, 3.6.10, 3.15.14, 3.23.29, and in Aulus Gellius' *Attic Nights* see 5.1, 9.2.8–11, 16.1.1–2, 18.2.1). As we might expect, the teachings of Epictetus display a distinct affinity with those of his own teacher; Oldfather (1926, viii n.2) goes so far as to state that:

> So many passages in Epictetus can be paralleled closely from the remaining fragments of Rufus (as Epictetus always calls him) that there can be no doubt but the system of thought in the pupil is little more than an echo, with changes of emphasis due to the personal equation, of that of the master.

A conjecture I find hard to resist is the possibility that as a boy Epictetus may have met Seneca. His master, Epaphroditus, as one of Nero's secretaries, would almost certainly have invited all members of the court, including Seneca, to his private residence at some time or another, and it is undoubtedly the case that Epaphroditus would have had frequent business with Seneca at an official level. This at least makes it feasible – so long as Epictetus was not born any later than the early to mid-fifties AD, and was acquired by Epaphroditus before AD 68 – that Seneca and Epictetus actually met on one of Seneca's visits to Epaphroditus' house. The boy of about ten who served wine to the elderly statesman may well have been Epictetus. And it is not beyond the bounds of possibility that Seneca sparked Epictetus' interest in Stoic philosophy. After all, we know from Seneca's writings (*Ep.* 47) that he urged people to treat their slaves as friends, and in contrast to many of the visitors to the house it is easy to imagine Seneca engaging the slave-boy in friendly conversation.

There is a story told by the author Celsus (probably a younger contemporary of Epictetus) – quoted by the early Christian Origen (*c.* AD 185–254) at *Contra Celsum* 7.53 – that when still a slave, Epictetus was tortured by his master who twisted his leg. Enduring the pain with complete composure, Epictetus warned that his leg would soon break, and when it did break, he said, 'There, did I not tell you that it would break?' And from that time Epictetus was lame. The *Suda* (tenth century), however, although confirming that Epictetus was lame, attributes his affliction to rheumatism (see *Discourses* 1.8.14, 1.16.20). Simplicius (commentary to Chapter 9) also confirms Epictetus' lameness, but does not identify any cause.

At some point Epictetus was manumitted, and in about AD 89, along with other philosophers then in Rome, was banished by the Emperor Domitian. He went to Nicopolis in Epirus (in north-western Greece) where he opened his own school which acquired a good reputation, attracting many upper-class Romans. One such student was Flavius Arrian (*c.* AD 86–160) who would compose the *Discourses* and the *Handbook*, and who later served in public office under the Emperor Hadrian and made his mark as a respected historian (some of his historical writings survive). Origen (*Contra Celsum* 6.2) observed that whilst Plato's books were to be found only in the hands of those who professed to be learned, it was the ordinary person desiring to be benefited and improved who instead admired the writings of Epictetus. Aulus Gellius (*c.* AD 125–*c.*165) reports that one of Marcus Aurelius' teachers, Herodes Atticus (*c.* AD 101–177), considered Epictetus to be 'the greatest of Stoics' (*Attic Nights* 1.2.6; for further references to

Epictetus in *Attic Nights* see 1.2.6–13, 2.18.10, 15.11.5, 17.19, 19.1.14–21: Epictetus is mentioned a third time in *Contra Celsum* at 3.54).

Our sources report that Epictetus did not marry, had no children, and lived to an old age. With respect to marriage and children we may note the story from Lucian (*Demonax*) about the Cynic philosopher Demonax who had been a pupil of Epictetus. On being exhorted by Epictetus to marry and have children (for it was a philosopher's duty to provide a substitute ready for the time when they would die), he sarcastically asked Epictetus whether he could marry one of his daughters. Demonax' criticism may be somewhat mitigated by the story of Epictetus late in life adopting the child of a friend who, under the pressure of poverty, was going to expose it, and also taking in a woman to serve as the child's nursemaid (Simpl. D116).

Writings

It appears that Epictetus wrote nothing himself. The works we have that present his philosophy were written by his student, Arrian (Lucius Flavius Arrianus, *c.* AD 86–160). We may conjecture that the *Discourses* and the *Handbook* were written some time around the years AD 104–107, at the time when Arrian was most likely to have been a student.

Dobbin (1998), though, holds the view that the *Discourses* and the *Handbook* were actually written by Epictetus himself; the *Suda* does say, after all, that Epictetus 'wrote a great deal'. Dobbin is not entirely convinced by Arrian's claim in his dedicatory preface that he wrote down Epictetus' words verbatim; first, stenographic techniques at this time were primitive, and anyway were the preserve of civil servants; second, most of the discourses are too polished, and look too much like carefully crafted prose to be the product of impromptu discussions; and third, some of the discourses (notably 1.29, 3.22 and 4.1) are too long for extempore conversations.

There is no way to resolve this question with certainty. Whether the texts we have do indeed represent a serious attempt to record Epictetus at work verbatim, whether draft texts were later edited and rewritten (as seems wholly likely), possibly by Epictetus, or whether Epictetus did in fact write the texts himself, drawing on his recollections as a lecturer with only occasional attempts at strictly verbatim accuracy, we shall never know. But what we can be certain of, regardless of who actually wrote the words onto the papyrus to make the first draft of the text as we have it today, is that those words were intended to present Stoic moral philosophy in the terms and the style that Epictetus employed as a teacher intent on bringing his students to philosophic enlightenment as the Stoics had understood this enterprise.

The Discourses

A *diatribê* is a short ethical treatise or lecture, and '*Discourses*' translates the plural Greek *diatribai*. Written in Koine Greek, the everyday contemporary form of the language, the *Discourses* appear to record the exchanges between Epictetus and his students after formal teaching had concluded for the day. Internal textual evidence confirms that the works of the early Stoic philosophers (Zeno, Cleanthes and Chrysippus) were read and discussed in Epictetus' classes, but this aspect of Epictetus' teaching is not recorded by Arrian. What we have, then, are intimate and earnest discussions in which Epictetus aims to make his students consider carefully what the philosophic life – for a Stoic – consists in, and how to live it oneself. He discusses a wide range of topics, from friendship to illness, from fear to poverty, on how to acquire and maintain tranquillity, and why we should not be angry with other people.

It is possible that not all of the *Discourses* have survived: Aulus Gellius informs us that once a fellow traveller brought out and read from the *fifth* book of the *Discourses* (*Attic Nights* 19.1.14 = Epictetus, *Fragment* 9), whereas today all we have are four books.

The Handbook

'*Handbook*' or '*Manual*' translates the Greek title of this work, *Encheiridion*, which is cognate with the adjective *encheiridios*, meaning 'in the hand' or 'ready to hand', and with the verb *encheireô*, meaning 'to take something in hand; to undertake or attempt something'. This little book, my translation of which features in the present volume, appears to be an abstract of the *Discourses*, focusing on key themes in Epictetus' teaching of Stoic ethics. Some of the text is taken from the *Discourses*, but the fact that not all of it can be correlated with passages in the larger work further supports the view that some of the *Discourses* have indeed been lost.

Fragments

Modern editions of Epictetus from Matheson and Oldfather onwards, include 36 fragments comprising sayings of Epictetus that survive in the writing of other authors: Arnobius, Aulus Gellius, Marcus Aurelius, and

Stobaeus (who preserves by far the most). Earlier editions included a much larger collection of aphorisms purporting to come from Epictetus which Oldfather rejects as spurious, whose inclusion 'would scarcely serve any useful purpose' (1928, 439), though his last eight fragments intriguingly follow the heading 'Doubtful and Spurious Fragments'.

Epictetus' Stoicism

The writings of the early Stoics, of Zeno (335–263 BC), the founder of the school, of Chrysippus (*c.* 280–*c.* 207 BC), the extremely influential third head of the Stoa, and of others, survive only as quoted fragments found in later works. The question arises as to what extent Epictetus preserved the original doctrines of the Stoic school, and to what extent, if any, he branched out with new emphases and innovations of his own. The nineteenth-century Epictetan scholar Adolf Bonhöffer (1998, 3) remarks: '[Epictetus] is completely free of the eclecticism of Seneca and Marcus Aurelius; and, compared with his teacher Musonius Rufus ... his work reveals a considerably closer connection to Stoic doctrine and terminology as developed mainly by Chrysippus.'

Evidence internal to the *Discourses* indicates that Epictetus was indeed faithful to the early Stoics. At 1.4.28–31, Epictetus praises Chrysippus in the highest terms, saying of him, 'How great the benefactor who shows the way! ... who has discovered, and brought to light, and communicated, the truth to all, not merely of living, but of living well' (trans. Hard). It would be inconsistent, if not wholly ridiculous, to laud Chrysippus in such terms and then proceed to depart oneself from the great man's teaching. At 1.20.15, Epictetus quotes Zeno, and at 2.6.9–10 he quotes Chrysippus, to support his arguments. Aulus Gellius (*Attic Nights* 19.1.14) says that Epictetus' *Discourses* 'undoubtedly agree with the writings of Zeno and Chrysippus'.

Scholars are agreed that the 'doctrine of the three *topoi* (topics, or fields of study)' which we find in the *Discourses* originates with Epictetus (see Bonhöffer 1996, 32; Dobbin 1998, xvii; Hadot 1998, 83; More 1923, 107). Oldfather (1925, xxi, n. 1), in the Introduction to his translation of the *Discourses*, remarks that 'this triple division ... is the only notable original element ... found in Epictetus, and it is rather a pedagogical device for lucid presentation than an innovation in thought'. Our enthusiasm for this division being wholly original to Epictetus should be tempered with a reading of extracts from Seneca's *Moral Letters* (75.8–18 and 89.14–15) where we also find a threefold division of ethics which, although not exactly similar to Epictetus' scheme, suggests the possibility that both Seneca and Epictetus drew on work by their predecessors that, alas, has not survived (see LS 56 with commentary). Suffice it to say, *what* Epictetus teaches by means of his threefold division is wholly in accord with the principles of the early Stoics, but *how* he does this is uniquely his own method. The programme of study and exercises that Epictetus' students adhered to was in consequence different from the programme that was taught by his predecessors, but the end result, consisting in the special Stoic outlook on oneself and the world at large and the ability to 'live the philosophic life', was the same.

Key concepts

The promise of philosophy

Epictetus, along with all other philosophers of the Hellenistic period, saw moral philosophy as having the practical purpose of guiding people towards leading better lives. The aim was to live well, to secure for oneself *eudaimonia* ('happiness' or 'a flourishing life'), and the different schools and philosophers of the period offered differing solutions as to how the *eudaimôn* life was to be won.

No less true of us today than it was for the ancients, few people are content with life (let alone wholly content), and what contributes to any contentment that may be enjoyed is almost certainly short-lived and transient.

The task for the Stoic teacher commences with the understanding that (probably) everyone is not *eudaimôn* for much, or even all, of the time; that there is a reason for this being the case and, most importantly, that there are solutions that can remedy this sorry state of affairs.

Indeed, Epictetus metaphorically speaks of his school as being a hospital to which students would come seeking treatments for their ills (*Discourses* 3.23.30). Each of us, in consequence merely of being human and living in society, is well aware of what comprise these ills. In the course of daily life we are beset by frustrations and setbacks of every conceivable type. Our cherished enterprises are hindered and thwarted, we have to deal with hostile and offensive people, and we have to cope with the difficulties and anxieties occasioned by the setbacks and illnesses visited upon our friends and relations. Sometimes we are ill ourselves, and even those who have the good fortune to enjoy sound health have to face the fact of their own mortality. In the midst of all this, only the rare few are blessed with lasting and rewarding relationships, and even these relationships, along with *everything* that constitutes a human life, are wholly transient.

But what is philosophy? Does it not mean making preparation to meet the things that come upon us?

(*Discourses* 3.10.6, trans. Oldfather)

The ills we suffer, says Epictetus, result from mistaken beliefs about what is truly good. We have invested our hope in the wrong things, or at least invested it in the wrong way. Our capacity to flourish and be happy (to attain *eudaimonia*) is entirely dependent upon our own characters, how we dispose ourselves to ourselves, to others, and to events generally. What qualities our characters come to have is completely up to us. Therefore, how well we flourish is also entirely up to us.

What is really good

The central claim of Stoic ethics is that only the virtues and virtuous activities are good, and that the only evil is vice and actions motivated by vice (see *Discourses* 2.9.15 and 2.19.13). When someone pursues pleasure or wealth, say, believing these things to be good, the Stoics hold that this person has made a mistake with respect to the nature of the things pursued and the nature of their own being, for the Stoics deny that advantages such as pleasure and health (wealth and status, and so forth) are *good*, because they do not benefit those who possess them in all circumstances. Virtue, on the other hand, conceived as the capacity to use such advantages wisely, being the only candidate for that which is always beneficial, is held to be the only good thing (see DL 7.99/103; LS 58A; Plato, *Euthydemus* 278e–281e and *Meno* 87c–89a).

Thus, the Stoics identify the *eudaimôn* ('happy') life as one that is motivated by virtue. The term we translate as 'virtue' (from the Latin *virtus*) is *aretê*, and means 'excellence'. To progress towards excellence as a human being, for Epictetus, means understanding the true nature of one's being and keeping one's *prohairesis* (moral character) in the right condition. Epictetus uses the term *aretê* only occasionally in the *Discourses* (and not once in the *Handbook*), and whereas the early Stoics spoke of striving for excellence as what was proper for a rational creature and required for *eudaimonia* ('happiness' or well-being), Epictetus speaks instead of striving to maintain one's *prohairesis* in proper order (see *Discourses* 1.4.18, 1.29.1, and *Handbook* 4, 9, 13, 30, 33.1, 48).

Although things such as material comfort, for instance, will be pursued by the Stoic student who seeks *eudaimonia*, they will do this in a different way from those not living the 'philosophic life' – for Stoics claim that everything apart from virtue (what is good) and vice (what is bad) is *indifferent*, that is, 'indifferent' with regard to being good or bad.

It is how one *makes use* of indifferent things that establishes how well one is making progress towards *aretê* (moral excellence) and a *eudaimôn* ('happy') life.

Indifferent things are either 'preferred' or 'dispreferred'. Preferred are life, health and wealth, friends and family, and pretty much all those things that most people pursue as desirable for leading a flourishing life. Dispreferred are their opposites: death, sickness and poverty, social exclusion, and pretty much all those things that people seek to avoid as being detrimental for a flourishing life. Thus, the preferred indifferents have value for a Stoic, but not in terms of their being *good*: they have an instrumental value with respect to their capacities to contribute to a flourishing life as the objects upon which our virtuous actions are directed (see *Discourses* 1.29.2). The Stoic does not lament their absence, for their presence is not constitutive of *eudaimonia*. What is good is the virtuous use one makes of such preferred things should they be to hand, but no less good are one's virtuous dispositions in living as well as one may, even when they are lacking.

What is in our power

To maintain our *prohairesis* (moral character) in the proper condition – the successful accomplishment of this being necessary and sufficient for *eudaimonia* ('happiness') – we must understand what is *eph' hêmin* ('in our power' or 'up to us'; see *Handbook* 1 and *Discourses* 1.22.9–16). If we do *not* do this, our *prohairesis* will remain in a faulty condition, for we will remain convinced that things such as wealth and status are good when they are really indifferent, troubled by frustrations and anxieties, subject to disturbing emotions we do not want and cannot control, all of which make life unpleasant and unrewarding, sometimes over-whelmingly so. This is why Epictetus remarks: 'This is the proper goal, to practise how to remove from one's life sorrows and laments, and cries of "Alas" and "Poor me", and misfortune and disappointment' (*Discourses* 1.4.23, trans. Dobbin).

> No one is master of another's *prohairesis* [moral character], and in this alone lies good and evil. No one, therefore, can secure the good for me, or involve me in evil, but I alone have authority over myself in these matters.
>
> (*Discourses* 4.12.7–8, trans. Dobbin)

What is in our power, then, is the 'authority over ourselves' that we have regarding our capacity to judge what is good and what is evil.

Outside our power are 'external things', which are 'indifferent' with respect to being good or evil. These indifferents, as we saw in the previous section, constitute those things that are conventionally deemed to be good and those that are conventionally deemed to be bad. Roughly, they are things that 'just happen', and they are not in our power in the sense that we do not have absolute control to make them occur just as we wish, or to make them have exactly the outcomes that we desire. Thus, for example, sickness is not in our power because it is not wholly up to us whether we get sick, and how often, nor whether we will recover quickly or indeed at all. Now, it makes sense to visit a doctor when we feel ill, but the competence of the doctor is not in our power, and neither is the effectiveness of any treatment that we might be offered. So generally, it makes sense to manage our affairs carefully and responsibly, but the ultimate outcome of any affair is, actually, not in our power.

What *is* in our power is the capacity to adapt ourselves to all that comes about, to judge anything that is 'dispreferred' not as bad, but as indifferent and not strong enough to overwhelm our strength of character.

The *Handbook* of Epictetus begins with these words:

> On the one hand, there are things that are in our power, whereas other things are not in our power. In our power are opinion, impulse, desire, aversion, and, in a word, whatever is our own doing. Things not in our power include our body, our possessions, our reputations, our status, and, in a word, whatever is not our own doing.
> (*Handbook* 1.1)

That is, we have power over our own minds. The opinions we hold of things, the intentions we form, what we value and what we are averse to are all wholly up to us. Although we may take precautions, whether our possessions are carried off by a thief is not up to us (but the intention to steal, *that* of course is in the power of the thief), and our reputations, in whatever quarter, must be decided by what other people think of us, and what they do think is *up to them*. Remaining calm in the face of adversity and controlling our emotions no matter what the provocation (qualities of character that to this day are referred to as 'being stoical') are accomplished in the full Stoic sense, for Epictetus, by making proper use of impressions.

Making proper use of impressions

An impression (*phantasia*) is what is impressed into the mind by any of the senses, in a way directly analogous to a signet ring imprinting its image into wax. To have an experience of anything is at one and the same time the same thing as having an impression *of* something. The interpretation of what any one impression is an impression *of* is almost invariably spontaneous and immediate. The fact *that* I see a cat on the mat is usually a good guide as to whether there is a cat on the mat, though this automatic interpretative faculty is not infallible, since I may really be seeing my screwed-up jacket on the mat. The interpretative faculty takes us from having an impression *of* something to having an impression *that* something is the case, and the content of this second stage can always be expressed in terms of a proposition: in this case, 'A cat is on the mat.' This is what I believe (with more or less conviction) to be the case, and Epictetus, following the Stoic tradition, talks of our *assenting* to impressions, which is to say, our assenting to *that* which our spontaneous interpretation takes the impression to reveal to be the case. How we view what is happening and what we decide to do next are dependent upon what we assent to, and thus the relevance of all this for moral conduct.

But over and above our being aware that something is the case, there is another stage of interpretation, and this occurs when we *evaluate* what we believe we are experiencing, and this allows for a different sort of assent – namely, our assenting to whether something is good or bad. Let us imagine that I am not fooled by my screwed-up jacket lying on the mat, and thus I do not assent to its being a cat, and instead I assent (correctly) to its being my jacket. But now the second type of assent comes into play when I *evaluate* what I take to be the case, and this is the sort of assent that most interests Epictetus. If I were not a Stoic *prokoptôn* (trainee) already making fair progress, I may well evaluate this situation as *bad*, and to do so will occasion a range of further responses: I may, for instance, be driven by anger to punish the person who dropped my nice new jacket on the floor, and this in itself constitutes feeling upset and losing my equanimity, and quite obviously undermines my hope for leading a *eudaimôn* (happy) life.

> In the first place, do not allow yourself to be carried away by [the] intensity [of your impression]: but say, 'Impression, wait for me a little. Let me see what you are, and what you represent. Let me test you.' Then, afterwards, do not allow it to draw you on by picturing what may come next, for if you do, it will lead you wherever it pleases.

But rather, you should introduce some fair and noble impression to replace it, and banish this base and sordid one.

(Discourses 2.18.24–5, trans. Hard)

So when Epictetus tells us not to be 'carried away' by our impressions he means to urge us not to make faulty evaluations. In 'waiting' we need to stick merely at our factual interpretation without progressing to a faulty evaluative interpretation: we need to base our actions solely upon this – and if we can, we will probably rescue the jacket from the floor to prevent further harm, find out what happened so as to avoid a recurrence, and possibly admonish any wrong-doing. But even admonishing the guilty party will not be done in anger. For having 'tested' the impression we know that nothing bad has happened, we have not been harmed in any way, and *this* evaluation has a completely different character to the one we might have made prior to Stoic enlightenment. We recognise that accidents sometimes happen, and perhaps even that malicious people will seek to make mischief, but that nothing that happens can disturb us. Making such an evaluation correctly, according to Stoic principles of value, is what we need to do to 'make proper use of impressions'.

Thus, our attaining the *eudaimôn* ('happy') life requires that we judge things in the right way, for 'it is not circumstances themselves that trouble people, but their judgements about those circumstances' (*Handbook* 5).

Remember that the insult does not come from the person who abuses you or hits you, but from your judgement that such people are insulting you. Therefore, whenever someone provokes you, be aware that it is your own opinion that provokes you. Try, therefore, in the first place, not to be carried away by your impressions, for if you can gain time and delay, you will more easily control yourself.

(Handbook 20)

The three topoi

The three *topoi* (fields of study) establish activities in which the *prokoptôn* applies their Stoic principles; they are practical exercises or disciplines that when successfully followed are constitutive of the *eudaimôn* ('happy') life which all rational beings are capable of attaining.

There are three areas of study, in which a person who is going to be good and noble must be trained. That concerning desires and aversions, so that he may never fail to get what he desires nor fall into what he would avoid. That concerning the impulse to act and not to act, and, in general, appropriate behaviour; so that he may act in an orderly manner and after due consideration, and not carelessly. The third is concerned with freedom from deception and hasty judgement, and, in general, whatever is connected with assent.

(Discourses 3.2.1–2, trans. Hard)

Our capacity to employ these disciplines in the course of daily life is *eph' hêmin* ('in our power' or 'up to us') because they depend on our opinions, judgements, intentions and desires – which concern the way we regard things – over which our *prohairesis* (moral character) has complete control.

The discipline of desire

The first discipline concerns what someone striving for excellence as a rational being should truly believe is worthy of desire, which for the Stoics is that which is truly good, virtue and action motivated by virtue.

Of these [three areas of study], the principle, and most urgent, is that which has to do with the passions; for these are produced in no other way than by the disappointment of our desires, and the incurring of our aversions. It is this that introduces disturbances, tumults, misfortunes, and calamities; and causes sorrow, lamentation and envy; and renders us envious and jealous, and thus incapable of listening to reason.

(Discourses 3.2.3, trans. Hard)

Epictetus remarks: 'When I see a man anxious, I say, What does this man want? If he did not want something which is not in his power, how could he be anxious?' (*Discourses* 2.13.1, trans. George Long). Those things that most of us, most of the time, seek after as being desirable, what we consider will make our lives go well, are things that are not in our power, and thus the hope we have for securing these things is placed in the hands of others or in the hands of fate. And when we are thwarted in our efforts to gain what we desire we become frustrated (or depressed or envious or angry, or all of these things). To be afflicted with such 'passions', says Epictetus, is the only real source of misery for human beings. Instead of trying to relieve ourselves of these unpleasant emotions by pressing all the harder to secure what we desire, we should rather place our hope not in 'external' things that are not in our power, but in our own dispositions and moral character. In short, we should limit our desire to virtue and to becoming (to the best of our capacities) examples of 'excellence'. If we do not do this, the inevitable result is that we will continue to desire what we may fail to obtain or lose once we have it, and in consequence suffer the unhappiness of emotional disquiet (or worse). And as is the common experience of all people at some time or other, when we are in the grip of such emotions we run the risk of becoming blind to the best course of action, even when construed in terms of pursuing 'external' things.

The Stoic *prokoptôn*, in contrast, sets their hopes on excellence, recognising that this is where their power over things lies. They will still pursue those 'preferred indifferent external' things that are needed for fulfilling both those functions and projects that they deem appropriate for them as individuals, and those they have obligations to meet. But they will not be distressed at setbacks or failure, nor at obstructive people, nor at other difficulties (illness, for instance), for none of these things is entirely up to them, and they engage in their affairs in full consciousness of this fact. It is in maintaining this consciousness of what is truly good (virtue), and awareness that the indifferent things are beyond their power, that makes this a *discipline* for the Stoic *prokoptôn*.

The discipline of action

The second discipline concerns our 'impulses to act and not to act', that is, our motivations, and answers the question as to what we each should do as an individual in our own unique set of circumstances to successfully fulfil the role of a rational, sociable being who is striving for excellence.

The outcomes of our actions are not wholly in our power, but our inclination to act one way rather than another, to pursue one set of objectives rather than others, *this is in our power*. The Stoics use the analogy of the archer shooting at a target to explain this notion. The ideal, of course, is to hit the centre of the target, though accomplishing this is not entirely in the archer's power, for they cannot be certain how the wind will deflect the arrow from its path, nor whether their fingers will slip, nor whether (for it is within the bounds of possibility) the bow will break. The excellent archer does all within their power to shoot well, and they recognise that doing their best is the best they can do. The Stoic archer strives to shoot excellently, and will not be disappointed if they shoot well but fail to hit the centre of the target. And so it is in life generally. The non-Stoic views their success in terms of hitting the target, whereas the Stoic views their success in terms of having shot well (see Cicero, *On Ends* 3.22).

> The [second area of study] has to do with appropriate action. For I should not be unfeeling like a statue, but should preserve my natural and acquired relations as a man who honours the gods, as a son, as a brother, as a father, as a citizen.
>
> (*Discourses* 3.2.4, trans. Hard)

> The actions that are appropriate for us can generally be determined by our relationships. He is your father. This tells you to take care of him, to yield to him in all things, to put up with him when he abuses you or beats you.
>   'But he is a bad father.'
>   Nature did not provide for you a good father, but a father. Your brother wrongs you? Well then, maintain your relationship to him. Do not think about what he is doing, but about what you will have to do if you want to keep your moral character in accordance with nature.
>
> (*Handbook* 30)

The actions we undertake, Epictetus says, should be motivated by the specific obligations that we have in virtue of who we are, our natural relations to others, and what roles we have adopted in our dealings with the wider community (see *Discourses* 2.10.7–13). Put simply, our interest to live well as rational beings obliges us act virtuously, to be patient, considerate, gentle, just, self-disciplined, even-tempered, dispassionate, unperturbed, and when necessary, courageous. This returns us to the central Stoic notion that the *eudaimôn* ('happy') life is realised by those who are motivated by virtue. The Discipline of Action points out to the *prokoptôn* how this should be applied in our practical affairs.

Epictetus sums up the first two disciplines:

> We must have these principles ready to hand. Without them we must do nothing. We must set our mind on this object: pursue nothing that is outside us, nothing that is not our own, even as He that is mighty has ordained: pursuing what lies within our will [*prohairetika*], and all else [i.e. indifferent things] only so far as it is given to us. Further, we must remember who we are, and by what name we are called, and must try to direct our acts [*kathêkonta*] to fit each situation and its possibilities.

We must consider what is the time for singing, what the time for play, and in whose presence: what will be unsuited to the occasion; whether our companions are to despise us, or we to despise ourselves: when to jest, and whom to mock at: in a word, how one ought to maintain one's character in society. Wherever you swerve from any of these principles, you suffer loss at once; not loss from without, but issuing from the very act itself.

(*Discourses* 4.12.15–18, trans. Matheson)

The loss here is, of course, loss of *eudaimonia*.

Failing to 'remember who we are' will result in our failing to pursue those actions appropriate to our individual circumstances and commitments. Epictetus says that this happens because we forget what 'name' we have (son, brother, councillor, etc.), 'for each of these names, if rightly considered, always points to the acts appropriate to it' (*Discourses* 2.10.11, trans. Hard). To progress in the Discipline of Action, then, the *prokoptôn* must be conscious, moment by moment, of (a) which particular social role they are playing, and (b) which actions are required or appropriate for fulfilling that role to the highest standard.

The discipline of assent

This exercise focuses on 'assenting to impressions', and continues the discussion already introduced in the section 'Making proper use of impressions' above. 'Assent' translates the Greek *sunkatathesis*, the verb being *sunkatatithesthai*, which means 'approve', 'agree', or 'go along with'. Thus, when we assent to an impression (*phantasia*) we are committing ourselves to it as a correct representation of how things are, and are saying, 'Yes, this is how it is.' The Discipline of Assent, then, is an exercise applied to our impressions in which we interpret and judge them in order to move from having the impression *of* something or other, to a declaration *that* such-and-such is the case.

The third area of study has to do with assent, and what is plausible and attractive. For, just as Socrates used to say that we are not to lead an unexamined life [see Plato, *Apology* 38a], so neither are we to accept an unexamined impression, but to say, 'Stop, let me see what you are, and where you come from', just as the night-watch say, 'Show me your token.'

(*Discourses* 3.12.14–15, trans. Hard)

Straightaway then, train yourself to say to every unpleasant impression, 'You are an impression, and by no means what you appear to be.' Then examine it and test it by the rules that you have, firstly (in this way especially) by asking whether it concerns things that are in our power or things that are not in our power: and if it concerns something not in our power, have ready to hand the answer, 'This is nothing to me.'

(*Handbook* 1.5)

And we should do this with a view to avoiding falling prey to subjective (and false) evaluations so that we can be free from deception and from making rash judgements about how to proceed in the first two disciplines. For if we make faulty evaluations we will end up (with respect to the first discipline) having desires for the wrong things (namely, 'indifferents'), and (with respect to the second discipline) acting inappropriately with regard to our duties and obligations. This is why Epictetus remarks that the third topic 'concerns the security of the other two' (*Discourses* 3.2.5, trans. George Long).

Epictetus runs through a number of imaginary situations to show how we should be alert to the dangers of assenting to poorly evaluated impressions:

… We ought … to exercise ourselves daily to meet the impressions of our senses … So-and-so's son is dead. Answer, 'That lies outside the sphere of the moral purpose, it is not an evil.' His father has disinherited So-and-so; what do you think of it? 'That lies outside the sphere of the moral purpose, it is not an evil.' Caesar has condemned him. 'That lies outside the sphere of the moral purpose, it is not an evil.' He was grieved at all this. 'That lies within the sphere of the moral purpose, it is an evil.' He has borne up under it manfully. 'That lies within the sphere of the moral purpose, it is a good.' Now if we acquire this habit, we shall make progress; for we shall never give our assent to anything but that of which we get a convincing sense-impression. His son is dead. What happened? His son is dead. Nothing else? Not a thing. His ship is lost. What happened? His ship is lost. He was carried off to prison. What happened? He was carried off to prison. But the observation: 'He has fared ill,' is an addition that each man makes on his own responsibility.

(*Discourses* 3.8.1–5, trans. Oldfather)

What we must avoid, then, is adding to our impressions immediately and without proper evaluation any notion that something good or bad is at hand. For the only thing that is good is moral virtue, and the only harm that anyone can come to is to engage in affairs motivated by vice. Thus, to see the loss of a ship as a catastrophe would count as assenting to the wrong impression, for the impression that we have is that of just a ship being lost. To take the extra step of declaring that this is a misfortune and harmful would be to assent to an impression that is not in fact present, and would be a mistake. The loss of a ship, for a Stoic, is nothing more than a dispreferred indifferent, and does not constitute a harm.

God

For Epictetus, the terms 'God', 'the gods', and 'Zeus' are used interchangeably, and they appear frequently in the *Discourses*. In the *Handbook*, God is discussed as the 'captain' who calls us back on board ship, the subsequent voyage being a metaphor for our departure from life (see *Handbook* 7). God is also portrayed as 'the Giver' to whom we should return all those things we have enjoyed on loan when we lose close relatives or friends who die, and when we lose our possessions through misfortune or wear (see *Discourses* 4.10.16 and *Handbook* 11).

If the Stoic making progress (*ho prokoptôn*) understands God, the universe, and themselves in the right way, they 'will never blame the gods nor accuse them of neglect' (*Handbook* 31.1):

> Will you be angry and discontented with the ordinances of Zeus, which he, with the Fates who spun in his presence the thread of your destiny at the time of your birth, ordained and appointed?
>
> (*Discourses* 1.12.25, trans. Hard)

Indeed, they will pray to God to lead them to the fate that He has assigned them:

> 'Lead me, Zeus, and you too, Destiny,
>   Wherever you have assigned me to go,
>   and I'll follow without hesitating; but if am not willing,
>   because I am bad, I'll follow all the same.'
>   'Whosoever properly with necessity complies
>   we say is wise, and understands things divine.'
>   'Well, Crito, if this pleases the gods, let it happen this way.'
>   'Certainly, Anytus and Meletus may put me to death, but they cannot harm me.'
>
> (*Handbook* 53)

[For] God has stationed us to a certain place and way of life.
                                        (*Discourses* 1.9.24, trans. Dobbin)

Epictetus presents orthodox Stoic views on God. His justification for believing in God is expressed essentially along the lines of what we recognise as an argument from design. The order and harmony that we can perceive in the natural world (from astronomical events to the way plants grow and fruit in season) is attributed to a divine providence that orders and controls the entire cosmos intelligently and rationally (see *Discourses* 1.6.1–11, 1.14.1–6, 1.16.7–8 and 2.14.11/25–7). The Stoics were materialists, and God is conceived of as a type of fiery breath that blends perfectly with all other matter in the universe. In doing this, God transforms matter from undifferentiated 'stuff' into the varied forms that we see around us. This process is continuous, and God makes the world as it is, doing what it does, moment by moment. Just as the soul of a person is understood to bring alive and animate what would otherwise be dead and inert matter, so God is thought of as the 'soul of the world', and the universe is thought of as a sort of living creature (see LS 44B–C, F, 54A–B). Diogenes Laertius (7.137 = LS 44F) remarks that the Stoics use the term 'world' (*kosmos*) in three ways: it can denote God Himself, the orderly arrangement of bodies manifest in the world, or that which comprises both (i.e. the disposition that matter has plus God, who animates and shapes matter). Thus, 'God, intelligence, fate, and Zeus are all one' (DL 135 = LS 46B1).

Stoics hold that the mind of each person is quite literally a part (*meros*) or fragment (*apospasma*) of God (see *Discourses* 1.17.27, 2.8.11), and that the rationality that we each possess is in fact a fragment of God's rationality; and this Epictetus primarily identifies as the capacity we have to make proper use of impressions (see *Discourses* 1.1.12). Epictetus expresses this in terms of what God has 'given us'; He is conceived of as having constructed the universe in such a way that we have in our possession all that is within the compass of our own character or moral choice *and nothing else*, but this is no reason for complaint:

What has He given me for my own and subject to my authority, and what has He left for Himself? Everything within the sphere of the moral purpose He has given me, subjected them to my control, unhampered and unhindered. My body that is made of clay, how could He make that unhindered? Accordingly He has made it subject to the revolution of the universe—[along with] my property, my furniture, my house, my children, my wife. ... But how should I keep them? In accordance with the terms upon which they have been given, and for as long as they can be given. But He who gave also takes away. …

And so, when you have received everything, and your very self, from Another [i.e. God], do you yet complain and blame the Giver, if He take something away from you?

(*Discourses* 4.1.100–3, with omissions, trans. Oldfather)

The capacity that the *prokoptôn* has for understanding, accepting, and embracing this state of affairs, that this is indeed *the nature of things*, is another of the main foundation stones of Stoic ethics.

On living in accordance with nature

The outlook adopted and the activities performed by the Stoic student in pursuit of excellence, as detailed in the sections above, are frequently referred to collectively by Epictetus (following the Stoic tradition) as 'living in accordance with nature', 'living in harmony with nature', 'following nature', or 'following God'. The Stoic *prokoptôn* maintains his harmony with nature by being aware of why he acts as he does in terms of both (a) what his appropriate actions are and (b) accepting what fate brings. If, for example, the *prokoptôn* is berated unfairly by his brother, he will not respond with angry indignation, for this would be 'contrary to nature', for nature has determined how brothers should rightly act towards each other (see *Discourses* 3.10.19–20). The task the Stoic student shoulders is to pursue actions appropriate to him as a brother, *despite all and any provocation to act otherwise* (see *Handbook* 30). This, for Epictetus, is a major component of what it means to keep one's *prohairesis* (moral character) in harmony with nature (see *Discourses* 1.6.15, 3.1.25 and 3.16.15).

Keeping ourselves in harmony with nature requires that we focus on two things. First, we must pay attention to our own actions so that we respond appropriately, and second we must pay attention to the world in which our actions take effect and which prompts those actions in the first place.

When you are about to undertake some task, remind yourself what sort of business it is. If you are going out to bathe, bring to mind what happens at the baths: there will be those who splash you, those who will jostle you, some will be abusive to you, and others will steal from you. And thus you will undertake the affair more securely if you say to yourself from the start, 'I wish to take a bath, but also to keep my moral character in accordance with nature.' Do likewise with every undertaking. For thus, if anything should happen that interferes with your bathing, be ready to say, 'Oh well, it was not only this that I wanted, but also to keep my moral character in accordance with nature, and I cannot do that if I am irritated by things that happen.'

(*Handbook* 4)

In this extract about going to the baths, Epictetus focuses more on accepting what fate brings, saying that we should anticipate the sorts of things that can happen, so that when they do we will not be surprised and will not be angry. In other situations, anticipation of trouble or misfortune is impossible, but all the same, the Stoic will accept their fate as what God has ordained for them, and this for Epictetus is the very essence of keeping in harmony with nature (see *Discourses* 1.4.18–21).

It is circumstances (difficulties) which show what men are. Therefore when a difficulty falls upon you, remember that God, like a trainer of wrestlers, has matched you with a rough young man. For what purpose? you may say. Why, that you may become an Olympic conqueror; but it is not accomplished without sweat. In my opinion no man has had a more profitable difficulty than you have had, if you choose to make use of it as an athlete would deal with a young antagonist.

(*Discourses* 1.24.1–2, trans. George Long)

Every problem we face in life should be understood as a new opportunity to strengthen our moral character, just as every new bout for the wrestler provides an opportunity for them to train their skill in wrestling.

To be instructed is this, to learn to wish that every thing may happen as it does. And how do things happen? As the disposer [i.e. God] has disposed them. And he has appointed summer and winter, and abundance and scarcity, and virtue and vice, and all such opposites for the harmony of the whole; and to each of us he has given a body, and parts of the body, and possessions, and companions.

Remembering then this disposition of things, we ought to go to be instructed, not that we may change the constitution of things,—for we have not the power to do it, nor is it better that we should have the power,—but in order that, as the things around us are what they are and by nature exist, we may maintain our minds in harmony with the things which happen.

(*Discourses* 1.12.15–17, trans. George Long)

> The wise and good man ... submits his own mind to him who administers the whole [i.e. God], as good citizens do to the law of the state. He who is receiving instruction ought to come to be instructed with this intention, How shall I follow the gods in all things, how shall I be contented with the divine administration, and how can I become free? For he is free to whom every thing happens according to his will [*prohairesis*], and whom no man can hinder.
>
> (*Discourses* 1.12.7–9, trans. George Long)

In this last extract we see Epictetus refer to the ideal Stoic practice as that of 'following the gods'. This means essentially the same as 'following nature', for God, who is immanent in the world (as the Stoics understand it), is identified with the way the world manifests, so if one follows nature, one must also be following God (see *Discourses* 1.20.15, 1.30.4, 4.7.20 and 4.10.14).

Metaphors for life

Epictetus employs a number of metaphors to illustrate what the Stoic attitude to life should be.

Life as a festival

Epictetus encourages us to think of life as a festival, arranged for our benefit by God, as something that we can live through joyously, able to put up with any hardships that befall us because we have our eye on the larger spectacle that is taking place. Epictetus asks his students:

> Who are you, and for what purpose have you come? Was it not he [i.e. God] who brought you here? ... And as what did he bring you here? Was it not as a mortal? Was it not as one who would live, with a little portion of flesh, upon this earth, and behold his governance and take part with him, for a short time, in his pageant and his festival?
>
> (*Discourses* 4.1.104, trans. Hard)

The whole thrust of Stoic ethics aims to persuade us that we should ourselves contribute to the festival by living as well as we may and fulfilling our duties as sociable citizens of God's 'great city' (*Discourses* 3.22.4; see also *Discourses* 1.12.21, 2.14.23 and 4.4.24–7/46).

Life as a game

At *Discourses* 2.5.2, in encouraging his students to appreciate that external things are indifferent (being neither good nor bad), Epictetus says that we should imitate those who play dice, for neither the dice nor the counters have any real value; what matters, and what is either good or bad, is the way we play the game. Similarly at 2.5.15–20, where Epictetus discusses the example of playing a ball game, no one considers for a moment whether the ball itself is good or bad, but only whether they can throw and catch it with the appropriate skill. What matters are the faculties of dexterity, speed and good judgement exhibited by the players, for it is in deploying these faculties effectively that any player is deemed to have played well (see also *Discourses* 4.7.5/19/30–1). Epictetus also uses the metaphor of playing games when discussing suicide, for just as someone stops playing a game when they are no longer amused by it, so it should be in life generally: if life should become unbearable, no one can force us to keep living it.

> To summarize: remember that the door is open. Do not be more cowardly than children, but just as they say, when the game no longer pleases them, 'I will play no more,' you too, when things seem that way to you, should merely say, 'I will play no more,' and so depart; but if you stay, stop moaning.
> (*Discourses* 1.24.20, trans. Hard; see also 1.25.7–21 and 2.16.37)

Life as weaving

In this metaphor, the wool that the weaver uses to make cloth takes the place of the ball in the game; that is, whatever material comes our way, it is our duty to make proper use of it, and if possible make it into the best thing of its kind as we can (see *Discourses* 2.5.21–2).

Life as a play

We have already seen, when discussing the Discipline of Action, that Epictetus urges us to 'remember who we are' and what 'name' we have, because what role we play in life will determine which actions are appropriate for us. Obviously, the metaphor of life as a play expands on this idea, but also brings in the notion of our having to accept our fate, whatever that may be, since we do not ourselves choose the role we must play (for although we may aim for one role rather than another, we must recognise that our attaining it is not, in fact, 'in our power').

Remember that you are an actor in a play of such a kind as the playwright chooses: short, if he wants it short, long if he wants it long. If he wants you to play the part of a beggar, play even this part well; and so also for the parts of a disabled person, an administrator, or a private individual. For this is your business, to play well the part you are given; but choosing it belongs to another.

(*Handbook* 17)

Life as an athletic contest

This metaphor invites us to see an analogy between one's training in Stoic ethics as preparatory for living the philosophic life and someone's training in athletics as preparatory for entering the contest in the arena. Epictetus addresses someone who has become distressed at not having enough leisure to study their philosophy books, saying:

For is not reading a kind of preparation for living, but living itself made up of things other than books? It is as if an athlete, when he enters the stadium, should break down and weep because he is not exercising outside. This is what you were exercising for; this is what the jumping-weights, and the sand and your young partners were all for. So are you now seeking for these, when it is the time for action? That is just as if, in the sphere of assent, when we are presented with impressions, some of which are evidently true and others not, instead of distinguishing between them, we should want to read a treatise *On Direct Apprehension.*

(*Discourses* 4.4.11–13, trans. Hard)

Training to live a life that befits someone who strives for the Stoic ideal is directly compared to athletic training. Such training is difficult, demanding, and unpleasant; there is little point in showing eagerness for any endeavour if we have not properly assessed the demands that will be placed upon us, and in inevitably losing our original enthusiasm we will look foolish. This applies to philosophic training no less than to training as a wrestler in preparation for competing in the Olympic Games (see *Handbook* 29 = *Discourses* 3.15.1–13). Elsewhere, Epictetus declares that delay is no longer possible, that we must meet the challenges that life throws at us:

From this moment commit yourself to living as an adult, as someone who is making progress, and let everything that appears best to you be a law that you cannot transgress. And if you are presented with anything laborious, or something pleasant, with anything reputable or disreputable, remember that the contest is *now*, that the Olympic Games are *now*, that it is no longer possible to put them off, and that progress is won or lost as the result of just once giving in.

(Handbook 51.2;
see also Discourses 1.4.13–17, 1.18.21–3, 1.24.1–2, 3.25.3)

Life as military service

This metaphor returns us to the Stoic idea that the universe is governed by God, and that, like it or not, we are all in service to God. The Stoic *prokoptôn* (student making progress) should understand that they should live life attempting to discharge this service to the highest standards. Epictetus addresses the person who is upset that they are obliged to travel abroad, causing their mother to be distressed at their absence:

> Do you not know that life is a soldier's service? One man must keep guard, another go out to reconnoitre, another take the field. It is not possible for all to stay where they are, nor is it better so. But you neglect to fulfil the orders of the general and complain, when some severe order is laid upon you; you do not understand to what a pitiful state you are bringing the army so far as in you lies; you do not see that if all follow your example there will be no one to dig a trench, or raise a palisade, no one to keep night watch or fight in the field, but every one will seem an unserviceable soldier.
>
> … So too it is in the world; each man's life is a campaign, and a long and varied one. It is for you to play the soldier's part—do everything at the General's bidding, divining his wishes, if it be possible.

(Discourses 3.24.31–5, trans. Matheson;
see also 1.9.24 and 1.16.20–1)

Making progress

In making progress, the Stoic *prokoptôn* will pay a price. In standing to God, the world, society, themselves and their undertakings in this new way (by accepting the Stoic notions of what is truly good, what is truly up to them, where their proper duties lie, and in considering their life to be one of service to God), the *prokoptôn* separates themselves from the rest of society in fairly marked, if not profound, ways. For example, Epictetus wants his students to enjoy and participate in the 'festival of life', yet at the public games (for instance) they must not support any one individual, but must wish the winner to be the one who actually wins; they must refrain entirely from shouting or laughing, and must not get carried away by the spectacle of the contest (*Handbook* 33.10). So whilst the *prokoptôn's* friends immerse themselves fully in the games, cheering on their favourite and jeering at their opponent, the Stoic stands aloof and detached. Deliberately separating themselves from the crowd is the price they pay for well-being (*eudaimonia*), dispassion (*apatheia*), tranquillity and imperturbability (*ataraxia*), along with the conviction that they are living as God intends.

But having declared their hand, the *prokoptôn* will pay in other ways also, for those around them will rebuke and ridicule them (*Handbook* 22), for in abandoning the values and practices common to the wider community, they will provoke hostility and suspicion. Yet there remains the hope that some at least will see the *prokoptôn* as someone whose wisdom has value for the community at large, as someone who serves as an example of how one may get along in the world without being overwhelmed by it, as someone with specific skills to offer, such as mediating family disputes and suchlike (see *Discourses* 1.15.5).

Epictetus characterises the differences between the non-philosopher and someone making progress in these terms:

> The condition and character of the uneducated person is this: they never look for benefit or harm to come from themselves, but from external things. The condition and character of the philosopher is this: they look for every benefit and harm to come from themselves. The signs that someone is making progress are these: they blame no one, they praise no one, they find fault with no one, they accuse no one, they never say anything of themselves as though they amount to something or know anything. When they are impeded or hindered, they blame themselves. If someone praises them, they laugh inwardly at the person who praises them, and if anyone censures them, they make no defence. They go about as if they were sick, cautious not to disturb what is healing before they are fully recovered. They have rid themselves of all desires, and have transferred their aversion to only those things contrary to nature that are in our power. They have no strong preferences in regard to anything. If they appear foolish or ignorant, they do not care. In a word, they keep guard over themselves as though they are their own enemy lying in wait.
>
> (*Handbook* 48)

Epictetus' life as a Stoic teacher can perhaps be regarded as a personal quest to awaken to true philosophic enlightenment that person who will stand up proudly when his teacher pleads:

> Pray, let somebody show me a person who is in such a good way that he can say, 'I concern myself only with what is my own, with what is free from hindrance, and is by nature free. That is what is truly good, and this I have. But let all else be as god may grant; it makes no difference to me.'
>
> (*Discourses* 4.13.24, trans. Hard)

For having approached so closely to such enlightenment himself (for surely this we must suppose), Epictetus devoted his life to raising up others from the crowd of humanity who could stand beside him and share in a perception of the universe and a way of life that any rational being is obliged to adopt in virtue of the nature of things (see *Discourses* 2.19.29–34).

Extracts from Epictetus' *Discourses* in this Introduction to Epictetus have been taken from the following translations:

Dobbin, Robert. 1998. *Epictetus: Discourses Book 1*. Oxford: Clarendon Press.

Hard, Robin. 1995. *The Discourses of Epictetus*. ed. with introduction and notes by Christopher Gill. London: Everyman/Dent.

Long, George. 2004. *The Discourses of Epictetus with the Encheiridion and Fragments*. Whitefish, MT: Kessinger Publishing. [Facsimile reprint of the George Bell edition of 1877. The first edition of this translation was published in 1848.]

Matheson, P. E. 1916. *Epictetus: The Discourses and Manual*. 2 vols. Oxford: Clarendon Press.

Oldfather, W. A. 1925, 1928. *Epictetus: The Discourses as Reported by Arrian, The Manual, and Fragments*. 2 vols. Cambridge, MA: Loeb Classical Library, Harvard University Press.

The *Handbook* of Epictetus
Translation and commentary

Chapter 1

[1] On the one hand, there are things that are in our power, whereas other things are not in our power. In our power are opinion, impulse, desire, aversion, and, in a word, whatever is our own doing. Things not in our power include our body, our possessions, our reputations, our status, and, in a word, whatever is not our own doing.

[2] Now, things that are in our power are by nature free, unhindered, unimpeded; but things not in our power are weak, slavish, hindered, and belong to others. [3] Remember, therefore, that whenever you suppose those things that are by nature slavish to be free, or those things that belong to others to be your own, you will be hindered, miserable and distressed, and you will find fault with both gods and men. If, however, you suppose to be yours only what is yours, and what belongs to another to belong to another (as indeed it does), no one will ever compel you, no one will hinder you; you will find fault with no one, reproach no one, nor act against your own will; you will have no enemies and no one will harm you, for no harm can touch you.

[4] Thus, when aiming at such great things remember that securing them requires more than a modest effort: some things you will have to give up altogether, and others you will have to put aside for the time being. If you want such great things but at the same time strive for status and wealth, you may well not even obtain these latter things because you are seeking the former; at any rate, you will certainly fail to secure those former great things which alone bring freedom and happiness.

[5] Straightaway then, train yourself to say to every unpleasant impression, 'You are an impression, and by no means what you appear to be.' Then examine it and test it by the rules that you have, first (in this way especially) by asking whether it concerns things that are in our power or things that are not in our power: and if it concerns something not in our power, have ready to hand the answer, 'This is nothing to me.'

Commentary

Key terms

aversion (*ekklisis*)
belonging to another (*allotrios*)
body (*sôma*)
desire (noun) (*orexis*)
distress, trouble, or agitate
    the mind (*tarassô*)
enemy (*ho echthros*)
examine (*exetazô*)
find fault with (*memphomai*)
free (adjective) (*eleutheros*)
freedom (*eleutheria*)
gods (*theoi*)
happiness (*eudaimonia*)
harm (verb) (*blaptô*)
hinder (*empodizô*, *kôluô*)
impression (*phantasia*)
impulse (*hormê*)
in our power (*eph' hêmin*)

miserable, to be (*pentheô*,
    lament)
not in our power
    (*ouk eph' hêmin*)
opinion (*hupolêpsis*)
possession (*ktêsis*)
reproach (verb) (*enkaleô*)
reputation (*doxa*)
rule (*kanôn*)
status (*archê*, the office that
    one holds) [1.1]
status (*archô*, to hold office)
    [1.4]
test (verb) (*dokimazô*)
train (verb) (*meletaô*)
unhindered (*akôlutos*)
unimpeded (*aparapodistos*)
wealthy, to be (*plouteô*)

Epictetus' characterisation of philosophy as preparing us for meeting the things that happen in life (*Discourses* 3.10.6; see Introduction to Epictetus, 'The promise of philosophy') implies that in a pre- or non-philosophical condition we will be, in at least some sense, ill-equipped to face life. To be better equipped, says Epictetus, we will need not to change any of the things that 'come upon us', but to change our *outlook upon* the things that 'come upon us' (*Discourses* 1.12.17). The point of Epictetus' Stoic ethics is to show us how to effect this change.

Standing at the door to Epictetus' school, so to speak, wondering whether it will be worth our while to go in and start on new studies, the choice we will actually make is that of either remaining an *idiôtês* (an 'uneducated person') or of endeavouring to become a *philosophos* (a philosopher; see *Handbook* 29.7). Marcus Aurelius couches this in even more striking terms, possibly attempting a free paraphrase of Epictetus' *Discourses* 1.22.17 (Haines 1930, 319), or of 3.25.3 (Hadot 1998, 68), saying that the study of philosophy is 'no casual matter, for what is at stake is deciding whether we will be sane or insane (*mainesthai*)' (MA 11.38).

Indeed, the prize is great. If we are successful, we can secure for ourselves **freedom** and **happiness** (*Handbook* 1.4); in the midst of troubles we will **find fault** with no one, neither with other people nor with the **gods** (*Handbook* 1.2); we will have no **enemies** and, astonishingly, we will be impervious to **harm** (*Handbook* 1.2).

The term Epictetus uses for **happiness** (*Handbook* 1.4) (the only time it occurs in the *Handbook*, though the term is used not infrequently in the *Discourses*) is *eudaimonia*, whose meaning is not that well conveyed by the English term 'happiness'. *Eudaimonia* means 'supremely blessed', and conveys the notion of someone who is flourishing fully, someone who is happy not just in the sense that they are having a good time, or enjoying some temporary pleasure, but whose happiness is of a special kind: it is stable and enduring, it is a persistence of flourishing that pervades their whole life. Zeno defined it as a 'good flow of life' (*euroia biou*) (DL 7.88; Stob. 2.7.6e = LS 63A; see *Handbook* 8). Deciding what this flourishing consists in and how one may secure it was the task of ancient ethics. It was conceived of as the *telos*, as the end or goal of living, for whose sake everything in life is done such that it is not itself pursued for the sake of anything else (see LS 63). The early Stoics formulated the *telos* in several different but related ways (see Glossary A), but focused on the notions of 'living in accordance with virtue' and 'living in agreement with nature', which Epictetus conveys in terms of maintaining one's 'moral character' (*prohairesis*) in accordance with nature or of 'using impressions' in accordance with nature (see *Handbook* 4, 6, 13, 30), though he also talks of following nature and following **God** (*Handbook* 49, 53.1).

If we want to secure for ourselves this special sort of flourishing and make the transition from *idiôtês* (someone for whom freedom and happiness are perpetually elusive) to *philosophos* (someone who understands what freedom and happiness are, and what is required to make progress towards securing them), the first and essential step is to understand Epictetus' notion of what is **'in our power'**. This is the most important concept in Epictetus' moral teaching.

When Epictetus talks of things being **in our power** or **not in our power** (*Handbook* 1.1–2) he means this in an absolute sense. For Epictetus, for something to depend on us, to be in our power, in our control, or up to us, this must be so invariably and always. Let us look firstly at the things that are *not* in our power: in the second sentence of 1.1 we are told that these things include our **bodies**, our **possessions**, our **reputations** and **status**, and 'whatever is not our own doing' (comprising, I take it, the actions of other people, and such things as the weather, the atomic weight of gold, and so forth). To state that our **bodies** are not in our power at first sight seems odd, because as agents we are well practised in using our bodies to perform a whole variety of actions on a minute-by-minute and day-by-day basis. Quite obviously, if my own body were not in my power I would not be able to write these words. And if your body were not in your power, you would not be able to read what I have written. This, Epictetus accepts. But it remains the case that anything we might try to do is dependent upon factors that are *not* in our control, and this is Epictetus' key point. Even if our bodies continue to function normally (and this being so, although probable, is not actually up to us), other factors may intervene to obstruct our intentions. Here is a simple example: we intend to switch on the TV to watch our favourite soap. Potential obstructions to our accomplishing this come from many quarters, because so many factors are necessary for our success. The door to the room we plan to use may be locked; the TV may not come on if the power is off; the TV may be broken; the show may have been rescheduled; and more alarmingly we may suddenly be taken ill so that we cannot even make the attempt to enter the room and turn on the TV – the list is clearly extensive.

And similarly for our **possessions**. The condition they are in, whether we retain possession of them, and whether they will function as we hope, do not ultimately depend on us. It makes sense to look after our possessions just as it makes sense to care for our **bodies**, but whether a thief gets away with the TV, or whether we fall ill (*despite taking every precaution*) is not up to us. Of course, it makes sense to visit the doctor when we are ill, but whether we get ill or not in the first place, and whether the doctor's competence is good enough to provide us with the best and most appropriate treatment, or even whether such treatment will work – all these things are not in our power. This is even more obvious for our **reputations** and our **status** in society generally. We may strive to maintain good reputations, but whether we succeed or not is down to what other people think of us, and what *they* think is *up to them*. And as for **status** (which for Epictetus means public office, but for us may be construed in far wider terms), well, no matter what efforts we make ourselves to come across as we would prefer, whether we succeed in gaining an appointment in employment or in attaining some other status in a social context, this is entirely in the hands of other people.

In contrast to all these things that are not wholly within our control are capacities of our minds which, so Epictetus claims, *are* always and invariably in our power. In *Handbook* 1.1 these are identified as opinion, impulse, desire and aversion. **Opinion** covers our beliefs and judgements, how we regard things, and *especially how we evaluate things*, generally. An **impulse** is what motivates action, and was conceived of as a 'motion of the soul towards something' (Stob. 2.7.9). The Stoics understood that nature has endowed all creatures with impulses that direct them to what is appropriate (DL 7.85–6 = LS 57A; Stob. 2.7.5b3), thus, for example, gazelles eat grass and lions eat gazelles, and this general fact about what is specific to different kinds of creature is also true of human beings. But humans differ because we also have a capacity for reason which means that, unlike animals, we do not simply instinctively respond to stimuli, but can reflect on what is in our best interests, form intentions, and act accordingly. **Desire** means exactly what we would expect: to desire something is to want it for one's own, to have it present with one, and to have power over it, as well as simply wanting something to be a certain way. **Aversion** is simply the opposite of desire: to be averse to something is to desire that it remain absent, or if it is already present, to desire that it go away or otherwise change its character to become something less disagreeable.

Epictetus' fundamental claim is that no outside agency has power over these capacities of the mind (not even Zeus; see *Discourses* 1.1.23; see also 1.6.40, 3.3.10, 4.12.12). They are entirely in our power. What we think of things, how we respond to events, what we desire and what we are averse to, are all wholly and entirely in our own power.

In *Handbook* 1.2, Epictetus stresses the stark dichotomy between what is in our power and what is not. Our mental capacities are in and of their own nature '**free, unhindered, unimpeded**', whereas things not in our power are 'weak, slavish, **hindered**, and **belong to others**'. They belong to others not because other people have complete control over our bodies, possessions, reputations and status (obviously they do not), but because the actions of other people are instrumental in determining how matters go (excepting, perhaps, those cases involving exclusively natural phenomena – though even here, it is most likely that Epictetus would want to place the responsibility for natural phenomena in the hands of **God**, so that even events wholly independent of human agents do all the same 'belong to another').

The significance of this distinction is pressed in *Handbook* 1.3. If we fail to understand and appreciate the difference between what is in our power and what is not, believing that and desiring that (for example) our possessions will be entirely safe whilst we are away on holiday only to come home to find most of them stolen and most that remain trashed, then of course we will be **miserable** and **distressed**. On the other hand, if we do understand and appreciate the distinction between what is in our power and what is not, then, we are told, no one can ever compel us, no one can **hinder** us; we will **find fault** with and **reproach** no one; and somewhat more obscurely, we will not act against our own will, we will have no **enemies** and we will be immune to **harm** (see *Handbook* 30, and commentary to *Handbook* 3). Why should understanding this distinction confer such benefits?

Well, simply to understand the distinction will not be enough. The Stoic student, says Epictetus in *Handbook* 1.4, will be *aiming* at these 'great things' (to live in such a way that they never find fault with anyone, never act against their own will, never encounter an enemy, and find that no harm ever befalls them) – and 'aiming' implies a process of training and progress towards this end. Indeed, Epictetus tells us that this training will require more than a modest effort (see *Handbook* 29). In particular we will have to decide what we want most, because, we are told, we cannot want and strive for the 'great things' at the same time as striving for **status** and **wealth** – the attempt to do both will make it *likely* that we fail to obtain the status and wealth that we seek, and make it *certain* that we will fail to secure the 'great things' that bring **freedom** and **happiness** (see *Discourses* 1.1.14–15, 4.10.25–6, 4.2; *Handbook* 13). But why does Epictetus say that we must give up some things altogether and put others aside *for the time being*? As we will see in the course of discussing the *Handbook*, the Stoic *prokoptôn* (one who is making progress in their Stoic training) will indeed have to give up all sorts of practices commonly pursued by the *idiôtês* (uneducated person), but some (though by no means all) may be picked up again once progress has become substantial and enduring, for in this new condition, these practices will have a new significance and meaning and, in contrast to how they were engaged in earlier, pursuing them will no longer run the risk of stirring up the violent emotions (*pathê*) and undermining the successful Stoic's 'good flow of life' (*euroia biou*). (For an extended treatment of the notion of what is in our power, see *Discourses* 4.1.62–82.)

In the concluding phrase of *Handbook* 1.4, '**freedom**' describes the *eudaimôn* person's state of mind, and is characterised by a range of qualities that identify what the *eudaimôn* person is *free from* in a complete and enduring manner. At *Discourses* 4.6.16 we are told that such a person is free from distress (*alupos*), free from fear (*aphobos*), free from the violent emotions (*apathês*), and free from hindrance (*akôlutos*). The *akôlutos* person aims for nothing that is not in their power (*Discourses* 4.1.129). Recognising that external events (including their own bodies) and other people (the condition they are in, what they do, and how they experience the world) are not in their control, makes possible the avoidance of assenting to false judgements about what is truly good and bad, and thereby attaining a state of *ataraxia* (peace of mind) and *apatheia* (dispassion). This is what Epictetus means when he says that only the educated person is truly free (see *Discourses* 2.1.21–2), and by 'educated' he means being trained in Stoic theory and practice: 'Why did you go to the philosophers? To be as unfortunate and miserable as always? No – but to be free from fear and troubles' (*Discourses* 4.1.83–4). When we express these states of mind enjoyed by the *eudaimôn* person as adverbs, we describe the way in which this person engages with affairs: they carry out their tasks serenely (*alupôs*), fearlessly (*aphobôs*), dispassionately (*apathôs*), and freely (*akôlutôs*). **Happiness** and **freedom** are won by the person who adjusts their inner disposition according to Stoic **rules**. Chief amongst these in Epictetus' educational system is the practice of 'making proper use of **impressions**' (see for instance *Discourses* 1.20.7/15).

An **impression** (*Handbook* 1.5) is an awareness of how something stands, both factually and evaluatively. Thus, for example, we can talk of someone having an impression of paint having been spilled all over the carpet. They are prepared to assent to the proposition *that* the paint is all over the carpet, and this is what Epictetus means when he talks about 'assenting to impressions'. Assenting to *this* impression is fine – it correctly represents the world as it is. But Epictetus warns against assenting to the further impressions that (1) '*this is something bad for me,* (2) *to which an emotional response is appropriate*'. To do so would be to make a false evaluation. The Stoics hold that the only good is virtue and action motivated by virtue (and conversely that the only evil is vice and action motivated by vice; see *Discourses* 2.9.15, 2.19.13; DL 7.101–3 = LS 58A) – and if this is so, no quantity of paint on the carpet, however large, can ever be truly bad. Such an occurrence is something *indifferent* – indifferent with respect to being good or bad – and it is something that is not in our power.

This, then, is the first exercise we need to **train** in (*Handbook* 1.5) – to respond to every unpleasant **impression** by **testing** and **examining** it (*Discourses* 2.18.24). So if we see that the paint has been spilled all over the floor, instead of getting angry or otherwise reacting emotionally (for this is *really* the cause of happiness eluding us), we should actually stand back from what has happened and commence a discourse and ask the **impression** whether it concerns anything that is **in our power**, and when we understand that it does not, the proposition that we assent to is '*this is nothing to me*'. The successful Stoic student, upon facing such a decorating catastrophe, will be able to calmly attend to what needs doing, dispassionately clearing up the mess and moving on.

The **rules** that Epictetus refers to are meant to extend the one basic rule emphasised here, '**examine** and **test** every **impression** to see if it concerns what is **in our power**' (see *Discourses* 2.18.24–5), and these will encompass the entirety of Stoic doctrine to provide the necessary conceptual foundation for being able to apply the test and understanding what we are doing, and why. The overarching Stoic rule is 'live in accordance with nature' (*Discourses* 4.4.43, 4.5.5), which is partly unpacked in the following three rules: 'keep one's "ruling principle" (*hêgemonikon*) in accordance with nature' (*Discourses* 1.15.4); 'keep one's moral character (*prohairesis*) in accordance with nature' (*Discourses* 3.4.9); and 'keep one's desires and aversions in accordance with nature' (*Discourses* 1.21.2). Others include: 'live virtuously to secure happiness, impassivity, and a good flow of life' (*Discourses* 1.4.1–11); 'only virtue is good – everything else is indifferent' (*Discourses* 2.9.15); 'follow the gods in all things' (*Discourses* 1.12.8, 4.1.89–90/98–9); 'wish for everything to happen just as it does' (*Discourses* 1.12.15; *Handbook* 8, 53); and 'endeavour to direct your actions to the appropriate performance of your duties to fulfil your social roles by "remembering who you are" [father, brother, teacher, etc.]' (*Discourses* 4.12.16; *Handbook* 30).

Chapter 2

[1] Remember that, on the one hand, desires command you to obtain what you long for and, on the other, aversions command you to avoid what you dislike. Those who fail to gain what they desire are unfortunate, whilst those who fall into what they seek to avoid are miserable. So if you seek to avoid only those things contrary to nature amongst the things that are in your power, you will accordingly fall into nothing to which you are averse; but if you seek to avoid sickness, or death, or poverty, you will be miserable. [2] Therefore, remove altogether your aversion for anything that is not in our power, and transfer it to those things contrary to nature that *are* in our power. For the time being, completely restrain your desires, for if you desire any of those things not in our power you are bound to suffer misfortune. For of those things in our power, which it would be proper to desire, none is yet within your grasp. Use only impulse and repulsion, but use even these lightly, with reservation, and without straining.

Commentary

Key terms

aversion (*ekklisis*)	**not in our power**
contrary to nature (*para phusin*)	(*ouk eph' hêmin*)
death (*thanatos*)	poverty (*penia*)
desire (noun) (*orexis*)	repulsion (*aphormê*)
impulse (*hormê*)	reservation (*hupexhairesis*)
in our power (*eph' hêmin*)	restrain (*anaireô*)
miserable (*dustuchês*)	sickness (*nosos*)
miserable, to be (*dustucheô*)	unfortunate (*atuchês*)
misfortune, to suffer (*atucheô*)	

In *Handbook* 2.1 Epictetus offers a diagnosis of human **misfortune** and misery. We are **unfortunate** and **miserable**, he says, when our **desires** are frustrated and when we have to suffer that to which we are **averse**. The slip into medical analogy with the term 'diagnosis' is deliberate. Epictetus specifically states that the philosopher's school is a doctor's surgery (*iatreion*; *Discourses* 3.23.30; see also 4.8.31), to which their students come to be cured of their ills. It is the task of Stoic ethics to provide diagnosis, prognosis, and treatment. The prognosis is clear and stark: we will be **miserable** so long as we continue seeking to avoid **sickness**, **death**, and **poverty** (and by implication anything else to which we are averse). And in 2.2 we are told the cure – we must give up our **aversion** to anything that is **not in our power**; and we must completely **restrain** our **desires**.

How we should manage our **desires** and **aversions** is the first topic in Epictetus' educational system (see 'The promise of philosophy' in the Introduction to Epictetus; *Discourses* 3.2.1), and is referred to as the 'most important and most urgent' of the three topics (*Discourses* 3.2.3). The fact of the matter, something to which we can all assuredly admit, is that when our **desires** are frustrated, or our **aversions** incurred, we react with a range of emotions whose occurrence diminishes or entirely undermines any 'good flow of life' (*euroia biou*) we may have been enjoying (however impoverished a 'flow' this might be in comparison with the Stoic ideal) – or else makes an already unsatisfactory situation even worse. These emotions (anger, frustration, disappointment, fear, or what have you) are what constitute our **misfortune** and **misery**. If our desires could be thwarted whilst we retained an unshakable equanimity, or if we could withstand that to which we are **averse** with complete calm and composure, we would surely count ourselves blessed (*eudaimôn*, no less), and if we already enjoyed such a disposition we would not accept or need Epictetus' invitation to attend his philosopher's surgery. But we simply cannot resist the charge that we are in need of the therapy that Stoic ethics offers. (For more on the medical model of ancient ethics, including Stoicism, see especially Nussbaum 1994.)

And this is what we must train ourselves in: we must let everything happen as it will with an open acceptance (*Discourses* 1.12.15–17), even those things to which we are usually **averse**, seeking to avoid *only* 'those things **contrary to nature** amongst the things that are **in our power**', and these are the passions (*pathê*), the 'disturbing or violent emotions' that constitute our **misery**. Passions are excessive impulses, '**contrary to nature**' because they are 'contrary to correct and natural reasoning' (Stob. 2.7.10a), in that any one passion is, or is dependent upon, a false judgement concerning what is good and bad for us (see DL 7.111; LS 65G3); they are 'excessive' because they are 'disobedient to the choosing reason or an irrational motion of the soul' (Stob. 2.7.10, trans. Pomeroy; see also DL 7.110); and they are '**in our power**' because it is entirely up to us how we evaluate things, and whether we assent to the judgements that sanction (or comprise) the passions (see the commentary to *Handbook* 1.5). (For more on the question as to whether we should regard a passion as identical with the false judgement to which we assent, or whether we should regard the passion as a result or consequence of assenting to a false judgement, see Inwood 1985, 130–2 and Sellars 2003, 157 n. 51.)

Are the passions alone in the category of 'those things **contrary to nature** amongst the things that are **in our power**'? Probably not. Stoics describe the disposition of the non-virtuous person as *kakos*, bad or vicious. All of us – excepting only the Stoic *sophos* – are susceptible to assenting to false judgements about what is good and bad, and what truly benefits us (virtue), and these assents are, or give rise to, the passions which are impulses to act in ways that are non-virtuous and contrary to our own interests (and thus contrary to nature – that is, contrary to our own human nature, obviously, but also contrary to cosmic nature, since it is our failure to accept the way the world goes that makes us prone to assenting to false judgements). Thus someone who is prey to the passions must necessarily be vicious, and someone who is vicious has got into that state by falling victim to the passions. This gives us reason to place the vices, alongside the passions, in the category of what is **contrary to nature** amongst the things that are **in our power**. Although it is not really the *vices* and being vicious that are directly in our power (though vicious behaviour, to be sure, is contrary to nature), but the *judgements* to which we assent that either are themselves passions, or give rise to passions (and it is the passions, conceived of as impulses, that motivate vicious actions) – it is assuredly the case that *if we can master our faculty of assent we will at one and the same time master our vicious behaviour*. When Epictetus tags on the phrase 'whatever is our own doing' to the list of items that are in our power at *Handbook* 1.1, he probably means to include virtuous and vicious behaviour. The Stoic enterprise of making progress towards virtue would be pointless or even meaningless if 'being virtuous' were not in some pretty clear-cut fashion 'up to us'. But Epictetus never asserts in so many words that 'being virtuous is in our power'. 'Virtue' is *not* one of the items specifically listed as being in our power at *Handbook* 1.1, and at *Discourses* 1.30.4 he identifies good things as 'proper moral character and proper use of impressions', which contrasts with orthodox Stoic doctrine which reserves 'good' for the virtues exclusively.

Epictetus links goodness to virtue through the notion of 'moral character' (*prohairesis*; see commentary to Chapter 4), since a proper moral character is one that manifests virtue and whose disposition is virtuous. So in saying that being virtuous or being vicious is in our power, we must be careful not to ignore the way in which Epictetus couches his own exposition. The focus of our attention for Epictetus is making proper use of impressions, and our being able to do so is necessary and sufficient for our acting virtuously, and only in this sense is being virtuous up to us. In *Fragment* 4 (= Stob. 2.8.30 = Musonius Rufus, *Fragment* 38, Lutz 1947, 135–7) Epictetus tells us that making proper use of impressions is at one and the same time freedom (*eleutheria*), a 'good flow' (*euroia*), cheerfulness (*euthumia*), and steadfastness (*eustatheia*); and these qualities of character are identified as 'the sum and substance of virtue' (trans. Oldfather).

In *Handbook* 2.2 we are told to 'completely restrain' our **desires**. Certainly, if we desire things that are not **in our power**, sooner or later our desires will be obstructed and we will be prone to frustration, annoyance, anger, or some other *pathos*, or possibly a cocktail of several *pathê* all at once. This then is the first task for the Stoic *prokoptôn* – to simply desire nothing (*Discourses* 1.4, 3.12.8, 3.22.13, 4.4.33/39, 4.8.33). In the penultimate sentence of *Handbook* 2.2 Epictetus tells us not even to desire those things '**in our power** which it would be proper to desire' – and these are the virtues, the components of a wholly virtuous disposition enjoyed by the fully wise person – because at such an early stage of training we simply do not properly understand what that disposition is like: we cannot direct our desire towards an object that we cannot represent to ourselves.

If we let our **aversion** stand guard against only assenting to false judgements and to the *pathê*, and if we suspend the faculty of **desire** completely, that leaves us needing to function practically in the world. 'How am I to eat, for example, if I do not allow myself any *desire* to eat? Must I not *desire* to do everything that I do?' No. To engage in the practical tasks of daily living we are to use **'impulse** and **repulsion'** (*Handbook* 2.2). Nature has already supplied us with what we need to get by in the world without desire – for we have in-built impulses to pursue what is appropriate for us.

The Stoic concept of **impulse** (*hormê*) was introduced briefly in the commentary to *Handbook* 1.1, and we have just seen that a passion is an 'excessive and irrational' impulse. All animals, including human beings, are driven by impulses. In the case of any animal, the occurrence of an impression gives rise immediately and automatically to an impulse for acting in a way that is appropriate for the type of animal that it is (and this is what Epictetus refers to as merely '*using* impressions'; *Discourses* 1.6.13): thus, for example, a camel that has trekked for several days across the parched desert, upon having the impression of the pool of water at an oasis, will have the impulse to drink and, if nothing intervenes to prevent this action, that is what it will do. The same applies to all actions throughout the animal kingdom, and the term 'instinct' is not an inappropriate synonym for the Stoic notion of 'impulse'. Animals are driven by their instincts. Human beings, of course, are different. Our impulses, as they do in animals, direct us often enough to what is appropriate – thus we drink when we are thirsty and eat when we are hungry – but we have a further faculty that animals lack: that of reason. And this allows us to convert any action that an impulse might urge into an *intentional* action, something we do on purpose and deliberately, in full consciousness of what we are doing and why (and this is what Epictetus refers to as '*understanding the use* of impressions' and '*making proper use* of impressions'; see *Discourses* 2.8.6 and 2.14.15–16, for instance: see also '*phantasia*' in Glossary A for many further references). In order for any action to be intentional, we have to understand the background of the situation against which we intend to act, what we hope to accomplish and why it is reasonable to suppose that *this* action will produce *that* result. For human beings, our impulses do not usually move us around as if we were puppets having our strings pulled (though that image does illustrate the nature of animal action and of people in the grip of passions) – because as self-conscious agents we can step in to change the propositions we assent to, thereby cancelling or modifying an impulse prior to any action occurring. For Epictetus, what is important is that we have to assent to the interpretations and evaluations that our impressions suggest.

Take the simple example of someone having an impression of a cake on the table before them. If they are to eat the cake, it seems that two acts of assent are required: (1) they must assent to the proposition that 'a cake is present', and (2) they must assent to the proposition that 'it would be appropriate for me to eat this cake'. Commonly, most people unacquainted with Stoic ethics take the eating of the cake to be something that is not just appropriate but something that is *good and desirable* for them. This is why being frustrated in their action to eat the cake – if it is suddenly snatched from their grasp, say – would count as something *bad and undesirable*; trivial enough, to be sure, but all the same possibly taken so seriously as to occasion an angry outburst and a sense of annoyance (or worse), for now they have assented to something extra, that being deprived of the cake is something bad for them to which an emotional response is appropriate. The Stoic *prokoptôn*, on the other hand, assents only to the judgement that eating the cake would be *appropriate* – if it is (if it is on *their own* plate and not on someone else's, amongst other things) – *and also preferred*. For the Stoic recognises that the eating of cakes (and indeed anything and everything that can happen excepting only acquiring and maintaining a virtuous disposition) is something indifferent: it is something neither good nor bad, but is preferred because it is appropriate, being in accordance with (human) nature, for nature has so arranged matters that human beings require a certain type and quantity of sustenance.

In the final sentence of *Handbook* 2.2, Epictetus urges his students to make use of their faculty of **impulse** (*hormê*) – and its opposite, **repulsion** (*aphormê*) – but 'lightly' and 'without straining', which means not taking the successful outcome of any action as really important, and not attaching their emotional well-being to what actually happens, one way or the other (see for example *Discourses* 3.24.84).

There is a technique for engaging in affairs generally that breaks our attachment to the outcome of our actions, and this is 'acting with **reservation**'. The Stoic *prokoptôn* recognises that what is in their power is not the outcome of any action, no matter how competently performed, but the intention to do virtuously what is appropriate.

[The Stoics] say that nothing happens to the good man which is contrary to his inclination (*orexis*) or his impulse or his intention, on account of the fact that he does everything of this kind with a reservation (*hupexhairesis*), and nothing which he would not want can happen unexpectedly.

(Stob. 2.7.11s, trans. Donini, Inwood and Donini 1999, 737)

To undertake something 'with **reservation**' is like contracting with oneself and saying, 'This, I believe, is what is appropriate for me, and doing it this way (to the best of my understanding) satisfies the requirements of virtue – and if this is what Zeus has planned for the world, then my action will succeed. Either way, I will have acted as I should.' Seneca says this about acting with reservation:

The safest policy is rarely to tempt [Fortune], though to keep her always in mind and to trust her in nothing. Thus: 'I shall sail unless something happens'; and 'I shall become praetor unless something prevents me'; and 'My business will be successful unless something interferes.' That is why we say that nothing happens to a wise man against his expectation.

(*On Tranquillity of Mind* 13, trans. Costa 1997, 51–2)

The wise man sets about every action with reservation: 'if nothing happens which might stop him'. For this reason we say that he always succeeds and that nothing unexpected happens to him: because within himself he considers the possibility that something will get in the way and prevent what he is proposing to do.

(*On Benefits* 4.34.4, trans. Donini, Inwood and Donini 1999, 737)

So in the face of apparent failure, the Stoic will be conscious of having done what was required, and that the failure does not in the least reflect upon them individually but indicates that what they had aimed for was not in fact what Zeus had planned for the world. And now they must move on and continue to live wisely, focusing their commitment upon what truly depends on them, and avoiding becoming attached to things that are not in their power, including the preferred outcomes of their actions. (See especially Inwood 1985, 119–26, who offers a comprehensive treatment of 'reservation'.)

Chapter 3

With respect to any of those things you find attractive or useful or have a fondness for, recall to mind what kind of thing it is, beginning with the most trifling. So if you are fond of an earthenware pot, say, 'I am fond of an earthenware pot.' Then you will not be upset if it gets broken. When you kiss your child or wife, say that you are kissing a human being; then, should they die, you will not be distressed.

Commentary

Key terms

child (*paidion*)
distress (noun) (*tarachê*)
earthenware pot (*chutra*)
human being (*anthrôpos*)

fondness for something,
  to have (*stergô*)
wife (*gunê*)

The notion of 'reservation' introduced in *Handbook* 2.2 underpins the outlook that Epictetus presents in Chapter 3. Not only can we *act* with reservation, but we can face life in a completely general sense *with reservation*. The training that we are embarking upon, as we have seen, has as its aim the proper use of impressions so that we do not assent to false judgements in consequence of which we will inevitably fall prey to the disturbing emotions (*pathê*) which, in turn (because they are excessive impulses, 'contrary to nature'; see commentary to *Handbook* 2.1) inevitably propel us into vicious actions – and this is to lose what we understand to be the goal of living (*telos*), our capacity to fully flourish and be happy (*eudaimonia*) and experience a 'good flow of life' (*euroia biou*).

Losing what we value, the topic of Chapter 3, is obviously a significant source for a range of disturbing emotions. Everything in the world is transient, from the flower that blooms for but a day, to the very mountains of the earth that are doomed eventually, in the fullness of time, to be ground into dust and washed away. All our possessions, from the most lowly, whose loss occasions merely a moment's inconvenience, to those we most treasure, can be ours only temporarily: they wear, they break, they get lost, they get stolen. And so too for the people that we love – they too are transient, destined by the way that Zeus has made the world to be our companions only temporarily, for like all living creatures, every **human being** must one day die.

The disposition that the Stoic *prokoptôn* is in training to perfect is one that can withstand, with equanimity and with no diminution of their 'good flow of life' (*euroia biou*), even the loss of loved ones. Clearly we have a long way to travel, for in all likelihood within a short time of reading this sentence, something will happen – a plate will be broken, the washing-machine will break down, or some such triviality will occur

– in response to which we will get upset. Our emotional response is what undermines our 'good flow of life', for a 'good flow of life' is broken and disrupted even by occasional upsets. Facing the ups and downs of daily life 'with reservation' will arm us against assenting to false judgements that anything bad has happened to which an emotional response is appropriate.

With respect to Epictetus' example of the **earthenware pot**, I can contract with myself and say, 'I will have the use of my earthenware pot until such time as it gets broken (or lost, or stolen).' Its eventually being lost to me, sooner or later, is pretty much inevitable, and if I can accept the way things are in a deep and wholehearted fashion, I can preserve my 'good flow of life' (*euroia biou*) with respect to any misfortune. For as we have seen, **distress** is the result of failing to obtain what is desired or of having to incur that to which one is averse. If we can successfully apply the lesson of *Handbook* 2.2 and completely restrain our desires, we will cease to be vulnerable to any of the things that can happen, and this is why in *Handbook* 1.3 Epictetus holds out the promise that Stoic training will make his students immune to all harm.

The Stoic *prokoptôn*, in 'living with reservation', can accept anything that happens, for the things that happen always do so in accordance with the will of Zeus: these things lie in the province of things that are not in our power, and our concern should never be to inappropriately desire that they should happen otherwise or that we should be able to make them happen otherwise (see for instance *Discourses* 4.7.20). Our task is to judge matters properly, to 'make proper use of impressions', and to respond appropriately to *whatever does happen.*

And this includes our accepting the loss of **human beings** generally, and of our **wives**, husbands, **children**, and other loved ones. Here, we live with reservation by saying to ourselves, 'So-and-so, whom I dearly love, will be my companion in life for so long as they live, for so long as this is the will of Zeus.' And should we lose them before they lose us, we will know that this is what Zeus has planned for the world all along, and now we must live without them, and if our progress is substantial and enduring, such a blow will have no power to compromise our *eudaimonia.*

As we start out on our training, it seems astonishing that such an outlook could ever be realised, and progress towards it, as Epictetus says in *Handbook* 1.1, will 'require more than modest effort'. This is why Epictetus suggests a training programme, one in which we begin with the 'most trifling' of things to acquire the capacity to use our impressions properly and not to get upset at the loss of **earthenware pots** and the like, for this is the nature of things, to be broken and lost – and then to move on to other things, and of course people, of which we are far more **fond**.

The end of this training is to make ourselves immune to the shock of unexpected events, for they are unexpected only in terms of their details (what, who, when, how); in general terms we have known all along that **earthenware pots** get broken and that **human beings** die. This is why on being told that his son had died Anaxagoras said, 'I knew my child was mortal' (*TD* 3.30/58; cf. *Discourses* 3.24.105), why Epictetus says of mortality, 'For such is the world we live in' (*Discourses* 3.24.29, trans. Hard), and why he says more generally, 'Whenever you grow attached to something, do not act as though it were one of those things that cannot be taken away' (*Discourses* 3.24.84, trans. Oldfather; see also *Discourses* 3.24.11/27–8/58–60/84–8; *MA* 11.34).

It is important to stress that the background against which the Stoic *prokoptôn* endeavours to be prepared for the worst and never to be overwhelmed by anything unexpectedly is that of *never finding fault with anything that Zeus bestows*, always bearing willingly everything that is inevitable, for our *eudaimonia* and 'good flow of life' (*euroia biou*) depend not at all on what we possess, or with whom we travel on life's road, but exclusively on the character of our inner dispositions (see *Discourses* 1.12.15/17/21, 1.14.16, 2.6.10; *Handbook* 53; the earthenware pot example also occurs at *Discourses* 3.24.84–8, 4.1.111–13; and for more on the general topic of this commentary, see especially *Discourses* 3.24; *Fragment* 4; Inwood 1985, 119–26; Stephens 1996).

(The theme of this chapter is picked up again at *Handbook* 11, 14 and 26.)

Chapter 4

When you are about to undertake some task, remind yourself what sort of business it is. If you are going out to bathe, bring to mind what happens at the baths: there will be those who splash you, those who will jostle you, some will be abusive to you, and others will steal from you. And thus you will undertake the affair more securely if you say to yourself from the start, 'I wish to take a bath, but also to keep my moral character in accordance with nature.' Do likewise with every undertaking. For thus, if anything should happen that interferes with your bathing, be ready to say, 'Oh well, it was not only this that I wanted, but also to keep my moral character in accordance with nature, and I cannot do that if I am irritated by things that happen.'

Commentary

Key terms

irritated, to feel (*aganakteô*)	**moral character** (*prohairesis*)
in accordance with nature	**task, undertaking** (*ergon*)
(*kata phusin*)	

Many of Epictetus' students probably visited the public baths in Nicopolis as a matter of daily routine, and those who did not would nevertheless have gone fairly regularly. Over and above the practical business of attending to washing the body, the public baths offered a venue where one would meet one's friends and associates, take a snack, and indulge in light exercise. Everyday, at the conclusion of Epictetus' classes (possibly as early as lunch-time), it is undoubtedly the case that a group of students would make their way to the baths where – at least sometimes we may presume – they would continue to debate their lessons, discuss their essays, or gripe about the hardships of student life far from home (that students wrote essays is suggested by *Discourses* 2.1.34, 3.26.3, 4.4.14/17, 4.5.36; that students sometimes complained about their lot is suggested by 2.21.14).

The fact that what happens at the public baths – like much in life – can constitute a source of **irritation** cannot have escaped the notice of even the most dirty student who bathed there only infrequently (but see *Discourses* 4.11, 'On Cleanliness'). Epictetus' example of the baths would have related directly to the personal experience of every student, for there is no denying that attending the baths hoping for a pleasant, relaxing afternoon only to fall victim to other people's splashing, jostling, abuse and stealing will annoy and **irritate**. Some students will recall feeling intensely irritated by even the most feeble abuse, let alone by finding that all their clothes have been stolen. And this is something we seek to avoid, for this is to fall prey to a passion (anger, annoyance, **irritation**, or what have you), to judge that something is bad when it is really indifferent, and to lapse into vice (to threaten or even hit someone, return the abuse, or curse the gods). When that happens we lose our *euroia* ('good flow'), and *eudaimonia* is as far away as ever.

We have already seen that the competent *prokoptôn* will enjoy their bath 'with reservation' – 'if nothing prevents me, and if this is the will of Zeus, then I will enjoy my bath' – and in Chapter 4 Epictetus expands further on the exercise of preparing ourselves in advance for the things that happen (introduced in *Handbook* 3). If, in this sense, we expect them, we will not be surprised and taken unawares should any of them happen. And so with anything that we **undertake**. For the Stoic sets about their **tasks** with two objectives: in this case (1) to have a relaxing bath, but also (2) to keep their '**moral character**' **in accordance with nature**. If we are thwarted with respect to the first, well, that is the way of things, that is how things sometimes work out; but with respect to the second, we need never fail, and never to fail is to enjoy a *euroia biou*, a 'good flow of life', to be *eudaimôn*, to flourish and be happy in a complete sense.

Just twice does Epictetus mention the orthodox Stoic principle that only virtue is good, vice is evil, whilst everything else is indifferent (at *Discourses* 2.9.15 and 2.19.13). *Aretê*, 'excellence' or 'virtue', is not used at all in the *Handbook*, and only fairly sparingly in the *Discourses*. Instead, to explain where the good for human beings lies, he employs the concept of '**moral character**', *prohairesis* (see Table 4 in Appendix 2 for alternative translations). This concept plays a central role in Epictetus' exposition of Stoic ethics, and 'is the most noteworthy feature of his entire philosophy' (Long 2002, 28). Our **moral character** is the faculty (*dunamis*) we use to make proper use of impressions, given to us by God (*Discourses* 1.17.27, 2.23.6–7, 4.1.100) to be the one thing that is wholly in our power (1.22.10, 2.5.4) that cannot be taken away (3.26.24), and whose nature is such that it cannot be harmed (3.19.2, 4.5.23). The good for human beings lies in this one thing alone, for each of us to perfect our **moral character**, to bring it into harmony with nature, making it 'elevated, free, unhindered, unimpeded, trustworthy, and honourable' (*hupsêlos, eleutheros, akôlutos, anempodistos, pistos, aidêmôn*; 1.4.18). In the passages where he discusses *prohairesis*, Epictetus implicitly identifies virtue – the only good thing – with having one's **moral character** manifest the proper disposition (see especially 1.8.16, 1.29.1–3, 3.10.18, 4.12.7–8); and with respect to the practical business of getting through life, instead of expounding dryly that 'only virtue is good', he explains virtue in terms of the proper functioning or quality of one's **moral character**, the chief function being, of course, to make proper use of impressions – do that consistently, and you have attained virtue. At *Discourses* 2.23.5–29, Epictetus tells us that *prohairesis* is the faculty that oversees and makes use of all our other faculties. What we should look at, what we should believe, how we should speak, and how we exercise *all* our faculties, is determined by our *prohairesis*, or more precisely, by the disposition of our *prohairesis*, for if we can maintain this one ruling faculty in the right condition, then everything else we do by means of the other faculties will be done well – if not, they will be done badly, and we will ourselves be bad (see 2.23.28). And upon this depends our securing happiness (*eudaimonia*; 2.23.29).

Epictetus identifies *prohairesis* with our very selves. At *Discourses* 3.1.40 he says to his student: 'You are not flesh, nor hair, but *prohairesis*' (see also 2.22.20). It is the locus of our self-conscious experience of the world, of our agency, of our power to act, to form intentions on the basis of our judgements and understanding of what is happening, and to carry them through. The task of the Stoic *prokoptôn* is to make their *prohairesis* beautiful (*kalos*), accomplished by disregarding their worthless (*phaulos*) judgements (*Discourses* 3.1.42; see also 4.8.3), and in the most general of senses this means giving up our concerns for 'external things' (*ta ektos*; *Discourses* 3.3.8, 4.7.10, 4.10.1, 4.12.15).

External things are specifically identified as being *aprohairetos*, outside the scope of our *prohairesis*, not in our power (see *Discourses* 2.5.4–5, 3.12.5), and these things are 'nothing to us' (1.30.3), neither good nor evil (2.1.4, 2.13.10, 2.16.1). Seeing that this is the case is the first step towards maintaining our *prohairesis* **in accordance with nature**. Although external things are beyond our power to influence directly and completely, obviously we should do our best to do things responsibly, appropriately and to the best of our abilities (*virtuously*, no less; see especially *Discourses* 2.5.6–9). But it is not the outcomes of our actions that matter, but the attitudes, outlooks and intentions that find their expression in our actions, and constitute our own experience of being.

Keeping one's *prohairesis* **in accordance with nature** is to maintain it in a state that is best suited for living – as a human being – as nature intends (and for the Stoics, nature, construed as intelligible, intelligent, rational and purposive, is identical with Zeus), and this can be accomplished by anyone who models their outlook and their conduct on Stoic principles. For one's *prohairesis* to be **in accord with nature** means accepting and being always mindful of a specific set of judgements – that some things are in our power and that those that are not are 'nothing to us' (*Handbook* 1.5), that everything happens as Zeus wills with respect to which we are wholly accepting, that only the disposition of our *prohairesis* is truly good or bad, and that harm to our **undertakings** and possessions is absolutely no harm to *us* (and further, that as sociable creatures with obligations to others we should set about fulfilling our responsibilities in ways appropriate to the roles we have, and to do this in good spirits, understanding that doing so is how we should discharge our service to God; see for example *Handbook* 17, 30, 43; see Introduction to Epictetus, 'The Discipline of Action').

Back at the baths things are not going well. We have been splashed, jostled, insulted, and now we find that our clothes have been stolen. For today at least, we have failed in the first thing we aimed at: a relaxing bath. But shall we also fail at the second thing the Stoic *prokoptôn* must always strive to secure – a well disposed *prohairesis*? Whether other people splash us, bump into us, behave rudely, or steal our possessions is not in our power. Sometimes such things happen, for no matter how puzzling this might seem from our individual perspectives, this is the will of Zeus. But how we respond *is* in our power. Thus we can do as most people are apt to do: hurl abuse back at those who splash us or insult us, give a good shove to the person who jostles us, and curse the gods as much as the thief when our clothes are stolen. But where does that get us? About as far away from a 'good flow of life' (*euroia biou*) as is possible.

The worst thing that can happen is that we fall prey to the passions and become angry, frustrated and **irritated**; *that* is the only harm we need ever fear. So when we face **irritation**, disappointments and failures, such as what happened at the baths, we should be able quite spontaneously to affirm that what we prefer is for our **undertakings** to succeed, but what we want is for affairs to transpire as Zeus wills, even if this frustrates our preferences, and for our **moral characters** to maintain a disposition unaffected by passion (*apatheia*), distress (*alupia*), fear (*aphobia*), and troubles (*ataraxia*), and therefore free (*eleutheros*; *Discourses* 4.3.8). All we have to do to achieve this state of mind is to use our impressions properly, and upon hearing an insult, or seeing that our clothes have gone, to immediately and automatically refuse to assent to the judgement that anything bad is at hand, for it is not.

(Bathing will appear again in Chapter 45. For more on baths and bathing, see Balsdon 2002, 26–32; Carcopino 1991, 277–86; Dupont 1992, 263–4; Fagan 1999; Guhl and Koner 1989, 396–406, 507–11; Johnston 2002, 265–77; Shelton 1998, 309–14. For Epictetus on why the Stoic *prokoptôn* should care for their body and keep it clean, see *Discourses* 4.11. For references to *prohairesis* in the *Discourses*, see the entry in Glossary A. For more on *prohairesis*, see Brittain and Brennan (*Simplicius*) 2002a or 2002b, 22–4; Dobbin 1991 and 1998, 76–7; Inwood 1995, 123, 240–2; Kahn 1996, 251–5; Long 1996c, 162; Long 1996g, 275–7, 281; Long 2002, 210–20; Rist 1969, 228–32. For a table of various translations of *prohairesis* adopted by scholars and translators, see Table 4 in Appendix 2.)

Chapter 5

It is not circumstances themselves that trouble people, but their judgements about those circumstances. For example, death is nothing terrible, for if it were, it would have appeared so to Socrates; but having the opinion that death is terrible, *this* is what is terrible. Therefore, whenever we are hindered or troubled or distressed, let us never blame others, but ourselves, that is, our own judgements. The uneducated person blames others for their failures; those who have just begun to be instructed blame themselves; those whose learning is complete blame neither others nor themselves.

Commentary

Key terms

agitate, disturb, or trouble the mind (*tarassô*)
blame (verb) (*aitiaomai*)
death (*thanatos*)
distressed, to be (*lupeô*)

hinder (verb) (*empodizô*)
judgements (*dogmata*)
Socrates (*Sôkratês*)
terrible (*deinos*)
uneducated (*apaideutos*)

Our 'good flow of life' (*euroia biou*) is disrupted by the **disturbing** or violent emotions (*pathê*) which arise when we assent to false **judgements**. As we saw in the discussion of Chapter 1, the shift from assenting to an interpretive **judgement** (that, at the baths for example, our clothes are missing) to an evaluative **judgement** (that this is bad for me and it is appropriate for me to respond emotionally) is virtually automatic. Interrupting this movement from correct interpretation to false evaluation is the chief task of Stoic training. So Epictetus reminds us again in Chapter 5 that our **troubles** stem not from *what* actually happens, but from our (evaluative) **judgements** *about* the things that happen.

Epictetus appears now to offer a proof of this. The second sentence offers the following argument: (1) If **death** is **terrible** it would have appeared so to **Socrates**; (2) **Death** did *not* appear to be **terrible** to **Socrates**; (3) Therefore **death** is not **terrible**. The value of this argument lies not in the fact that there is at least one person who does not find **death terrible**, for we may suppose that not finding **death terrible** is indeed actually shared by a variety of people, including sometimes insane people, we may be sure, and others who subscribe to any number of outlooks and beliefs. This argument has no weight at all were we to learn that **Socrates** was in fact mad. The value of the argument lies in the *personal qualities of Socrates as a philosopher*, and I think Epictetus means to offer a more general proof that **troubles** result from faulty **judgements** with the following tacit syllogism: (A) If **Socrates** (a fully wise person) holds a doctrine to be true, then we will be wise to hold that doctrine ourselves; (B) **Socrates** holds to be true the doctrine that **troubles** result from the **judgements** that people have about circumstances (and not from the circumstances themselves); (C) therefore we should ourselves hold to this very doctrine. Premiss (B) is supported by considering how **Socrates** himself faced what is commonly taken to be the most **terrible** of all catastrophes: one's own **death**.

'**Socrates** is the philosopher with whom the Stoics most closely aligned themselves' (Long 1996h, 16), and interestingly Epictetus mentions, quotes or paraphrases **Socrates** (who, of course, was not a Stoic) over 50 times in the *Discourses* (and seven times in the *Handbook*), slightly exceeding the total number of times he makes references to Zeno, Chrysippus and Cleanthes, his own Stoic predecessors. At the age of 70 in 399 BC **Socrates** was found guilty of impiety and corrupting the youth by an Athenian jury, and sentenced to death by poison. **Socrates** does not believe that his own death can harm him, and Epictetus paraphrases Plato's account (at *Apology* 30c–d) four times (at *Discourses* 1.29.18, 2.2.15, 3.23.21, and *Handbook* 53.4): 'Anytus and Meletus can kill me, but they cannot harm me.' Indeed, **Socrates** declares that his accusers, Anytus and Meletus, harm themselves far more by putting someone to death unjustly (see *Discourses* 4.1.123), and he says this in his concluding remarks in the *Apology*:

> You too must be of good hope as regards death, gentlemen of the jury, and keep this one truth in mind, that a good man cannot be harmed either in life or in death, and that his affairs are not neglected by the gods.
>
> (Plato, *Apology* 41c–d, trans. Grube
> in Brickhouse and Smith 2000, 235)

Other helpful and interesting extracts include *Apology* 29a–b, where **Socrates** points out that no one knows the truth about death, and that perhaps it is the greatest of blessings, and *Apology* 40c–41a, where **Socrates** points out that death is either 'nothing' and the dead have no experience of anything but sleep a sound and dreamless sleep for all eternity, or a relocating of the soul to an afterlife where it may meet with all those who have already died (see Reeve 1989, 180–3 for **Socrates** on death and a discussion of this passage). In *Gorgias* 523a–524a, **Socrates** expounds the belief that the souls of the dead are conveyed to an afterlife that is commensurate with their moral standing in life. These passages are included by Brickhouse and Smith (2000, 252–61) in their discussion of **Socrates** on death and the afterlife. At the very end of the *Republic* (614b–621d), in the story of Er, **Socrates** presents a myth of the afterlife and reincarnation (see Appendix 1).

When we are **hindered**, **troubled** or **distressed** we have only ourselves to **blame**, for we have assented to a false **judgement** that something that has happened is either good or bad when really it is indifferent, and thus we undermine our 'good flow' (*euroia*).

The overall Stoic theory of how and why the **disturbing** or violent passions arise that we have been examining suggests that people fall into one of three types: (1) those who are **uneducated** in the theory, (2) those whose instruction is underway but not complete, and (3) the fully wise person whose instruction is complete and whose mindfulness of Stoic living is consistent and permanent, and who thereby lives wholly successfully as nature or Zeus intends.

The **uneducated** person thinks that when their undertakings fail they are in receipt of something bad (and conversely that an undertaking which succeeds constitutes something good; see *Handbook* 6 and commentary) such that when they are upset by a setback such as the loss of their clothes at the baths, they will **blame** their passions on the thief. The thief, we may suppose, really is responsible for taking the clothes, but the Stoic denies that they are on that account also responsible for the emotional reaction of the person who suffers the loss. This is why the person whose training is underway will **blame** *themselves* for any upset they experience; they realise that their disturbance results from their false evaluation that something bad has occurred, and this gives them the chance to rectify their error. The fully wise person whose Stoic training is complete will never be in a position to **blame** anyone at all (not even themselves), because this person has secured a 'good flow' (*euroia*) that is stable and enduring – they simply do not assent to false evaluations, but pass through life calmly accepting and responding appropriately to every circumstance, *such that nothing ever happens to occasion blame*. This person is wholly *apathês*, 'without passion'.

(See *Discourses* 3.17.9. For further references to the notion of troubles being caused by false judgements, see *Discourses* 1.19.8, 2.1.13, 2.16.22–6, 3.3.18–19, 3.17.9, 3.19.3, 4.5.28. For more on the distinction between the educated and the uneducated person, see Kerford 1978. See MA 8.47. Socrates appears in the *Handbook* five times, in this chapter and at 5, 32.3, 33.12 and 46.1; he is quoted twice, in 53.3 and 53.4. For the numerous references to Socrates in the *Discourses*, see the very end of the commentary to *Handbook* 51.)

Chapter 6

Do not take pride in any excellence that is not your own. If a horse were to say proudly, 'I am beautiful,' one could put up with that. But when you say proudly, 'I have a beautiful horse,' remember that you are boasting about something good that belongs to the horse. What, then, belongs to *you*? The use of impressions. Whenever you are in accordance with nature regarding the way you use impressions, then be proud, for then you will be proud of a good that is your own.

Commentary

Key terms

excellence (*proterêma*)   use of impressions
good (adjective) (*agathos*)   (*chrêsis phantasiôn*)
in accordance with nature
   (*kata phusin*)

Having just discussed in Chapter 5 how people respond to circumstances they take to be bad, Epictetus in Chapter 6 addresses the converse alternative of how people respond to circumstances they take to be **good**. Sometimes, to be sure, the possessions we have about us may exhibit features of **excellence** and qualities of various kinds. We may, for example, possess a fine house, a superb car, or even an **excellent** horse. The mistake that the uneducated person makes is to think that owning such things constitutes something truly good, that they are thereby truly benefited.

Assenting to the false judgement that the beauty of one's horse is a good results in the first instance, obviously, not in any disturbing or violent passion, but does result in a *pathos* nevertheless – in this case, pride, which is a species of pleasure, 'an elation of the soul disobedient to reason [occasioned] by forming a fresh opinion that a good is present, in the face of which it is appropriate to be elated' (Stob. 10b, trans. Pomeroy).

The horse and its beauty are external things which do not depend on us, and the judgement that they can be of real value is a mistake, and going about our affairs feeling proud of the horse, over and above simply being a misrepresentation of how the world is, and detrimental in that sense, it is possible that under the influence of this pride we may lapse into vice, declaring for example, 'My horse is more beautiful than yours, therefore I am better than you' (see *Handbook* 44), and that would be to render an injustice (a trivial enough example, admittedly, but the point is sound) – for *our* **excellence**, if our efforts to make moral progress should bear fruit, cannot possibly have anything to do with the horse, no matter how wonderful it is. And in judging incorrectly that the beauty of the horse is really something good for us, we also expose ourselves to the possibility of falling into disturbing passions, as would happen when the horse becomes sick, or gets injured, or dies, or is abused by someone, or is stolen; for in our error, any of these things happening will arouse in us passions of various sorts, including disappointment, anxiety, frustration, grief, and anger, and again we will have ruined our 'good flow of life' (*euroia biou*).

Epictetus suggests that the pride we should feel is that whose object is our own Stoic practice, directed at our capacity to **use impressions in accordance with nature** and never make false evaluations as to what is **good** and bad for us. This pride must be of a different character to that concerning the horse, and cannot be a *pathos*; it is constituted by an awareness of our own progress and arises in response to the Stoic mindfulness we are trying to cultivate, and Epictetus may be implying that it is a species of *chara* ('joy'), one of the *eupatheiai* ('good feelings') experienced habitually by the fully wise person (see Glossary A).

Chapter 7

Just as on a voyage, when the ship has anchored, if you go ashore to get water you may also pick up a shell-fish or a vegetable from the path, but you should keep your thoughts fixed on the ship, and you should look back frequently in case the captain calls, and, if he should call, you must give up all these other things to avoid being bound and thrown on board like a sheep; so in life also, if instead of a vegetable and a shell-fish you are given a wife and a child, nothing will prevent you from taking them – but if the captain calls, give up all these things and run to the ship without even turning to look back. And if you are old, do not even go far from the ship, lest you are missing when the call comes.

Commentary

Key terms

child (*paidion*)	**wife** (*gunaikarion*,
captain (*kubernêtês*)	diminutive of *gunê*)

This story of coming ashore from a sea voyage is the sole instance of a parable or fictional narrative (such that it is) in the whole of Epictetus' thought, though whether there were other examples in those portions of

Arrian's writings that are now lost to us we will never know. The **captain**, whose ship has conveyed us to this spot, is of course God, the 'pilot of the universe' (Simpl. 33.40 = Brittain and Brennan 2002a, 77) who remains aboard the ship, ever-present, preparing for the moment of His own choosing when He will summon us back on board. The parable obviously intends to represent symbolically, and in the simplest of terms, what living a life amounts to. The shore we are taken to represents the time and place in which we will live, and the arrival and departure of the ship represent our coming into life and our eventual leaving it. God is in charge of our entering upon life and our departure from it, but between those two points how we conduct ourselves is entirely up to us. Whatever we direct ourselves to, whatever possessions may come our way upon which we engage ourselves (symbolised by the shell-fish and the vegetable and later interpreted as a **wife** and **child** by Epictetus who appears not to be able to resist making a basic analysis of his own parable), we must always bear in mind that the **captain** will soon enough call us back to the ship.

Life, then, is merely a sojourn, for however long we may remain on the shore, our stay here is all the same temporary, and all of the people we come to know, including our own families and those most dear to us, are of course fellow sojourners brought here by God, destined to be carried off again by God when that suits His plans.

The point of the parable is to encourage us to adopt the right attitudes to our lives, to God, our possessions, and those with whom we live. We must be ready to give up everything freely and willingly. Our final illness, however brief or extended, must of course be a trauma to the body, but it need not be a trauma to our minds, that is, to our moral character (*prohairesis*), for we must welcome and embrace everything that God does, even when this includes His designs on how and when we must leave life, 'run to the ship', and be carried off across the sea and into that mystery whence we came. We know that when the time comes we must willingly make room for those who must come ashore after us, so that they too will have the opportunity to flourish as rational beings should and participate in and enjoy the great festival that is the world God has made (see *Discourses* 1.9.16, 3.13.14, 3.26.28–31, 4.1.103–8).

As we have seen, Stoics hold that the things in life with which we occupy and concern ourselves are indifferent with respect to being good or bad for us; indeed, having life itself is nothing more than a preferred indifferent. Our good fortune to have been given life, to have been brought ashore by God, consists wholly and exclusively in virtue, in the disposition of our moral character (*prohairesis*), and the way in which we exercise our powers of agency, in virtuous activity.

Chapter 8

Do not demand that things should happen just as you wish, but wish them to happen just as they do, and all will be well.

Commentary

Key terms

flow well (*euroeô*)   **wish** (verb) (*thelô*)

'All will be well' translates the verb *euroeô*, meaning 'to flow well' (the only time this expression occurs in the *Handbook*), and refers specifically to Zeno's definition of happiness as the end or goal of human life being *euroia biou*, a 'good flow' of life' (Stob. 2.7.6e = LS 63A2). One's 'good flow' of life' is realised by living in accordance with nature, that is, by living in accordance with one's own human nature (by pursuing what is appropriate, virtuously, rationally and consistently), but also by living in accordance with cosmic nature, and it is the latter objective that Epictetus alludes to in Chapter 8.

The world will take the course that it will, and the vast majority of events will occur just as they do regardless of our **wishes**, though of course there remains a small proportion of events that turn out to be authored by us. But even here, as we have seen, the outcomes of our actions are not in our power, and even when we aim with confidence at a specific outcome, what results, for whatever reason, may not actually be what we had wanted. Only sometimes will events beyond our control (or over which we attempt to exert no influence) accord with our **wishes**, and similarly with respect to events that follow upon our actions – only sometimes will we get what we want.

Obviously, there is plenty of room for events to frustrate our **wishes** and distress us, and this observation also applies to events brought about by other people, for here we are liable, at least occasionally, to be angered by these people and suffer a *pathos* (a disturbing or violent emotion) in addition to other *pathê* that merely express dissatisfaction with events generally. And as we have seen, falling prey to any of the *pathê* is how we lose our 'good flow' of life' (*euroia biou*). To protect ourselves we need only to resist assenting to unpleasant or false impressions by making 'proper use of impressions' and testing them (see commentary to

Handbook 1.5; *Discourses* 2.18.24, 2.22.5, 3.2.8, 3.12.15, 3.24.108, 4.3.7).

But if we **wish** positively for everything to occur just as it does – by contracting in advance so to speak with each event to say to it 'this is what I want' or 'this is what God wants, so I want it also' – we can forestall having to defend ourselves against impressions that urge an incorrect evaluation that something bad or unwanted has occurred that sanctions a *pathos* (this is something bad for me to which it is appropriate to react emotionally), because in adopting this outlook we are declaring in advance that nothing bad ever happens, and this, in effect (for the Stoic *sophos*, at any rate), is already to have evaluated every impression in advance of its occurring as representing something good, desirable, and in accordance with the will of God. But in striving to adopt the role of the Stoic *prokoptôn*, responding to events that constitute the destruction of our property, the humiliating collapse of our enterprises and other sorts of dispreferred eventualities, we may be doing well merely to accept the inevitable without going so far as to declare them positively desirable; these are things that must happen if God is to make the world according to His plan, and suffering this fate is how we contribute to that plan – the leap to embracing these things as *good* is at this stage a leap too far for us, though we know that the more we can sustain our dispassion the closer we approach a '**good flow** of life' (*euroia biou*).

If something happens that frustrates an action that we believe is appropriate (without, of course, frustrating us emotionally) we must move on and do what is appropriate in the new circumstances, perhaps attempting to do something for a second time, or admonishing a wrong-doer (but dispassionately and 'with reservation', not hoping for any particular outcome). We must invest our hopes not in the things that happen, but in our capacities to face them as human beings. Nothing that happens can prevent us from **wishing** that it should have happened just as it did, or prevent us **wishing** that *everything* should happen just as it will.

The topic of this chapter reminds me of something Seneca comments on in a letter to Lucilius:

> I discovered in the Stoic writer Hecaton [pupil of Panaetius, head of the Stoic school from *c.* 129 BC] his remark that removing one's desires is also an effective cure for fear. 'Cease to hope,' he says, 'and you will cease to fear.' … Although seemingly incongruous, hope and fear are really closely related … for fear follows hope. … Both belong

to a mind in suspense, a mind made anxious by thoughts about the future.

(Seneca, *Ep.* 5.7–8, with omissions)

Someone who desires, **wishes** or hopes for something in the future exposes themselves immediately to anxiety for fear that what they hope for will be frustrated by forces beyond their control. The way to prevent expectation from developing into a *pathos* and undermining our '**good flow**' (*euroia*) is to await only that which actually occurs, for whatever does occur we already know that we have the faculties we need to cope, and need not hesitate to address God and say:

Bring on me now, O Zeus, whatever difficulty you will, for I have the means and the resources granted to me by yourself to bring honour to myself through whatever may come to pass.

(Epictetus, *Discourses* 1.6.37, trans. Hard)

Epictetus seems to be saying in Chapter 8 that **wishing** for what actually happens is *sufficient* for a '**good flow** of life' (*euroia biou*). If so, and I think this is the correct interpretation, one may wonder whether all the paraphernalia of Stoic ethics is really required if all we need to do is change our outlook on events. But here's the difficulty – changing our outlook in this way cannot be compared to putting on a different hat, or drinking tea instead of coffee; we cannot decide to do it and then just do it. To alter our outlook on the world in the way Epictetus advocates in this chapter means changing our very selves, it means shaping our own *prohairesis* (moral character; see Chapter 4 and commentary) to respond differently and automatically to our impressions, recognising that our own *aretê*, moral excellence, is the only good thing, and that our being free from troubles (*atarachos*) requires finding the insight that nothing is really troubling except our own response to things, which can be accomplished by embracing Stoic philosophy as both an intellectual exercise and a practical exercise that will call for a sustained effort analogous to that undertaken by an athlete in training (see Introduction to Epictetus, 'Metaphors for life'; *Discourses* 4.4.11–13, 3.15.1–13 = *Handbook* 29). We cannot just **wish** for things to happen as they do and marvel at how easy it is to be *apathês* (free from passion): we have to learn how to wish differently, and to do that we will have to transform our soul.

Chapter 9

Illness interferes with one's body, but not with one's moral character, unless one so wishes. Lameness interferes with one's leg, but not with one's moral character. Say this to yourself regarding everything that happens to you, for you will find that what happens interferes with something else, but not with you.

Commentary

Key terms

body (*sôma*)   **moral character** (*prohairesis*)

Some of the things that happen will, of course, concern our **bodies**, so in adopting the outlook discussed in Chapter 8, if this is to be accomplished in a thoroughgoing manner, the Stoic *prokoptôn* must also commit themselves to wishing for whatever happens concerning their health and physical constitution. Epictetus presses a strict dichotomy between what is truly ours, what is completely and always in our power, and everything else that is external to our agency; and our **bodies** are external to our agency, belonging to that part of Zeus' cosmic plan over which we have no direct control. The *prokoptôn* will, of course, make every effort to stay in good health and avoid physical harm to their **body**, but if, despite their efforts, they become sick or disabled (whether that be permanently or temporarily), they will not mind. They will not mind because their *prohairesis* (**moral character**) – their capacity to assent to impressions as they should, to form intentions to fulfil their duties and to virtuously pursue what is in accordance with nature – has not been harmed. As Epictetus says, and we believe he is talking from personal experience, lameness interferes with one's leg, and not with one's **moral character**.

The things external to our agency are the *adiaphora*, the indifferent things – indifferent with respect to being good or bad, because, so the Stoics say, the only thing that can be good or bad is the condition of our **moral character** and how we use it, how we exercise our power of agency in our disposition and conduct.

Illness and disability may affect what we do in a practical sense, but they cannot affect what we do in a moral sense and, as we have seen, it is what we do in the moral sense that constitutes our *eudaimonia*. Illness and disability cannot prevent us from striving to act wisely, from dealing with others justly, from maintaining self-restraint and facing our difficulties with courage. Similarly, no illness or disability, just in the fact of our suffering it, can cause us to lapse into any of the *pathê* (violent or disturbing emotions), and this means that a 'good flow of life' (*euroia biou*) is no less attainable by those who are sick or disabled than it is by those who are fully fit.

I am inclined to the thought that Epictetus needs to qualify his remarks in this chapter with the proviso 'all things being equal'. Sometimes they are not equal, as would be the case for the person who suffers the misfortune of an illness or accident that *does* affect their **moral character** – for surely that occurs in the case of advanced dementia, a head injury sufficiently traumatic to result in serious brain damage, or a major stroke. This person truly is unfortunate. Their condition is hopeless; *eudaimonia*, or progress towards it, is permanently beyond their grasp. The plight of this pitiable person is not discussed in Stoic writings, and the reason is perhaps a simple one – there is no point. The person whose mental faculties are diminished or disrupted beyond a certain point falls out of the moral sphere: they cannot make proper use of impressions because they cannot assent to their interpretative and evaluative judgements, and possibly they do not even have these judgements, but respond to events more in the manner of animals. We are all vulnerable to this catastrophe, but until it falls upon us, if ever it does, we must – when it is our lot – care for those who have already suffered it and support others who do so.

So, all things being equal, anything and everything that happens to us can never interfere with our **moral character**. The only harm that can occur is harm to our undertakings, and if we ever become frustrated at some undertaking being obstructed this is because we have made the error of failing to distinguish between what in essence we are, *agents*, and the objectives we strive to secure as *agents*. The only objective that truly matters is that of making progress towards *aretê*, moral excellence, the condition of our **moral character** that secures *eudaimonia*. If we conduct ourselves as we should, we have already attained complete success regardless of what happens in consequence of our actions and whether or not we obtain the results we had hoped for.

Chapter 10

On every occasion when something happens to you, remember to turn to yourself to see what capacity you have for dealing with it. If you are attracted to a beautiful boy or woman, you will find that self-control is the capacity to use for that. If hardship befalls you, you will find endurance; if abuse, you will find patience. Make this your habit and you will not be carried away by impressions.

Commentary

Key terms

abuse (noun) (*loidoria*)	endurance (*karteria*)
become accustomed or	hardship (*ponos*)
habituated to something	impression (*phantasia*)
(*ethizô*)	patience (*anexikakia*)
capacity (*dunamis*)	self-control (*enkrateia*)

One aspect of the Stoic wise person's wisdom is manifest in their correct use of **impressions**. Thus, to follow Epictetus' examples, the fully wise person, on seeing a sexually attractive individual, will not assent to the judgement that sex with this person would be something good or desirable, when facing **hardships** they will not assent to the judgement that anything truly bad is at hand, and when **abused** or insulted they will not assent to the judgement that they have been harmed in any way.

But we, on the other hand, who are not wise but hope to make progress towards wisdom do not always make proper use of our **impressions**; we know all too well how easily we can be lulled by lust into inappropriate thoughts and even perhaps questionable or immoral actions, oppressed by **hardships** into anxiety, frustration and depression, and provoked by **abuse** to respond with indignation and anger. There goes our 'good flow of life' (*euroia biou*) again.

In Chapter 10, Epictetus offers us some practical training that can help us step in to consciously expand the gap (which is usually so narrow as to be instantaneous) between having an impression of something and assenting to a false evaluative judgement about what we mistakenly take to be good or bad, desirable or undesirable with respect to our original **impression** and our interpretative evaluation.

Epictetus points out that we have **capacities** within us, powers of our *prohairesis* (our inner selves or moral character) that we can apply to the temptations and troubles of daily life which can help us prise apart the gap between having **impressions** and assenting to judgements: or if the worst comes to the worst, we can use these **capacities** to reject any false judgements we have already made and try again to assent to what is true, instead of what is false. If we are inappropriately sexually attracted to someone we can apply **self-control**; when facing **hardships** we need not succumb to despair and frustration if we bring to bear our **endurance**; and when **abused** by others we should marshal our **patience** (see for instance *Discourses* 1.25.28–9 for more on resisting abuse).

These **capacities** need to be trained and **habituated** so that their deployment becomes as automatic and instantaneous as was our assenting to false judgements previously (*Discourses* 2.18.26). Our training then becomes a matter of daily practice for, of course, daily life itself affords us with all the material we need to work upon – and if we sometimes feel overwhelmed by troubles and our *pathê* (violent or disturbing emotions) threaten to undermine us, then we will have to muster even more **endurance**. Either that, or give in and abandon our progress for a life (if devoid of Stoic insight or any other spiritual guidance) of anxiety, frustration and disappointment, whose objectives will lack true value, the living of which will demean us as self-conscious, rational beings.

This chapter mentions just three **capacities**: but to hold to our course we will need to deploy and develop a wide range of **capacities** to which Epictetus makes frequent reference in the *Discourses*. The *prokoptôn* making progress will need to exhibit magnanimity (*megalopsuchia*), courage (*andreia*; one of the four cardinal virtues), endurance (*karteria*; *Discourses* 1.6.28) and decency (*euschêmosunê*; 4.9.11) – they will need to be self-respecting (*aidêmôn*) and faithful (*pistos*; see entries in Glossary A for references); patient (*anektikos*), gentle (*praos*), kindly (*hêmeros*) and forgiving (*sungnômonikos*; 2.22.36); abstinent (*aphektikos*) and co-operative (*sunergêtikos*; 2.22.20, 4.4.18); well-behaved (*kosmios*) and moderate (*sôphrôn*; 4.9.17). (This list is representative rather than complete or wholly comprehensive; a careful reading of the *Discourses* will reveal frequent references to a wide range of **capacities** by which we may 'endure everything that happens' (1.6.28); for other inventories, see DL 7.92–3/126; LS 61H; Stob. 2.7.5b–5b2.)

With the exception of courage (*andreia*), which is itself one of the cardinal virtues, these **capacities** are, of course, aspects of, or are subordinated to, the four cardinal virtues that jointly constitute the excellence of character that the Stoic wise person exhibits and which the *prokoptôn* hopes to acquire – the four cardinal virtues being (1) wisdom (*phronêsis*), (2) moderation, temperance or self-restraint (*sôphrosunê*), (3) courage (*andreia*), and (4) justice (*dikaiosunê*) – whose possession and application are sufficient for *eudaimonia* ('happiness').

In summary, then, we need to watch ourselves (see *Handbook* 48.3) at all times to be ready to apply the appropriate **capacity** to forestall assenting to a false judgement and lapsing into vice or suffering the *pathê* (violent or disturbing emotions) and ruining our 'good flow of life' (*euroia biou*). Once we can do this consistently and completely reliably, our progress will have been perfected.

Chapter 11

Never say of anything, 'I have lost it,' but rather 'I have given it back.' Has your child died? It has been given back. Has your wife died? She has been given back. Has your land been taken from you? Well, that too has been given back. 'But the one who took it from me is a bad man!' What concern is it of yours by whose hand the Giver asks for its return? For the time that these things are given to you, take care of them as things that belong to another, just as travellers do an inn.

Commentary

Key terms

child (*paidion*)   the Giver (*ho dotêr*)
give back (*apodidômi*)   wife (*gunê*)

This chapter continues the topic started in *Handbook* 3 about loss and death, and how to develop the ideal Stoic outlook on the sorts of thing that almost everyone agrees constitute the worst of personal catastrophes. One of Epictetus' core objectives that forms a dominant theme in the *Discourses* is to nurture in his students the proper understanding of God and the formation of the right sort of relationship with God (for an outline of this programme, plus references, see *theos* in Glossary A; see Long 2002, 142–206, for a substantial analysis of how Epictetus' conception of God underpins and contributes to his ethical teaching).

In *Handbook* 11, God is identified as **'the Giver'** ('*ho dotêr*'), as the source from which everything we have and enjoy originates, and to whom everything, eventually, must be **given back**. The examples offered here, of suffering the loss of one's **child**, one's **wife** and one's land, are intended to be representative of anything and everything that we may lose. From the most trivial and insignificant to the most treasured and precious items, all that we have about us, including of course the people who are most dear, may be taken from us, perhaps without warning, or otherwise over periods of time, as would be the case for someone who eventually succumbs to an illness, or for a favourite garment that finally becomes so worn that we have to discard it. Some things like the favourite garment, although taken to be inconsequential, may be liked or even treasured, but not to the extent of seriously distressing us when their time comes. But for other things, perhaps almost exclusively other people whom we cherish and love, the story is quite different. The loss of these things and these people constitutes the greatest of calamities and upheavals.

Stoics claim that their special training offers not merely to insulate us from these distresses, but to transform our outlook so completely that we become *wholly immune* to them. Many people would retort that since losing someone we are close to is the worst possible of human misfortunes, for Epictetus to suggest that we should develop an outlook that will prevent us from being upset amounts to suggesting that we should strive to be less than human – for how can it be said that we really loved someone if we are not upset at losing them? Epictetus, of course, would refute that charge, and claim, paradoxically in the eyes of the 'uneducated person' to be sure (see *apaideutos* and *idiotês* in Glossary A), that it is people who get carried away by events and who get upset by losses who fall short of their potential humanity; for one essential component of a fully realised humanity is accepting one's fate as what is best and what is needed for the world to fulfil its end according to God's plan.

Our fate, inevitably, involves losing things and people – which means simply that some things will wear, deteriorate or be lost, and that some people will die before the time at which we ourselves must take leave of this world. But as we can see in this chapter of the *Handbook*, Epictetus wants us to think not in terms of loss, but in terms of returning willingly to God what we have been privileged to enjoy for however short or long a time this may have been. This requires us to give up thinking of anything as being our own possession, or being *ours* in any sense beyond being merely *on loan* to us.

Epictetus presents the example of a piece of land being stolen. From within the perspective of human affairs, this is something unjust, and the owner may well pursue a legal remedy to their plight. But from a wider perspective, the Stoic *prokoptôn* knows that having their land stolen *may* be the means by which God calls in what He has loaned, so any legal action will be undertaken 'with reservation' bearing this in mind, without their placing hopes on the outcome under which the thief has to give back the land. And so with anything whose loss or being taken from us benefits someone else – it is God's choice to call in His loan in such a fashion, and it is our task to accept it with good grace.

Understanding that everything we have is on loan from God does not reduce or undermine our commitments and duties to them. The Stoic does not love anyone less because this person is God's to dispose of as He wills, nor fail to take care of these objects to the highest standards because directed by the will of God they were brought into being by certain changes occurring in the world, and will find their end in different transformations that will unmake them, leaving their constituent elements ready to be made into yet other things (see

Discourses 3.24.10–11; MA 4.36, 5.13, 6.15, 7.18/23/25, 9.19, 12.21).
The whole of our lives, then, should be regarded as a temporary stopover
at an inn during which we have the use and enjoyment of, but also the
responsibility for, the items and facilities that are made available to us.
The capacity to transform our understanding of loss according to the
teaching of this chapter will be, at least in part, a measure of our progress
towards *eudaimonia* and a 'good flow of life' (*euroia biou*).

(The inn analogy is found again at *Discourses* 2.23.36–9; God as 'the
Giver' occurs at 4.1.103–7, 4.4.47, 4.10.14–16; for more on how the
Stoic wise person relates to other people, see especially Annas 1993a,
262–76, and Stephens 1996).

Chapter 12

[1] If you want to make progress, set aside all considerations like these: 'If I neglect
my affairs, I will have nothing to live on'; 'If I do not punish my slave-boy, he will be
bad.' For it is better to die of hunger, free from distress and fear, than to live
perturbed amidst plenty. It is better for your slave-boy to be bad than for you to be
wretched. [2] Begin therefore with little things. The olive oil is spilled. The wine is
stolen. Say to yourself, 'This is the price for peace of mind, and this is the price for
being free of troubles. Nothing can be had without paying the price.' And when
you call your slave-boy, bear in mind that it is quite possible he won't heed you, or
even if he does heed you it is quite possible that he won't do the things you tell
him to. But he is not in so fine a position that your peace of mind depends upon
him.

Commentary

Key terms

bad (*kakos*)
free from distress (*alupos*)
free from fear (*aphobos*)
freedom from troubles,
  serenity (*ataraxia*)
pay the price (*pôleô*, to exchange
  or barter goods)

peace of mind (*apatheia*, without
  passion, freedom from passion)
perturb the mind (*tarassô*)
plenty (*aphthonos*)
progress (noun) (*prokopê*)
slave-boy (*pais*)
wretchedness (*kakodaimonia*)

Progress is that process of transformation that the Stoic *prokoptôn* (one
making progress, trainee) endeavours to effect through the study,
understanding, and application of Stoic principles whose end is that
state of mind and way of life enjoyed by the Stoic *sophos* (wise person).

Such a way of life is characterised as one whose undertakings honour the wise person's relationship with God and their commitments to themselves – to flourish in ways that befit a rational creature – and to their family and friends, as well as the wider community. This way of life is conceived by the Stoics, and by Epictetus especially, as being in service to God, in which one's undertakings have objectives that are *never outcomes in the way we usually think of actions having objectives* (to acquire money, to find something lost, to lay a carpet, and so forth), but in which one *acts invariably with the primary purpose of expressing virtue* such that the success of any undertaking is judged never in terms of the practical results, but only ever in terms of the manner of its execution. The wise person will accordingly enjoy a different state of mind in contrast to the non-wise person: if, for example, it is appropriate to seek for something lost, they will not mind that they do not find it (since this, it turns out, is what fate had in store for them). To engage in affairs generally in this spirit results in the wise person being **free from passion** (*apathês*, tranquil, dispassionate, calm).

In this chapter, Epictetus identifies four specific qualities of the state of mind possessed by the person who lives this way: they will be *apathês* (**without passion**, tranquil, calm), *atarachos* (**free from troubles** or disturbance, **serene**), *alupos* (**free from distress**), and *aphobos* (**free from fear**); thus, at *Discourses* 1.4.3 Epictetus remarks that progress towards virtue is at one and the same time progress towards happiness (*eudaimonia*), **peace of mind** (*apatheia*) and a 'good flow' (*euroia*). So what are we doing wrong to prevent ourselves from enjoying these states? In Chapter 12.1 Epictetus offers two examples of how the non-wise person engages in their affairs with the wrong outlook.

In the first example, of the person who is worried about neglecting their affairs, we know from Epictetus' general tenor that he is not referring to those things that concern the Stoic *prokoptôn* (making proper use of impressions, in particular, and attending to one's moral duties; see especially *Discourses* 1.11, 2.10), but to concern for 'external things' (*ta ektos*, which are also *ta aprohaireta*, those things outside the scope of one's *prohairesis*), comprising all those things that are not in our power, over which we have no absolute control. With respect to these things, the *prokoptôn* will act appropriately and virtuously, and that is where their interest lies – they are not concerned with acquiring property, making money, showing themselves off in a big house, attaining political power, or exerting power over others in either a business or domestic setting. Pursuit of these things, imagining that they are the ends for which we live, is what **perturbs** the mind and sets a barrier to a 'good flow of life' (*euroia biou*). To suffer such a distraught state of mind amidst material **plenty**, Epictetus maintains, is worse than dying of hunger having attained philosophical enlightenment. It is not material goods and physical comforts, nor even dying of hunger, that matter, but the state of mind one enjoys whilst one is alive *whatever one's worldly circumstances.*

The second, more specific, example presents someone worried that their **slave-boy** will not do as they wish unless they punish him. The boy cannot be relied upon to follow instructions, and this person is **wretched** as a result. But to place one's hopes for **peace of mind** and **serenity** (*apatheia* and *ataraxia*) on the behaviour of someone else is folly, and demonstrates a fundamental mistake in the eyes of the Stoics; for one's own state of mind is something that is within one's own power and, as we have seen in the course of discussing the *Handbook*, depends not upon what other people do nor upon the events in which one is immersed, but solely upon the judgements that one makes (*Discourses* 3.19.3): and one's slave-boy misbehaving or misunderstanding instructions is not something that should be judged as **bad**. Indeed, maintaining one's **peace of mind** and **serenity** *even when* one's slave-boy is **bad** is the goal.

In 12.2, Epictetus offers a simple technique for maintaining this outlook and, as he did with respect to the exercise presented in Chapter 3, he instructs us to begin our practice 'with little things' – his intent, clearly enough, being to get us accustomed to responding appropriately to trivial and essentially inconsequential eventualities in preparation for facing larger frustrations and catastrophes with confidence as time goes by. Every difficulty or inconvenience that would have previously disturbed us should be regarded as the **price we pay** for our **peace of mind** and **serenity**. In practical terms, whenever something happens that threatens our equanimity, we must step in immediately to forestall assenting to the false judgement that something **bad** has happened, and remind ourselves that this very thing is the payment we have made to carry on **free from distress** (*alupês*). And the *prokoptôn* carries on, doing what is appropriate, virtuously, in the situation they find themselves facing.

(For more on **progress**, see especially *Discourses* 1.4 and Dobbin 1998, 88–98 for a commentary. For more on what is appropriate, see *Handbook* 30 and 33.13 with commentaries, and for references in the *Discourses*, see *kathêkon* in Glossary A.)

Chapter 13

If you want to make progress, submit to appearing foolish and stupid with regard to external things. Do not wish to appear knowledgeable about anything and, if others think you amount to something, distrust yourself. For you should know that it is not easy both to keep your moral character in accordance with nature and to keep secure external things, for in attending to one, you will inevitably neglect the other.

Commentary

Key terms

external things (*ta ektos*)   moral character (*prohairesis*)
foolish (*anous*)   progress (noun) (*prokopê*)
in accordance with nature   stupid (*hêlithios*)
    (*kata phusin*)

'**External things**' were introduced in the commentary to Chapter 12: *ta ektos* are coextensive with *ta aprohaireta*, those things that lie outside the scope of one's *prohairesis* (**moral character**), comprising *everything other than* one's own 'opinion, impulse, desire, and aversion' (Chapter 1.1), that are 'not in our power' (*ouk eph' hêmin*). To make **progress** (see commentary to Chapter 12) the Stoic *prokoptôn* will have to adopt an outlook towards **external things** that will make them vulnerable to appearing **foolish** and **stupid** in the eyes of uneducated people. And to this they will have to submit; being condemned, ridiculed, or just the object of puzzlement on the part of others are just minor items in the vast array of **external things** that contribute, just in themselves, nothing whatever of value or disvalue to the wise person's *eudaimonia* and 'good flow' (*euroia*) – thus, **external things**, including the jibes and criticisms of other people, are also *adiaphoros*, 'indifferent' with respect to being good or bad.

    The gulf in outlook between the Stoic wise person (whom the *prokoptôn* is striving to emulate and become) and the uneducated person arises from the fact that for the uneducated person **external things** are everything (or almost always so). Such people live their lives in pursuit of them, wishing to have possession and power over them; they measure their status against what and how many they have, and they believe that their well-being is determined by the success of this enterprise. When well-being eludes them (as, according to Stoic teaching it must often or always do), they immediately believe that this results from some deficiency in the **external things** over which they struggle to maintain power, or from a specific lack of this item or that which now they pursue, in the belief that in acquiring it they will also secure well-being. It is this desire for **external things** that the *prokoptôn* is trying to extinguish, and which is the subject of Epictetus' 'first topic' of study (see Introduction to Epictetus, 'The Discipline of Desire'; *Discourses* 1.4.1, 3.9.22, 3.13.21, 4.4.33).

Of course, if people generally measure their own value and the value of others in terms of their possessions and the attitude they have towards acquiring material goods, then in their eyes the Stoic *prokoptôn* will look very odd indeed. The *prokoptôn*'s training consists largely in the endeavour to throw off this outlook. And over and above looking odd with respect to their outlook on material possessions, the *prokoptôn* will also look odd with respect to their attitude towards their body and matters of health. Enduring poor health, for the uneducated person, is likely to be a matter of distress and possibly fear, and a serious injury, such as the loss of a limb, is likely to be judged a sheer catastrophe. Not so for the well-advanced *prokoptôn*. Sickness and injury, certainly, are dispreferred indifferents and are contrary to nature, but need not compromise one's 'good flow' (*euroia*); one's well-being – understood in terms of the condition in which one keeps one's **moral character** (*prohairesis*) by means of which one maintains one's service to God – is independent of the body and its health (see *Handbook* 9 and commentary).

When Epictetus warns against not wishing to appear knowledgeable about anything, he may mean this in a wholly general way – to have knowledge is one thing, but to have a desire to show it off and be regarded as a knowledgeable person is altogether something else, and is inappropriate for the Stoic *prokoptôn* – for placing one's well-being (to however small a degree) on the satisfaction of this desire is to rely on something that is not in one's power, something external and indifferent, and risks undermining one's 'good flow' (*euroia*). But I suspect Epictetus means 'knowledgeable' to refer only to knowledge of good and bad, moral excellence, the indifferent and **external things**, and of Stoic ethics as a whole. However advanced our **progress**, it is unlikely ever to be complete, and to impose our views on others is not fitting, for however severe their faults may be, even if our faults are less, our efforts should be applied to diminish our own faults, not theirs. (However, a different rule must apply, I am inclined to think, when other people specifically ask the *prokoptôn* for advice – and such advice will be offered not with even half an eye on appearing knowledgeable or as someone who amounts to something, but with a genuine concern for the other person's welfare and an alertness to the responsibility that one is taking up when responding to such a request.) The Stoic *prokoptôn* will demonstrate their Stoic outlook not in words, but in deeds, and those interested to learn will see for themselves how someone set on making Stoic **progress** goes about the business of living (see for instance *Discourses* 3.13.23, 3.24.118).

To conclude this chapter, Epictetus reminds us of something already stated (in Chapter 1.4), that one cannot have two objectives at the same time, to secure **external things** *and* to keep one's **moral character** (*prohairesis*) **in accordance with nature**: these aims are not compatible, and we must pursue either one or the other (*Discourses* 4.10.25–6). To attempt to perfect one's **moral character** requires abandoning one's belief that **external things** can be truly good and can have genuine value, and if one can do that, one no longer has a motive for pursuing **external things**, not as things that have primary value, to be sure, though even the Stoic Sage will – all things being equal – seek to obtain sufficient nourishment, and have clothing, shelter and friends, for these things are *preferred* indifferents, **in accordance with nature**, and number among a whole range of preferred indifferents that it will be rational for the wise person to pursue in relation to the roles and undertakings that they adopt. Obtaining these preferred indifferent external things is, of course, advantageous for the undertakings themselves; but the wise person's 'good flow' (*euroia*) does not depend upon the success of their undertakings, but only ever upon the disposition in which their undertakings are pursued (*Discourses* 2.16.15). The undertakings may be obstructed and frustrated, but never the wise person themselves.

To keep one's **moral character in accordance with nature** means for Epictetus, above all, making proper use of impressions and not assenting to any false evaluative judgements prompted by one's impressions. When something is evaluated incorrectly one immediately opens the door to the *pathê*, the violent or disturbing emotions that destroy one's *eudaimonia* and 'good flow' (*euroia*). A **moral character** that is maintained **in accordance with nature** will be elevated, free, unhindered, unimpeded, trustworthy, honourable (*hupsêlos, eleutheros, akôlutos, anempodistos, pistos, aidêmôn; Discourses* 1.4.18); unconstrained (*ananankastos*; 1.17.21); serene, fearless (*atarachos, aphobos*; 2.1.21, 4.1.84); patient, abstinent, co-operative (*anektikos, aphektikos, sunergêtikos*; 2.22.20, 4.4.18); gentle, kindly, forgiving (*praos, hêmeros, sungnômonikos*; 2.22.36); steadfast (*eustathês*; 3.3.9); dispassionate (*apathês*; 3.5.7); noble, magnanimous (*gennaios, megalopsuchos*; 4.7.8); tranquil, happy, secure, and reverent (*euroos,* *eudaimôn, ablabês, eusebês*; 4.7.9). Why are these qualities of **moral character** said by the Stoics to be '**in accordance with nature**'? Because in possessing them someone is better able to flourish as nature intends, is better able to approach their full potential as a human being, and is better able to align themselves to God's will and contribute to the unfolding of the universe as He plans. Stoic training (3.12) makes all these qualities of character available to us, and the degree to which we acquire them and maintain them consistently, no matter what comes our way, and no matter what provocations urge us to give them up, is the degree to which we approach the Stoic ideal of the *sophos*, the fully wise person blessed with unshakable *eudaimonia* and serenity (*ataraxia*).

Chapter 14

[1] It is foolish to wish that your children and your wife and your friends should live forever, for you are wishing for things to be in your power which are not, and wishing for what belongs to others to be your own. It is foolish in the same way, too, to wish that your slave-boy should never do wrong, for now you want badness not to be badness, but something else. However, if you wish not to fail in what you desire, this you are able to do. Exercise yourself, therefore, in what you *are* able to do. [2] A person's master is the one who has power over that which is wished for or not wished for, so as to secure it or take it away. Therefore, anyone who wishes to be free should neither wish for anything nor avoid anything that depends on others; those who do not observe this rule will of necessity be the slaves of others.

Commentary

Key terms

badness (*kakia*)
child (*teknon*)
desire (verb) (*oregô*)
exercise (verb) (*askeô*)
foolish (*hêlithios*)
free (*eleutheros*)

friend (*philos*)
master (*kurios*)
slave (*doulos*)
wife (*gunê*)
wish (verb) (*thelô*)

How the *prokoptôn* should regard his relationship with his **wife** and **children** is once again discussed (having already featured in Chapters 3, 7, and 11). Epictetus addresses *male* students – talking of *wives*, but never of husbands – because his students were male. There was every reason from within the Stoic tradition for Epictetus to admit female students to his school; his own teacher in Rome, Musonius Rufus, says this:

> Women as well as men ... have received from the Gods the gift of reason, which we use in our dealings with one another and by which we judge whether a thing is good or bad, right or wrong. ... Moreover, not men alone, but women too, have a natural inclination toward virtue and the capacity for acquiring it, and it is the nature of women no less than men to be pleased by good and just acts and to reject the opposite of these. If this is true, by what reasoning would it ever be appropriate for men to search out and consider how they may lead good lives, which is exactly the study of philosophy, but inappropriate for women?
>
> (Musonius Rufus, frag. 3 'That Women too Should Study Philosophy' = Stobaeus, *Anthologium* 2.31.126, trans. Lutz 1947, 39–41)

But it is doubtful that wives, sisters, or daughters would have been permitted to indulge in higher education except on the rarest of occasions. If Epictetus did teach women students in his long career, he probably did not do so at all often. The fact that Epictetus addresses male students does not mean that he would not have liked to address women too, and encourage them to the Stoic outlook.

It is foolish to wish for what is not in our power, because to do so invites anxiety, frustration and disappointment. We are all destined to perish before so very long, and if those most dear to us, our **wives** (or husbands), **children**, and **friends**, should depart this shore upon which we live for but a short while (see Chapter 7 and commentary) before we ourselves must leave, that is how things are. Similarly, to wish that our **slave-boy** (already met with in Chapter 12) should never be **bad** is just as **foolish**. The boy will have the capacities and disposition that are his own, and even though we may try to make him conform to our requirements, we obviously cannot guarantee success. But there is nothing to prevent our desire always succeeding in its objective if only we **desire** what we should – a moral character (*prohairesis*) in the right condition – and this we can accomplish by **exercising** ourselves in 'what we *are* able to do' (contrary to what we are *not* able to do: make people live forever, and make our **slave-boy** never do wrong), which is making proper use of impressions, and never assenting to false evaluative judgements, so never experiencing the *pathê* (violent or disturbing emotions).

In 2.1 Epictetus points out that in **wishing** for the wrong things we make ourselves the **slaves** of others. The person who has power over what we **wish** for becomes our **master**, and has our well-being in *their* power. To be **free** (to be free of anxieties, unfulfilled desires, troubles and frustrations generally) we must avoid **wishing** for anything that is in the power of other people. If we do not do that, we make ourselves **slaves** – at least in the sense that Epictetus means here: people whose enjoyment of life falls under the control of someone else.

(For more on the Stoic attitude towards women and philosophical training, see especially Nussbaum 1994, 322–4 and 54 n. 21.)

Chapter 15

Remember, you ought to behave in life as you would at a banquet. Something is carried round and comes to you: reach out and take a modest portion. It passes by? Do not stop it. It has not yet arrived? Do not stretch your desire towards it, but wait until it comes to you. So it should be concerning your children, your wife, your status, your wealth, and one day you will be worthy to share a banquet with the gods. If, however, you do not take these things even when they are put before you, but have no regard for them, not only will you share a banquet with the gods, but also rule with them. By acting in this way, Diogenes and Heraclitus, and people like them, were deservedly gods and were deservedly called so.

Commentary

Key terms

banquet (*sumposion*)
child (*teknon*)
desire (noun) (*orexis*)
Diogenes (*Diogenês*)
gods (*theoi*)

Heraclitus (*Hêrakleitos*)
status (*archê*, the office that one holds)
wealth (*ploutos*)
wife (*gunê*)

It is most doubtful that Epictetus intends the example of attending a **banquet** to serve as a general metaphor for life. Such an occasion, consisting of lying down a great deal, eating, drinking, talking, watching and listening to the entertainments, does not sit well with Epictetus' other metaphors for life which include attending a festival, playing a game, acting a part in a drama, training for and competing in an athletic contest, and engaging in military service, all of which suggest undertakings that are active and purposeful, in contrast to attending a **banquet**, which is largely a passive affair (see Introduction to Epictetus,

'Metaphors for life'). At *Discourses* 2.16.37, Epictetus uses the example of leaving the **banquet** as a metaphor for suicide, for leaving one's life; but this does not require that the **banquet** be regarded in any thoroughgoing sense as a metaphor for life – the **banquet** is something one may leave of one's own volition when the time comes, and the same is true of one's life, since when it becomes too burdensome one may simply take one's leave.

Rather, the **banquet** offers a more basic and simple parallel with living, and this concerns the attitudes we should adopt towards our hopes, expectations and **desires** for the things we would like to come to us, the things that – for whatever reason – we believe will make our lives better, more rewarding, more complete and more satisfying. At the **banquet**, we are obliged to abide by the usual rules of etiquette, and to do so honours our host as well as our fellow guests. What the dishes actually are, the timing of their arrival, and the order in which the guests are served, are all determined by the host. To demand that we be served first, or that our portion should be bigger than the host intended, or worse, to jump up and start stuffing ourselves from the platters the moment they are brought from the kitchens, would be wholly inappropriate. The platters will come when they come, and our share will be offered to us in good time. How are we to enjoy the present dish or attend to the conversation if we are distracted or consumed by **desire** for the dishes that have not yet arrived?

Epictetus could have made more of his metaphor by suggesting the parallel between the host and **God**, and hopefully he would not object to our taking this step for ourselves. In life it is **God** who determines which dishes will come our way, and how large the portions will be. Living a life is a good deal more active than attending a **banquet**, and of course we can take steps to procure the 'dishes' for ourselves. But whatever we pursue in life – excepting only the proper care of our moral character (*prohairesis*) – will always number amongst 'the externals' (*ta ektos*) that are indifferent with respect to being good or bad and which are not 'up to us'; their appearing at all, and coming to us (if they do), is up to **God**.

We will find the **banquet** more enjoyable and our equanimity more complete if we refrain from 'stretching our **desire**' towards what we hope for. And exactly the same is true of life in general. If, instead of 'stretching our **desire**' towards **children, wife, status** and **wealth** – which is in fact to press our hopes upon what may never come to us, or come to us in ways we had not anticipated, if, for instance, our **child** is disabled or if our **wealth** attracts the attention of greedy and petty people who cause us trouble – if we can wait patiently for what **God** brings to us and withhold our **desire** for those things that seem always to go to other people but never to us, we will improve our chances of sustaining a 'good flow of life' (*euroia biou*) and thereby enjoy the present moment free from anxieties about the future.

In his sentences about dining and ruling with the **gods**, Epictetus is alluding to two aspects of sagehood.

(1) Those who can wait patiently and restrain their **desire** for what has not yet arrived attain a special status of 'being worthy to share a **banquet** with the **gods**'. This first type of person is none other than the Stoic Sage, the fully wise person (*sophos*), whose training as a *prokoptôn* is successful and complete. This person has learned what is 'in their power' (the correct use of impressions and maintaining their *prohairesis*, their moral character, in the right condition), and that everything else is external and indifferent with respect to being good or bad; they know that only virtue is good, and that no matter what fortune may bring their way regarding **children**, **wife**, **status**, **wealth**, their undertakings generally, and any external things upon which they exercise their unshakable power of virtuous agency, they can never be harmed, and that their capacity to flourish fully, to be *eudaimôn*, is always in their power. Their ability to grasp these truths, to understand them and live by them in a complete and enduring manner, puts them on a level with the **gods** – their vision of the world and how Zeus has made it work, and of their own purpose in life, is essentially Zeus' own vision, and this capacity to participate in Zeus' reason places them in a community of the wise, comprising gods and men, and what better way to celebrate this community than to represent it as a **banquet**?

(2) Another aspect of sagehood is found in a second type of person who, even when they are offered the things that people usually **desire**, simply decline them, 'having no regard for them', and this makes them worthy *both* to share a **banquet** with the **gods** *and* to 'rule with them': this person doesn't just share a vision with Zeus, but shares the administration of the universe with Him. And Epictetus offers **Diogenes** as an example of such a person. (This is **Diogenes** of Sinope, *c.* 413–*c.* 323 BC, the Cynic philosopher who may have been a student of Antisthenes – whom Diogenes Laertius holds to be the founder of the Cynic movement at 6.2 – who in turn was a student of Socrates. **Diogenes** taught the Cynic Crates of Thebes, *c.* 368–*c.* 285 BC, who taught Zeno of Citium, 335–263 BC, the founder of the Stoic school.)

Diogenes Laertius (7.121) reports that the Stoic Apollodorus (late second century BC, pupil of Diogenes of Babylon) maintained that taking up the Cynic lifestyle was a shortcut to virtue (see also DL 6.104), and it is hard to see that Epictetus would not have endorsed this view (see especially *Discourses* 3.22). The Cynic, and especially **Diogenes**, has a special standing in Epictetus' eyes as an example of what dedicated training can achieve (and references to **Diogenes** in the *Discourses* are outnumbered only by those to Socrates). His is an example of what philosophical transformation can accomplish, and how a person thus transformed engages with the world, their fellows, and with **God**, in a new and different way. Epictetus understands the Cynic to be a messenger (*angelos*) in the service of **God**, whose message *is* the way of life he has adopted that proves to anyone who cares to consider it that complete autonomy can easily be won, and that good and evil lie in one's disposition and not in external things: his mission is to report these facts (*Discourses* 3.22.23–9). His duty to render this report imposes upon him the task of supervising and caring for humanity with respect to what is best (see 3.22.18/26, 3.24.64–5) and where a 'good flow' (*euroia*) and happiness (*eudaimonia*) may be found; and this obliges him to adopt the role of ruler and master – someone who instructs others from a privileged position constituted by his philosophical enlightenment:

> And how is it possible for a man who has nothing, who is naked, without home or hearth, in squalor, without a slave, without a city, to live serenely? [*euroôs*] Behold, God has sent you the man who will show in practice that it is possible. 'Look at me,' he says, 'I am without a home, without a city, without property, without a slave; I sleep on the ground; I have neither wife nor children, no miserable governor's mansion, but only earth, and sky, and one rough cloak. Yet what do I lack? Am I not free from pain and fear, am I not free? [*alupos, aphobos, eleutheros*] When has anyone among you seen me failing to get what I desire, or falling into what I would avoid? When have I ever found fault with either God or man? When have I ever blamed anyone? Has anyone among you seen me with a gloomy face? And how do I face those persons before whom you stand in fear and awe? Do I not face them as slaves? Who, when he lays eyes upon me, does not feel that he is seeing his king and his master?'
>
> Lo, these are the words that befit a Cynic, this is his character, and his plan of life.
>
> (*Discourses* 3.22.45–50, trans. Oldfather)

Epictetus conceives of the Cynic's caring and supervising role as a manifestation of Zeus' rule that harnesses the moral character (*prohairesis*) of the Cynic to the service of His divine plan, one aspect of which is that everyone should be happy, at least in the sense that the knowledge and means by which they may be so are always to hand and in our power. This, anyway, is how I am inclined to take Epictetus' remark about the person who is worthy to rule with the **gods** in conjunction with his presentation of **Diogenes** the Cynic, and his references to the Cynic being worthy of Zeus bestowing upon them the sceptre and diadem (*skêptron, diadêma*), symbols of autonomy, kingship, and authority over others (*Discourses* 3.22.63, 4.8.30–3).

It is tempting, though, to see the Cynic as superior to the ordinary Stoic *prokoptôn* who succeeds in becoming a *sophos* (wise person) yet does not, unlike the Cynic, give up his **wife**, **children**, property, business commitments, and what have you, to lead the Cynic life. But I don't think this can be right. The transformation for both the Cynic and the Stoic that their philosophical enlightenment has brought about is the same for both of them: each maintains their *prohairesis* (moral character) in the right condition (using impressions correctly), invariably acts virtuously, and fulfils their duties to the highest standard. The difference between them is found in the way they *made progress*, and the material upon which they exercised themselves. The Stoic, in continuing their old life with family and friends, and in maintaining old commitments (in business, for example), is essentially private, and their practice may be undertaken in secret, or almost so (see *Discourses* 4.8.17–20). In contrast, the Cynic is distinguished from the Stoic not so much by the philosophical doctrines they hold but by the conscious decision to take up a radically different way of life. In abandoning their old life and giving up literally everything to live without possessions and without a home, the Cynic is essentially public (4.8.32), maintaining their practice for all to see (how else could they set an example and 'rule over' everyone?) – and Epictetus sees this public life as one that is successfully and constantly dedicated to the service of **God** precisely because the Cynic is free from the distractions of private duties, relationships, and domestic chores (3.22.69–75). It is being free of such distractions – which without doubt will soon enough overwhelm the Stoic *prokoptôn*, resulting in their suffering passions (*pathê*) and acting viciously – that sets the Cynic on their shortcut to virtue; you cannot, for example, lapse into a passion about losing money if you don't have any. From this privileged position, the Cynic is qualified to rule over people, to tell them in what their unhappiness resides, and in what their salvation may be found.

In the final sentence, **Heraclitus** (fl. *c.* 500 BC) is a Presocratic philosopher who expounded doctrines of the *logos* and of cyclical cosmic conflagration (*ekpurôsis*) which influenced Stoic thought. The doxographer Diogenes Laertius was acquainted with texts which allude to the divine status of **Diogenes** of Sinope and the *sophos* in general (see DL 6.77, 7.119). This accords with the familiar drift we find in Epictetus that the *prokoptôn* in perfecting their rationality is in effect making themselves resemble (*exomoiazô*, make or become like) Zeus, to eventually share in His attributes, and this is what it means to attain wisdom and secure *eudaimonia* (*Discourses* 2.14.12). They must endeavour to emulate (*zêloô*) **God**: if the deity is faithful (*pistos*), free (*eleutheros*), beneficent (*euergetikos*), and high-minded (*megalophrôn*), they must strive to be just the same, and so forth for all of God's attributes (2.14.13). Epictetus declares the ideal practice to be one in which the *prokoptôn* 'wishes to be of one mind with God', 'has set his heart upon changing from a man into a god', and has 'his purpose set upon fellowship with Zeus' (2.19.26–7, trans. Oldfather).

(For more on banquets, see Epictetus *Fragment* 17. For references to **Diogenes** of Sinope, see *Discourses* 1.24.6–10, 2.3.1, 2.13.24, 2.16.35–8, 3.2.11–12, 3.21.18–19, 3.22.23–5/57–61/80/88/90–2, 3.24.40/63–76, 3.26.23, 4.1.29–32/111–17/152–8, 4.7.29, 4.11.21–4. For more on **Heraclitus**, see DL 9.1–17 and the items in the Bibliography including Barnes 1999, 57–81 and Kirk *et al.* 1983, 181–212; for **Diogenes** of Sinope, see DL 6 and especially Navia 1998; for more on Epictetus' allusions to **Diogenes**, see Long 2002, 58–60. For more on the relationship between Stoicism and the early Cynics, see Rist 1969, 54–80; and for a thorough treatment of the Cynic movement generally, see Branham and Goulet-Cazé 1996.)

Chapter 16

When you see someone weeping in grief because their child has gone abroad or because they have lost their property, take care not to be carried away by the impression that these external things involve them in anything bad, but be ready to say immediately, 'This person is not distressed by what has happened (for it does not distress anyone else), but by the judgement they make of it.' Do not hesitate, however, to sympathise with words, or if it so happens, to weep with them; but take care not to weep inwardly.

Commentary

Key terms

bad (*kakos*)	**external** (*ektos*)
child (*teknon*)	**judgement** (*dogma*)
distressed, to be (*thlibô*, to	**impression** (*phantasia*)
be burdened)	**weep** (*stenazô*)

As we have seen (especially in *Handbook* 2, 5, and commentaries),
Epictetus explains emotional disturbance as arising from (or possibly
being the affective component of) false evaluative **judgements** about
what is happening, which occur when someone fails to make proper use
of their **impressions**. If someone is upset in consequence of their **child**
going abroad or as a result of their property being lost, this is because
they have judged these things to be **bad** for them, and Epictetus says that
this is a mistake. Such occurrences, to be sure, may be detrimental to
certain objectives or undertakings that someone takes to be important,
but they cannot undermine the good spirits of the person who has set
themselves the task of maintaining their moral character (*prohairesis*) in
good order. As Epictetus points out, the source of one's **distress** and
emotional disquiet cannot be anything other than one's **judgement**
about what has happened (see *Handbook* 5). There are no *facts* about the
world with which we might be acquainted (about one's **child** having to
go abroad, or about the loss of one's property, for instance) that can *in
themselves* make someone upset. The **distress** that people experience can
arise only when those facts are evaluated one way rather than another.
The mere fact of my **child** going abroad doesn't **distress** anyone else; if
mere acquaintance with facts could **distress** us directly, then this would
upset dozens or even hundreds of people who happen to hear of it! Only
I am upset because I judge this occurrence differently from other people.
Stoic teaching and Stoic training will show me my mistake and
encourage me towards making a different response, namely: 'This is
something **external** to me – to my moral character (*prohairesis*) – and
cannot involve me in anything **bad**; it is my own faulty **judgement** that
distresses me.'

   The Stoic, inevitably, will encounter people who are subject to
distressing emotions, and although they understand each person's
remedy to lie within their own grasp (if only they will pay heed to Stoic
teaching), they do not condemn or abandon the person in **distress**. The
Stoic has a duty to care for everyone with whom they have contact
according to their role and station, and how they exercise their

responsibilities to other people is the subject of Epictetus' second 'topic' (see Introduction to Epictetus, 'The discipline of action'). The general thrust of Epictetus' position is found in his remark that the Stoic 'must maintain [their] natural and acquired relations, as a religious man, as son, brother, father, citizen' (*Discourses* 3.2.4, trans. Matheson). Sometimes it is enough just to be with someone who is **distressed**; at other times words of comfort may be required. But the *prokoptôn* must resist slipping into seeing the distressing calamity from the distressed person's point of view, central to which is the notion that something **bad** has happened – to do that would be to risk '**weeping** inwardly', to risk falling into a *pathos* of one's own and to mistakenly believe that the person in **distress** really has been harmed. They have been harmed by their own faulty judgement, and although this probably cannot be repaired quickly or easily, the general approach that the Stoic should take comes fairly readily to mind. They should point out that such things happen, and may even be fairly common, that down the ages many, many people have suffered this tragedy, and that they all – almost all, anyway – pull through to less troubled times in which they can view their catastrophe from a more objective perspective.

The Stoic might also point out that hidden strengths can often be roused by misfortune (see for instance Seneca's *On Providence*), and that an experience of a disaster such as this can often render someone fit to support others facing a similar peril. At other times harsh words may provide appropriate support: if someone is reacting with dismay to something essentially trivial, this needs to be pointed out – one is perhaps lucky to be afflicted by something so small and petty when many are brought low by disasters of a character far more severe. And possibly, just possibly – and here experience and subtle judgement are required – the Stoic may be able to use the occasion of some disaster to open someone's mind to the possibility that a conversion to Stoicism offers by far the best remedy for all and any trial.

(For more on 'sympathising with words', see *Discourses* 3.24.22–4. For more on whether emotions should be regarded as the affective component of false evaluative judgements, or as occurring in consequence of making such judgements, see *TD* 4.14–15; Inwood 1985, 130–2; Sorabji 1998. For more on how the Stoic relates to other people see especially Stephens 1996.)

Chapter 17

Remember that you are an actor in a play of such a kind as the playwright chooses: short, if he wants it short, long if he wants it long. If he wants you to play the part of a beggar, play even this part well; and so also for the parts of a disabled person, an administrator, or a private individual. For this is your business, to play well the part you are given; but choosing it belongs to another.

Commentary

Key terms

actor (*hupokritês*)	**play** (noun) (*drama*)
part, role (*prosôpon*)	**playwright** (*didaskalos*)

'Another', at the very end, and '**playwright**' in the first sentence, refer of course to God. It is God who brings us into the world when His plan requires our participation, and Epictetus' metaphor suggests that the whole world, with its millions of inhabitants, is one vast **play**, and we are all **actors** playing our **parts**. Many, I think, would object to this metaphor because it implies a thorough-going predestination in which God casts us ready-made, with capacities to exercise and tasks to fulfil according to a script already written, upon the world-stage whose character and history is also determined by His script. This way of thinking was perhaps more acceptable to people in times past, at least in some societies, where sons always followed in their father's footsteps, and where daughters were married not according to their own wishes, but according to the advantages that their fathers and other relatives were trying to secure. Today, much more prevalent, is the view that we are all masters of our own fate, that with hard work and determination *anything* can be achieved. I have personally known people who sincerely believe that those who fall ill and stay ill can be blamed for their own plight because they lack the will-power to recover. That view may be extreme and uncommon, but it reflects, I am sure, a general tendency to think that we all deserve our lot in life, and can change it if we so choose with action based on 'positive thinking'.

Such an outlook, I think, is held by people who fear loss of control: they fear illness, perhaps, or losing their jobs, or growing old and feeble, and they fortify themselves against such fears with the conviction that sheer will-power will see them through. To base one's well-being on this attitude will doom one to disappointment and misery, eventually. But as we know, Epictetus says that our security can be complete if we can accept that our well-being depends not at all on external things – on our control over external things, or our power to make things go as we wish – on how God's **play** happens to unfold. Our well-being is in fact identical with the condition of our moral character (*prohairesis*), and *that* does not depend upon – or at least need not depend upon – the external circumstances in which we find ourselves, nor upon the **role** we happen to be playing as **actors** in God's **play**. When we focus on the notion that what truly matters is developing the right sort of disposition of character, we can see that the *specific* **role** we play is fundamentally unimportant.

I am personally convinced that what we have and the stations we attain are altogether less in our control than almost everyone likes to think. And oddly, we will meet people who in candid moments tend to confirm this view – they will explain that but for this teacher (for example) who enthused them for their subject, or that friend who lent them such-and-such a book, or for some other completely chance coincidence or meeting, they would not now be doing what they do, or living where they live, or earning as much as they earn. How did each of us come to be living with our partners, or sharing our lives with friends we care about? Spouses and friends all, surely, came to us by chance, by forces and factors invisible to us and beyond our control.

Our task is to accept the **part** we have been given, no matter how desirable or undesirable this will be judged by the common mind, responsibly and enthusiastically – to face our hardships with courage, deal with others justly, and with life in general moderately; and within the bounds set for us by our **roles**, to act wisely with respect to which undertakings are feasible and befitting for us, as people who wish to live in the light of the philosophical enlightenment that Stoic teaching shines upon us. (For further instances of Epictetus' metaphor of acting in a **play**, see *Discourses* 1.29.41–7, 4.1.165, 4.7.12–14.)

Chapter 18

When a raven croaks inauspiciously, do not be carried away by the impression, but straightaway draw a distinction and say to yourself, 'This portent signifies nothing with respect to me, but only with regard to my body, my possessions, my reputation, my children or my wife. To me, however, all portents are auspicious, if I wish them so. For however the affair turns out, it is in my power to benefit from it.'

Commentary

Key terms

benefit (verb) (*ôpheleô*)	**possession** (*ktêseidion,*
body (*sôma*)	diminutive of *ktêsis*)
child (*teknon*)	**raven** or **crow** (*korax*)
impression (*phantasia*)	**reputation** (*doxarion,*
portent (*sêmeion*)	diminutive of *doxa*)
	wife (*gunê*)

Today, the student who turned up in class troubled by anxieties that the cawing of a bird **portended** some disaster would be ridiculed for their superstition. In Epictetus' time, such a dismissive response would most likely have been directed towards the person who *rejected* the validity of reading meaning and significance into natural events. In was widely accepted in the Greco–Roman world that the gods communicated to people through signs, omens and **portents**. The Stoics were especially happy to accept this traditional belief because they understood that the whole of the natural world is directed by a single, supreme intelligence – Zeus – such that all phenomena cohere into an intelligible pattern of interconnected events. Discovering the relation between signs and what they **portend** thus becomes less of a superstition and more of a science in which careful observation can reveal the correlations by which divination succeeds (see Frede 2003, 184; Ogilvie 1986, 19–20.)

To most of Epictetus' students, perhaps to all of them, the inauspicious croaking of a **raven** was a serious matter. Epictetus does not try to relieve his student's anxiety by denying the validity of the **portent**, but by saying that *even though* it is valid, it concerns the welfare of something external – any disaster, if disaster is foretold, can befall only one's **body**, one's **wife** or **child** or some other person, one's **reputation**, or one's **possessions**. All these things are external to one's moral character (*prohairesis*), and the successful Stoic's well-being is completely secure because it is completely independent of anything dispreferred happening to these external things.

This is, of course, an example of how one should use **impressions** correctly. In this case, the **impression** you have is of a raven croaking inauspiciously, which, due to your prior knowledge of such things, provokes the immediate conviction (let us suppose) that your possessions are in imminent danger. We know from the studies we have already made that as a well-advanced Stoic you will instantly prevent the occurrence of any *pathos* (violent or disturbing emotion) by simply not judging that anything bad is at hand. You remind yourself at once that the **portent** attaches to something *external*, something that is not in your power – something that has no bearing upon your *euroia biou* ('good flow of life') – except only to call upon whatever quality of character is appropriate for sustaining that 'good flow' (see *Handbook* 10). You know that the inner essence of your being, your very self, is always safe from harm no matter how disastrously events may turn out for your undertakings.

All **portents** are auspicious for the Stoic because no matter what happens, their serenity (*ataraxia*), equanimity (*apatheia*) and 'good flow' (*euroia*) can never be disturbed – indeed, their wish is always for the fate of the world and their own fate to unfold exactly as Zeus wishes it, knowing that it is in their power to **benefit** from whatever comes to pass by doing nothing more than maintaining a virtuous disposition and responding appropriately.

In his commentary to the next chapter, Simplicius offers the following argument (that he thinks Epictetus 'hints at') as proof for the lesson of Chapter 18, that nothing can be a sign of anything bad for the Stoic *prokoptôn* (its formulation, in slightly different wording, is put forward by Brittain and Brennan 2002a, 136 n. 241): (1) It is in your power never to desire or seek to avoid external things; (2) If you neither desire nor seek to avoid external things, you cannot be defeated (*hêttaomai*); (3) If you are not defeated, you cannot be in a bad situation; (4) If you are not in a bad situation, then nothing is a sign of something bad for you; (5) Therefore it is in your power to bring it about that nothing is a sign of something bad for you.

(For more on portents and divination in Roman culture, see Ogilvie 1986, 19–23 and 53–69. From the ancient sources see especially Seneca, *NQ* 2.32; Pliny *Natural History* 2.97, and 10.30/33 for remarks on crows and ravens. See also Cicero, *On Divination*. Epictetus discusses divination at *Discourses* 2.7 and at *Handbook* 32; he mentions ravens at *Discourses* 1.17.18–20 and 3.1.37.)

Chapter 19

[1] You can be invincible if you never enter a contest in which it is not in your power to win. [2] Beware that, when you see someone honoured before others, enjoying great power, or otherwise highly esteemed, you do not get carried away by the impression and think them happy. For if the essence of good lies in what is in our power, it is wrong to feel envy or jealousy, and you yourself will not wish to be praetor, senator or consul, but someone who is free. There is only one way to attain this end, and this is to have no concern for the things that are not in our power.

Commentary

Key terms

envy (noun) (*phthonos*)
essence of good (*ousia tou agathou*)
free (adjective) (*eleutheros*)
happy (*makarios*)
impression (*phantasia*)

in our power (*eph' hêmin*)
invincible (*anikêtos*)
jealousy (*zêlotupia*)
not in our power (*ouk eph' hêmin*)

Here is another example of how to use an **impression** properly. This time the **impression** in question is that of seeing someone greatly honoured, enjoying power, or being highly esteemed. When we see such people enjoying their status, we should not **envy** them and think them **happy**. The only sort of happiness worth attaining, or worth making progress towards if securing it in a thoroughgoing sense is beyond our ability (which it may well be), is *eudaimonia*; and whether or not these people who enjoy the sort of status that has attracted our eye are in any measure approaching *eudaimonia* is a question that should concern them *and not us*. Our concern is with our own *eudaimonia* and with transforming our moral character (*prohairesis*) so that we always make proper use of our **impressions**, for that is what is **in our power**, and in this lies the **essence of good**. It is in perfecting this capacity that we will progress towards being truly **happy**, and **free** from the **envy** or **jealousy** – or any of the passions (*pathê*) – that arise when we assent to a mistaken judgement about what is good or bad. Whether or not attaining the status of a praetor, senator, or consul is compatible with *eudaimonia*, only those who have assumed such positions are qualified to say – but what we do know is that attaining such stations is assuredly *not*, in itself, sufficient for happiness.

We cannot be overwhelmed by **envy** or **jealousy**, or any passion, to which we do not assent (that is, if we do not assent to the judgements that give rise to them), and in this lies our **invincibility**: in not wanting such status, and in not contending with others to acquire it. Our status, however lowly or exalted, ultimately depends upon other people, and is therefore **not in our power**. The Stoic *prokoptôn* recognises that having or lacking status has no direct bearing upon their well-being, but that being **jealous** of people who have it puts an end to their progress and returns them to a life governed by passion, disquiet, and unhappiness.

Chapter 20

Remember that the insult does not come from the person who abuses you or hits you, but from your judgement that such people are insulting you. Therefore, whenever someone provokes you, be aware that it is your own opinion that provokes you. Try, therefore, in the first place, not to be carried away by your impressions, for if you can gain time and delay, you will more easily control yourself.

Commentary

Key terms

abuse (verb) (*hubrizô*)   **insult** (noun) (*loidoria*)
control (verb) (*krateô*)   **judgement** (*dogma*)
delay (noun) (*diatribê*)   **opinion** (*hupolêpsis*)
hit (*tuptô*)   **provoke** (*erethizô*)
impression (*phantasia*)   **time** (noun) (*chronos*)

In this chapter we have yet another example of how to use an **impression** correctly, for now we have the **impression** of someone **insulting** us and perhaps even **hitting** us. The harm we suffer arises not from what has happened in a purely factual sense, but from our **judgement** of what has happened – that is, we have moved from an awareness of this person here meaning to **insult** us or **abuse** us, to the **judgement** that their attempting to do this is something bad for us. The irony is that for their action to succeed we must be complicit in it – their success depends upon *our* **opinion** that they have succeeded!

Merely to be aware that this person intends to **provoke** us cannot **provoke** us. So, if we *are* **provoked**, that is because we have allowed ourselves to be **provoked**. We can more easily **control** ourselves, that is not lapse into a *pathos* (violent or disturbing emotion), by **delaying** the shift from having an impression of an **insult** to the evaluative **judgement** as to whether we have actually been **insulted** (and thereby harmed). Splitting apart these two events, '*impression of*' from '*judgement that*', is the essence of using **impressions** correctly, required for maintaining an undisturbed 'good flow of life' (*euroia biou*) and being happy (*eudaimôn*). It is up to us to take the **time** we need to move from the initial **impression** to the correct evaluative **judgement** of what really has happened, and this requires a change in consciousness from that of our pre-enlightened state in which **judgements** (and their associated emotions) arise spontaneously upon having the **impression**, to that in which we ourselves mediate the movement from **impression** to **judgement**, fully aware of why our evaluation is justified and correct. The correct **judgement** is, of course, 'This person is setting out to insult me, purposefully trying to harm me: but this they cannot do, for my good lies wholly in the disposition of my moral character (*prohairesis*), and that is completely beyond this person's influence, if I so choose it.'

Chapter 21

Let death and exile, and all other things that seem terrible, appear daily before your eyes, but especially death – and you will never entertain any abject thought, nor long for anything excessively.

Commentary

Key terms

abject (*tapeinos*)	**exile** (*phugê*)
death (*thanatos*)	**terrible** (*deinos*)

Over and above the things that may trouble us and undermine our 'good flow of life' (*euroia biou*) – including perhaps dire portents (Chapter 18), envy at the good fortune of others (Chapter 19), the abuse and violence of other people (Chapter 20) – are those **terrible** things that frighten us the most. Epictetus offers the examples of **death** and **exile**, and for most people we may be sure, the prospect of the former stirs more terror than any other calamity, and close behind it come other terrors, differing in their names and characters according to whom we canvass. For the aristocratic elite (and sometimes for others) in the Roman culture that Epictetus knew, **exile** was an ever-present threat: indeed, our key sources for Stoic ethics in the first century were all **exiled**; Seneca was exiled to Corsica for eight years; Musonius Rufus, Epictetus' teacher, was banished from Rome twice – and on a third occasion went with his exiled friend Rubellius Plautus to Asia Minor; and of course, Epictetus was forced into exile when the Emperor Domitian banished all philosophers from Rome in about AD 89 (for more on Seneca's exile, see Griffin 1992, 59–63 and also Motto and Clark 1993a; whilst in exile Seneca wrote his *Consolation to Helvia* and *Consolation to Polybius*; for more on Musonius' exiles, see Dillon 2004, 6–7). The fear of **exile** or of being forced under duress to leave one's homeland still affects people today, and if we ourselves have the good fortune to be unaffected by this particular terror, then, no doubt, we will have other fears at the top of our lists of things most dreadful.

Dreadful things, no matter how dire, for the Stoic Sage and the advanced *prokoptôn*, are merely dispreferred indifferent things (*adiaphora*) that cannot impinge upon their 'good flow' (*euroia*) and happiness (*eudaimonia*). Even when these things are present or threaten with almost sure inevitability, the Sage remains completely untroubled (*atarachos*).

Epictetus tells us in this chapter to bring to mind daily what terrorises us the most. Why do that? If our Stoic progress is not yet sufficient for us to be free of our old fears, why remind ourselves continually that our progress is so limited? This, for most people, is probably an exercise too morbid. But the point seems to be that even if we cannot remove our worst fears, we can make use of their presence to eradicate lesser concerns, or at least to see them in a more realistic perspective such that they have less power to disturb our 'good flow' (*euroia*). Are not insults, the loss of a bit of money, a noisy neighbour, or a missed flight (for instance), in comparison to what we find most upsetting, but trivial inconveniences? To be sure, we will strive to avoid them 'with reservation', but if we fail to avoid them, what does that matter? They number among the things that can happen, that sometimes feature in the fate of the world, and in our own fate. Any **abject** thought concerning the things we have hitherto taken to be good or bad – that we will be distraught at the loss of wealth or possessions, envious at the good fortune of others, or devastated by bad health, for example – can thus be dismissed as unimportant, as attaching to things that in contrast with our worst terrors, are nothing at all.

And why long for something excessively? Our possessing it – if ever we do – can only be temporary, and will be ended soon enough by death or some other calamity. Seeing things in a more realistic perspective, which I think is what Epictetus means to suggest, in itself promotes a more steady flow of life, but also encourages the valuing of philosophy and its techniques for making moral progress as conceived by the Stoics, in which what we have or do not have, and what we think of other people and how they might regard us, are of no concern in comparison with the state of our own moral character (*prohairesis*) and the spirit with which we face what life serves up to us.

(For more on exile, see Balsdon 2002, 182–7. For Seneca's exile to Corsica between AD 41 and 49, see Griffin 1992, 59–63, and Motto 1973, 20–3; for his *Consolation to Helvia*, written around AD 42–3 to console his mother's grief over his exile, see Basore 1932, Costa 1997, or Hadas 1968. For Musonius Rufus' lecture on exile, 'That Exile is Not an

Evil', see Lutz 1947, 69–77 = Stobaeus, *Anthologium* 3.40.9. For further remarks from Epictetus concerning or mentioning exile, see for instance *Discourses* 1.1.21–5, 1.11.33, 1.29.6, 3.3.17–18, 3.24.29, 4.1.60/172, 4.7.13–14, 4.11.23, and *Fragment* 21.)

Chapter 22

If you set your heart on philosophy, be prepared from the very start to be ridiculed and jeered at by many people who will say, 'Suddenly he's come back to us a philosopher!' and 'Where do you suppose he got that supercilious look?' Now, for your part, do not show a supercilious look, but hold to the things that seem best to you, as someone who has been assigned to this post by God. And remember that if you persist in your principles, those who at first ridiculed you will later admire you. But if, on the other hand, you are defeated by such people, you will be doubly ridiculed.

Commentary

Key terms

admire (*thaumazô*)   jeer (*katamôkaomai*)
assign (*tassô*)   persist (*emmenô*)
best (*beltistos*)   philosopher (*philosophos*)
God (*theos*)   philosophy (*philosophia*)
hold to (*echô*)   ridicule (noun) (*katagelôs*)

If we turn to **philosophy** in the hope of eliminating or reducing our fears, tempering our desire, and finding a way to secure lasting happiness, we must be prepared to tread a stony path. The discipline that will bring the easing of our burdens has the potential to expose us to the **ridicule** and **jeering** of other people.

Epictetus now picks up again the topic already introduced in Chapter 13, of how the *prokoptôn* should maintain their relationships with other people, a central component of which is understanding, on the one hand, the differences between the *prokoptôn* and the Stoic Sage, and on the other, the differences between the *prokoptôn* and the uneducated person (see *apaideutos* and *idiôtês* in Glossary A), and what this means for our ongoing practice. The *prokoptôn* is, after all, setting themselves the task of changing from how they used to be into something different, and this will of necessity make them different from anyone else who happens not to take up the very same project (or engage upon some other spiritual path with a similar terminus).

It is the view of Zeno and his Stoic followers that there are two races of men, that of the worthwhile [*spoudaiôs*], and that of the worthless [*phaulos*]. The race of the worthwhile employ the virtues through all their lives, while the race of the worthless employ the vices.

> (Stob. 2.7.11g, trans. Pomeroy = LS 59N.
> See the entire sequence 2.7.11g–11k.)

The *prokoptôn* recognises that, of course, they as yet still number amongst the worthless (and probably always will), and are far from maintaining the insights of the Sage as permanent, stable, and ongoing dispositions in the course of daily life. But they are nevertheless distinguished from the 'uneducated' mass of the 'worthless' in striving to develop an understanding of what causes unhappiness, and the reasons why they lapse into vice and passion, endeavouring to learn and apply the remedies that promote a 'good flow of life' (*euroia biou*). The people around us who are aware (however dimly) of what we are trying to do in our quest for *eudaimonia* know at least this: we do not wish to be like them (but that is because we do not wish to remain as we were, and this they may not grasp). And if we make any progress, we will have changed, and some people will notice this – specifically, from their perspective, they will see that we have rejected their values, and we no longer care for what they care for.

> The one thing to be careful about beyond all others is this – not to get so involved with any of your former companions or friends, as to compromise your character for [their] sake.
>
> (*Discourses* 4.2.1, trans. Matheson)

Sandbach eloquently explains the difference between the wise person and others:

> The wise man is a rich man, not in money but in what is truly valuable, the virtues; he is beautiful, not with physical beauty but with that of the intellect; he is a free man, even if a slave, because he is master of his own thoughts. He alone is a king: for by 'king' is meant an ideal ruler, who must know what is good and evil. He alone is a prophet, a poet, an orator, a general, for he alone knows how to follow these professions as they should be followed to achieve acceptable results. The other side of the medal is that every man who is not wise is a slave, to his fears and cupidities; a madman, for his beliefs are hallucinations; a wretched man, for he has no true cause for joy. Nothing is useful for him, nothing belongs to him, nothing suits

him; for nothing is useful but virtue, which he lacks, nothing belongs unless it cannot be taken away, nothing that is not virtue is a suitable possession.

(Sandbach 1989, 43–4)

The *prokoptôn* must not be tempted off their path or intimidated by **ridicule**. They must **hold to** and **persist** in what they know is **best**, no matter how cruelly they may be **jeered**. Friends, family, and others who condemn the *prokoptôn* have abandoned the calling of their roles, *as* friends, *as* brothers, *as* fellow workers, and the fault of their own failing will be laid at the feet of the *prokoptôn* whose new values and demeanour so offends them. The Stoic **philosopher** may, of course, opt to work entirely in secret, to disclose nothing about their studies and their new beliefs (see, for example, *Discourses* 4.8.17–20). But if their work is to amount to anything, they will give themselves away, sooner or later, and perhaps only to the more perceptive eye, in their behaviour. Not being angered as they once were, for instance, may be accepted and even approved (though almost certainly not understood) by other people. But giving up the desire for wealth and possessions, power and status, and the pursuit of pleasures – these changes may not so easily be accepted.

However bad disapproval may become (and these warnings may have no relevance for *some* Stoic students) we should remember that our task has been **assigned** by **God** as the true purpose to which every rational being should devote themselves. The choice before us then is either to press on with the possibility of offending people around us but doing what **God** most wishes for us, or to abandon our work and fall back in line with the 'worthless', and like them succumb to our passions, value pleasures, possessions, wealth and power above peace of mind, and do what **God** least wishes for us – through sheer folly to expose ourselves to misery and dissatisfactions of all sorts.

Will those who first **ridiculed** us, if we hold unswervingly to our principles, later come to **admire** us, as Epictetus suggests? (Perhaps Epictetus is speaking more from experience than simply with hope, and perhaps he actually witnessed what he maintains.) This question, I am inclined to think, must be answered by each *prokoptôn* in turn, and I suspect that the answers will be varied. Knowing that the key to making progress is a proper understanding of what is in our power and what is not, we know that it is an error to persist in our training with the expectation of or desire for being approved of or **admired** by other people. It is to be preferred that we keep on good terms with others, but if, despite our efforts, this can be done only by compromising our principles, then it is better to keep to our course even if other people are hostile to our practice.

(For more on how the Stoic relates to other people, see especially *Discourses* 4.2; for the Stoic response to wrong-doers, see 1.18, 2.22.36, and also 2.12.3–4. See also 1.21 for the philosopher who wants to be admired, 1.22.17–21 for Epictetus' pretence of madness in reaction to a hostile critic, and 1.26.5–7 for the student who justifies his pursuit of philosophy to a critical parent. See also 3.23.7. Epictetus explains in 1.18 why the Stoic should not be angry with people whose faults offend us.)

Chapter 23

If at any time it should happen that you turn to external things with the aim of pleasing someone, understand that you have ruined your life's plan. Be content, then, in everything, with being a philosopher; and if you wish also to be regarded as such, appear so to yourself, and that will be sufficient.

Commentary

Key terms

external things (*ta ektos*)	**plan of life** (*enstasis*)
philosopher (*philosophos*)	**please** (*areskô*)

The Stoic's **plan of life**, if they have been successful in their training, is characterised by imperturbability, fearlessness, freedom (*ataraxia, aphobia, eleutheria*; *Discourses* 2.1.21), happiness, dispassion and serenity (*eudaimonia, apatheia, euroia*; 1.4.3; see also 3.22.19–22) – in particular, it is characterised by an unbroken persistence of these qualities. As we know, success in this endeavour requires that we make proper use of impressions, never assenting to false judgements about the things that happen, never judging anything good or bad when it is really 'indifferent' (*adiaphoros*). The Stoic treats other people well, striving to be patient (*anektikos*), gentle (*praos*), kindly (*hêmeros*) and forgiving (*sungnômonikos*; 2.22.36), and although other people may in fact be **pleased** by this treatment, the Stoic does not set out to **please** them.

Finding that people respond appreciatively when we treat them well may partly motivate our efforts to develop and sustain our moral character (*prohairesis*) in the right condition, and perhaps does no harm – so long as we do not lapse into thinking that our goal is specifically to please others. But our 'life's plan' will most definitely be undermined if we set out to **please** people, by buying them presents, for instance, in the hope of making them happy and of making them like us, or by our wearing certain clothes, eating at certain restaurants or taking a particular job with the intention of winning approval. If we do that, we will have chosen something over and above virtue as our goal in life, and we will have made our well-being dependent upon the reactions of other people. To be concerned about how they respond to our attempts to manipulate **external things** with the aim of **pleasing** them constitutes a slide into passion, for instead of watching our own conduct we will be watching theirs, and if they approve of what we do we will believe erroneously that something good is at hand and feel the pleasure of it, and if they disapprove of what we do we will believe erroneously that something bad is at hand and feel the distress of it. And that, of course, is to throw away our 'good flow of life' (*euroia biou*).

To be content with being a **philosopher** (a Stoic philosopher, of course) means satisfying our own requirements to the best of our understanding regarding the ways in which a wise person should conduct themselves, and being completely indifferent to the requirements of other people, excepting only the special case in which we take notice of a teacher or fellow student who values what we value, and understands, more or less clearly, in what a 'good flow of life' consists.

Now, to be completely indifferent to the requirements of other people does not mean that we do not fulfil our duties to them. But we must fulfil these duties in the right frame of mind. We do not, for example, honour our father's birthday by buying him a present *in order that* our duty should **please** him (though hopefully it will), but in order that we may fulfil our duty. The success of our actions, and our capacity to do what virtue requires, is never judged by the responses we elicit from other people. Though, we should remain alert to the possibility that the reactions of others may direct us to forming a more accurate self-evaluation; but even when we correct our behaviour, we do not do something differently *with the aim* of **pleasing** them.

Chapter 24

[1] Do not be troubled by thoughts such as these: 'I will be valued by no one my whole life long, a nobody everywhere!' For if lacking value is something bad (which it is), you cannot be involved in anything bad through other people any more than you can be involved in anything disgraceful. Is it any business of yours, then, to acquire status or to be invited to a banquet? Certainly not! How, then, can

this be regarded as lacking value? And how will you be a nobody everywhere, when all you have to be is a somebody concerning those things that are in your power, with respect to which you can be someone of the greatest value?

[2] 'But my friends,' you say, 'will lack support.'

What do you mean, 'lack support'? Certainly they won't get much cash from you, neither will you make them Roman citizens! Who told you, then, that these things are amongst those that are in our power, and not the business of other people? And who can give to others things they do not have themselves?

[3] 'Get some money, then,' someone says, 'so that we can have some too!'

If I can get it whilst also preserving my self-respect, my trustworthiness, my magnanimity, show me how, and I will get it. But if you ask me to forsake those things that are good and my own, in order that you may acquire those things that are not good, see for yourself how unfair and thoughtless you are. Besides, what would you rather have, money, or a friend who is trustworthy and has self-respect? Therefore help me towards this end, and do not ask me to do anything by which I will lose those very qualities.

[4] 'But my country,' you say, 'as far as it depends on me, will be without my help.'

I ask again, what help do you mean? It will not have colonnades and bathhouses on your account. But what does that mean? For neither is it provided with shoes by a smith, nor weapons by a shoemaker: it is enough if everyone properly attends to their own business. But if you were to provide it with another trustworthy citizen who has self-respect, would that not be of use to your country?

'Yes.'

Well, then, you also cannot be useless to it.

[5] 'What place, then,' you ask, 'will I have in the community?'

That which you may have whilst also preserving your trustworthiness and self-respect. But if, by wishing to be useful, you throw away these qualities, of what use can you be to your community if you become shameless and untrustworthy?

Commentary

Key terms

bad (*kakos*)
banquet (*hestiasis*)
good (*agathos*)
in our power (*eph' hêmin*)
lacking value or honour (*atimos*)
magnanimous (*megalophrôn*)
self-respect (*aidôs*)

self-respecting (*aidêmôn*)
status (*archê*, the office that one holds)
trustworthiness (*pistis*)
trustworthy (*pistos*)
useful (*ophelos*)
valuable, worthy (*axios*)

Chapter 24 develops the topic started in Chapter 23, about pleasing other people. Epictetus' student is judging matters from their old outlook when they were worried abou failing to acquire **status** being overlooked when the invitations to the **banquet** are being sent out, or when they worry about how much support they can give their friends. There certainly is a problem here. As we make progress in Stoic living, it is inevitable that some people we interact with will notice that instead of valuing their opinion of us we value instead our own conduct and disposition, and carry on regardless of how others judge us. What matters to the Stoic is maintaining their moral character (*prohairesis*) in the proper condition, and someone's disapproval of their doing this means nothing to them; to be of value, we know that we won't necessarily be deemed **valuable** by people, and in facing the choice of being approved of by others or keeping their **self-respect** (*aidôs*), the Stoic will always choose the latter (*Discourses* 4.2.8).

Lacking value is indeed something **bad**, as Epictetus points out, but this must be understood in the right way. There is nothing that other people can do that can bring disgrace upon us: the only disgrace that can befall us is that which we bring upon ourselves by abandoning our principles and throwing ourselves into a life of vice the doing of which is easily accomplished by merely recovering our old outlook in which we were deluded that our well-being is sustained by external things, wealth and possessions, **status** and power. No – to be of value as a Stoic is accomplished by devoting ourselves to those things that are **in our power**, our opinions, impulses, desires and aversions (see *Handbook* 1), and the correct use of impressions, thus saving ourselves from lapsing into vice and passions, and preserving our 'good flow of life' (*euroia biou*).

Epictetus' student is judging matters from their old outlook when they are worried about failing to acquire **status** or being overlooked when the invitations to a **banquet** are being sent out, or when they worry about how much support they can give to their friends. In one sense it is true that their friends will lack support, for the *prokoptôn* making progress will probably not be able to help their friends with loans and gifts of cash because they have given up the pursuit of riches. They have given up pursuit of office, also, so now they will not acquire the authority to make their friends – or anyone – Roman citizens. But there is nothing disgraceful in this. The Stoic will, of course, help their friends, even get money for them, for instance (*Handbook* 24.3), but never at the expense of their **self-respect** and **trustworthiness**.

Support cannot be rendered if this is to be at the price of the *prokoptôn's* throwing away their **self-respect** and **trustworthiness**. Self-respect (*aidôs*) and **trustworthiness** (*pistis*) are important concepts for Epictetus, and, although they appear in the *Handbook* only in this chapter (with *aidêmôn* putting in a brief appearance in Chapter 40), they occur frequently throughout the *Discourses* (see entries in Glossary A for references). *It is in these qualities of character that our value to our friends and community lies.*

Non-Stoics, and those bereft of a spiritual path which does not teach moral integrity, are liable to folly – for given the choice as to whether they would prefer a 'friend' who supports them with money and citizenship, yet who compromises their **self-respect**, **trustworthiness**, and **magnanimity** in the process, or a friend who holds to their principles, they are as likely as not to choose the money and the citizenship and a relationship with a 'friend' who lacks principles. To compromise one's moral integrity for the sake of friends and community, says Epictetus, is most definitely *not* to be **useful**. The **usefulness** that a Stoic has for their friends and community is always to be cashed in terms of their **self-respect** (*aidôs*) and **trustworthiness** (*pistis*).

Trustworthiness and **self-respect** are aspects of a perfected moral character (*prohairesis*) that is brought fully into harmony with nature (*Discourses* 1.4.18–20); these qualities cannot be taken from us (3.3.9), and their use cannot be hindered or put in the hands of other people (2.2.4, 4.1.161). They are 'our own' (1.25.4), we are harmed by losing them (2.10.21–30), and by losing them we make ourselves useless to society (2.4.1–7, 4.5.21). We preserve what is **good** (*agathos*) in us by preserving our **self-respect** (*aidôs*) and **trustworthiness** (*pistis*), and indeed we are charged by God to maintain these qualities (2.8.23). It is in attending to our impressions (and here is a doctrine unlikely to surprise) that we guard our **trustworthiness** (*pistis*) and **self-respect** (*aidôs*), along with our tranquillity (*eustatheia*), peace of mind (*apatheia*), immunity to distress (*alupia*), fearlessness (*aphobia*), imperturbability (*ataraxia*), or 'in a word', our freedom (*eleutheria*) (4.3.7). It is in preserving these characteristics that our capacity for true friendship is possible:

> For where else is friendship to be found than in trust [*pistis*] and respect [*aidôs*], and in giving and taking what is good, and nothing else?
>
> (*Discourses* 2.22.30)

In response to the query as to what **good** someone gains from their efforts to return to Stoic principles, Epictetus replies:

What greater good do you seek than this? From being shameless you will become self-respecting [*aidêmôn*]; from being undisciplined you will become disciplined [*kosmios*]; from being untrustworthy you will become trusted [*pistos*]; and from being dissolute you will become self-controlled [*sôphrôn*]. If you seek anything greater than these, go on doing what you are doing now – for even a god cannot save you.

(*Discourses* 4.9.17–18)

It is in caring for ourselves, in perfecting our moral character (*prohairesis*) because this is our ultimate **good**, that at one and the same time we render ourselves fit to serve as friends and to carry on the roles that we choose or which society lays upon us (*Discourses* 2.22.19–20). For the Stoic must face in two directions at once. They must direct their attention to their own well-being and happiness (*euroia, eudaimonia*), the doing of which is essentially self-centred; and they must be of use to their community by fulfilling their roles of father, son, friend, scholar, student, manager, worker, or what have you, the doing of which is essentially altruistic. But for the Stoic, there is no tension between these two objectives because it is in the manner of fulfilling their other-regarding (altruistic) undertakings that their self-regarding (self-centred) interest to enjoy a 'good flow of life' (*euroia biou*) has the possibility of being satisfied (see *Discourses* 1.19.13 and 2.10.4).

More specifically (following Kamtekar 1998) we can identify *aidôs* as the capacity of the *prokoptôn's* moral character (*prohairesis*) by which they may answer the question, 'What should I be like, what should I do, to be a morally accomplished human being who values *aretê* (excellence) above everything?' It is the capacity that evaluates and assents to judgements about which actions are appropriate and which satisfy the requirements of duty, and which more generally selects those undertakings and specific actions which satisfy the requirements of virtue.

(For more on the self-regarding and other-regarding aspects of Stoic ethics, see especially Annas 1993a, 223–6/262–76/302–11/322–5 and Long 2002, 189–204. For more on *aidôs* and *pistis*, see Kamtekar 1998, and Long 2002, 222–9.)

Chapter 25

[1] Has someone been honoured above you at a banquet, or in a greeting, or in being called in to give advice? If these things are good, you should be pleased for the person who has received them. If, on the other hand, they are bad, do not be

upset that you did not receive them yourself. Remember, with respect to acquiring things that are not in our power, you cannot expect an equal share if you do not behave in the same way as other people. [2] How is it possible, if you do not hang around someone's door, accompany them or praise them, to have an equal share with people who do these things? You will be unjust, therefore, and insatiable, if you refuse to pay the price for which these things are sold, but wish instead to obtain them for nothing. [3] For what price are lettuces sold? An obol, let's say. When someone else, then, pays an obol and takes the lettuce, whilst you, not paying it go without, do not imagine that this person has gained an advantage over you. Whereas they have the lettuce, you still have the obol that you did not pay.

[4] So, in the present case, if you have not been invited to someone's banquet, that is because you have not paid them the price for which a banquet is sold. They sell it for praise; they sell it for flattery. Pay the price, then, for which it is sold, if you think this will be to your advantage. But if at the same time you do not want to pay the one, yet wish to receive the other, you are insatiable and foolish.

[5] Do you have nothing, then, in place of the banquet? You have this – you have not had to praise the person you did not want to praise, and you have not had to bear the insolence of their doorkeepers.

Commentary

Key terms

bad (*kakos*)
banquet (*hestiasis*)
foolish (*abelteros*)
good (*agathos*)
not in our power (*ouk eph' hêmin*)
obol (*obolos*, a coin of low value)

pay/pay the price (*proïemai*, pay; *didômi*, give; '*dos to diaphoron*', 'give the balance')
praise (*epaineô*)
sell (*pôleô*)

In 25.1, Epictetus is alluding to the client–patron relationship that underpinned the social life of his times. Without doubt, each of his students would have had direct experience of how this relationship worked, either on account of their own social standing, or that of father, uncle, or some other close relative. This relationship, at its most basic, is characterised by reciprocal support and an exchange of services between client and patron. Clients would support their patrons by canvassing on their behalf at elections, by packing the audiences for their patron's political speeches or public recitations and leading the applause; when required, they would join the cortege of their patron on his visits, and accompany him to the baths. The degree of the patron's prestige was directly proportional to the number of clients pressing into his *atrium* for the morning *salutatio*. In return for this support, the patron is obliged to provide for his clients in a whole variety of ways: he will advise and support them in legal matters and provide loans or gifts of cash (and sometimes even land as a reward for lifelong commitment). The patron may also provide for his clients' lodgings, clothing, and in cases of need will dispense food, or cash in lieu of food (*sportula*, meaning 'little basket'). Indeed, the patron is honour bound to welcome his clients into his house, and is obliged at intervals to invite his clients to dinners or **banquets**.

It is within the dynamics of the client–patron relationship that clients would hope for social advancement, so Epictetus' student, seeing that someone else has been honoured in the seating arrangement by being shown to the place they had been expecting themselves (or that they have not been invited at all), or that someone else has been preferred as a source of advice, appears to have grounds for disappointment and distress, or even indignation and rancour. Such a snub was of serious concern, and the threat of such snubs a source of ongoing anxiety.

The Stoic Sage knows that not being invited to a **banquet**, or being accorded a lesser status than they had been expecting even if invited, are circumstances that number among the indifferent things (*adiaphora*) that inevitably sometimes happen: such turns of event are neither **good** nor **bad** (for the only **good** is virtue and the only evil is vice) and have absolutely no impact on their happiness (*eudaimonia*) and 'good flow of life' (*euroia biou*). To be sure, some of the Sage's undertakings can be harmed or disrupted by such inconsiderate behaviour, but the Sage knows that they themselves are *not* their undertakings, and that the wish that their undertakings will flourish has absolutely no bearing upon the condition in which they maintain their moral character (*prohairesis*; see commentary to *Handbook* 4). The Sage has habituated this outlook to the ups and downs of daily life so completely that they are never caught off guard, never provoked by anything (not even by the actions of cruel and malicious persons) into making the false value judgement that something **bad** has befallen them, and thus they never experience the *pathê*, the distressing or violent emotions or passions that are the affective components of such false value judgements (or in some other way arise in consequence of assenting to them).

The Stoic *prokoptôn*, on the other hand, knows no less than the Sage – they can rehearse the Stoic view that **good** and **bad** are reserved exclusively for virtue and vice, that harms to their undertakings are not harms for *them*, and that what ultimately matters is the state of their moral character (*prohairesis*) – but they have not accustomed themselves to applying this knowledge reliably and infallibly. Sometimes they succeed, and sometimes they fail. But even when they fail, not all is lost if a second line of defence can be held and, in this chapter, Epictetus seems to be offering a technique for defending this second line. We might have expected Epictetus, when faced with the student who is upset at having not been invited to a **banquet**, to take his usual line about making proper use of impressions – the impressions in this case being those of seeing someone else honoured more highly, or of not receiving an invitation. We already know how to make proper use of impressions, and in this chapter, we are shown a new technique for dissolving our discomfort.

This technique can be adopted even by those who are not Stoics, and who doubt the key principles of Stoicism. Epictetus is so firmly rooted in his Stoic perspective that he cannot refrain from reminding us (25.1) that someone's being honoured above us at a **banquet**, or in a greeting, or in being summoned to give advice, are of course **not in our power**, and therefore should not concern us (see *Handbook* 1.5, for instance). But even for people who think that being accorded these advantages really is **good** (and this will include the *prokoptôn* who has not yet gained full control of their judgements), there are two things of which they should remind themselves: (1) if truly **good**, these things must be **good** *for someone*, and it is possible to feel happy for the person who has them, and (2) to acquire such advantages *there is a price that must be paid*.

Clearly, when we are out at the market, we cannot go home with our **obol** *as well as* the lettuce, for the price of the lettuce *is* the **obol** that we pay if we prefer having the lettuce to having the **obol**. Which we have is for us to decide – but we cannot have both. Epictetus is suggesting that we can view many of the advantages we seek in the way we view the lettuce. If we **pay the price** that is asked for the advantage we desire, then we can have it. The invitation to the **banquet**, or being offered the higher status position, can be obtained by **paying** the appropriate **price** which typically, Epictetus suggests, is **praise** and flattery. Everything **sells** at one price or another; if we believe that something is an advantage to us, then all we have to do is **pay the price** at which it is **sold**. **Foolish** indeed, then, is the person who seeks some advantage, yet refuses to **pay the price** that it carries.

And if we abandon our desire and imitate the person who goes home with their **obol** but without the lettuce, have we not similarly retained the coin we would have had to spend to be invited to the **banquet**? Yes of course we have, for we have not incurred the expense of **praising** someone; we have not had to demean ourselves by stooping to whatever obsequious behaviour would have purchased our invitation.

Reminding ourselves of the **price** we must **pay** for something we want is a technique we can use generally, and gaining a proficiency in it will undermine our old, non-Stoic, habit of moving automatically from an awareness of a lack of something to making an evaluative judgement that we are thereby disadvantaged or harmed, causing us to suffer an attendant *pathos* and loss of 'good flow' (*euroia*). Instead, we will be aware of what we are able to retain, what we have not had to part with, to acquire something that we now realise was up for sale at an inappropriate or too high a **price**. No portion of our 'good flow' (*euroia*) should ever be given up for the supposed advantage of some external (*ektos*) thing.

(For more on the client–patron relationship in Roman society of Epictetus' time, see Balsdon 2002, 21–4; Carcopino 2003, 171–3; Dupont 1992, 18–20; Friedlander 1965, 195–202; Hornblower and Spawforth 1996, 348; and Shelton 1998, 11–15 for several primary source extracts that comment on clients. See also *Ep.* 19.4.)

Chapter 26

We can understand the will of nature from those things in which we do not differ from one another. For example, when our neighbour's slave has broken a cup, we are immediately ready to say, 'Well, such things happen.' Understand, then, that when your own cup gets broken you should react in just the same way as when someone else's cup gets broken. Apply the same principle to matters of greater importance. Has someone else's child or wife died? There is no one who would not say, 'Such is the way of things.' But when someone's own child dies they immediately cry, 'Woe is me! How wretched I am!' But we should remember how we feel when we hear of the same thing happening to other people.

Commentary

Key terms

child (*teknon*)	**the will of nature** (*to boulêma*
wife (*gunê*)	*tês phuseôs*)

'Nature' (*phusis*), in the context of this chapter, refers to universal nature conceived of as identical to Zeus; it is also the way Zeus' creation is manifest, what it is like generally and in specific detail, and in this sense it is also fate, the sequence of causal connections that constitute the history of the world and the explanation of each event in that history. (At other places, Epictetus uses the term *phusis* in other senses: at *Discourses* 2.16.7, for instance, he uses *phusis* to mean 'essence' or 'concept'; at 1.16.11, 3.1.3 and 4.1.121–2 the term denotes what is particular and specific to each person, creature, or plant; at 1.6.15 and 4.11.1 the term is used of human nature in general, and at *Handbook* 29.5 it is used to refer to the specific constitution of his interlocutor; see Stephens 1996, 24 n. 11.)

The phrase '**the will of nature**' (*to boulêma tês phuseôs*) occurs just this once in the *Handbook*, and twice in the *Discourses* at 1.17.14–15/17 and 3.20.13 (but see also 2.20.15). Epictetus talks about not understanding nature as such (its overall pattern and intricacies, laws and principles, as these things are investigated by modern-day scientists and theorists), but understanding the *will* **of nature** taken not as a metaphor, but meant literally as the intention and purpose of Zeus. For Epictetus and the Stoics, the world is consciously planned, and is continually unfolding towards its completion, and understanding the principle features of this plan, and how as individuals we relate to and contribute to it, is a major component of learning the meaning of 'living in accordance with nature'.

Seeing how we differ as individuals does not contribute to this endeavour – my noticing for instance that I have a hearing disorder, whereas most other people do not, will not help me make progress as a Stoic; rather, it has the potential to lead me to self-pity, frustration, envy of those not so afflicted and, in short, straight into a whole set of *pathê* (disturbing or violent emotions) that undermine my progress towards a 'good flow of life' (*euroia biou*). But if on the other hand I notice what I share with others, the potential to suffer such imperfections of health and all the other things common to the human condition, I can begin to foster an outlook in which afflictions and troubles are no longer viewed as irritations and disasters to be borne like punishments, but nothing more than manifestations of the divine plan for the world to which I contribute, at least in part, by living nobly, fulfilling my duties and striving for happiness (*eudaimonia*) just as I am, imperfections, afflictions and all.

We have all lived in the world quite long enough to be familiar, one way or another, with the things that happen. But most of us have yet to make the attempt to secure an interpretation of our experience that meets our need or wish for a satisfactory spiritual engagement with the world. Of course, Epictetus and the Stoics think that they can supply such an interpretation, and we have already seen in some detail how this is attempted. How to cope with the loss of one's **child** or **wife** has already been addressed in Chapters 3, 11, and 14. Here, in Chapter 26, Epictetus expands the discussion by instructing us to view our own calamities in exactly the same way as we view those of other people. The **will of nature** presides over the lives of everyone equally, showing no favour or bias: which is not to say that we all suffer adversity to the very same degree, or enjoy the very same advantages in exact proportion, but that we share in common with everyone the very same liabilities. Whatever has just now happened to me has happened to countless others, and will happen again to multitudes yet to come. But by the same token, we all share the same potential capacities, and although any one person cannot excel in all the things manifest by those most talented, when it comes to learning Stoic principles and making proper use of impressions, the race is that much more even. It is doubtlessly true that there is not a single person who, with the right teaching and training, would not be able to make some considerable progress towards the freedom and tranquillity that Epictetus commends.

To appreciate 'those things in which we do not differ from one another', and to be able to say of all turns of event, *even when they happen to us*, 'Such is the way of things', we must understand that the **will of nature** is that everything be as it is, and to see everything being as it is, without any favour towards the person we happen to be or bias towards our own life and against all others, requires perfecting a 'cosmic perspective', a perspective that does not privilege any individual point of view, but grasps, at least in imagination, the totality of Zeus' creation in which each component being and each specific event joins with and aligns with everything else to mutually bring about the harmony of the cosmos (see *Discourses* 2.14.7–8, for instance). The endeavour to secure this perspective and to maintain it unswervingly at all times, no matter how severe our adversities, is at the core of the discipline of desire (see Introduction to Epictetus, 'The Discipline of Desire').

> The discipline of desire essentially consists in re-placing oneself within the context of the cosmic All, and in becoming aware of human existence as being a part, one that must conform to the will of the Whole, which in this case is equivalent to universal Reason.
>
> The discipline of desire will therefore consist in refusing to desire anything other than what is willed by the Nature of the All.
>
> (Hadot 1998, 99 and 129)

At the very least, if finding and sustaining this cosmic perspective proves too elusive, there is nothing to prevent us saying when faced with any disaster, 'I will judge this as I please. Nothing bad has befallen me, because the only evil is vice. Only my undertaking has been harmed, only what I had hoped for. But what I hope for more than that, maintaining my moral character (*prohairesis*) in proper order, has not been touched.'

(God, nature, fate and providence are mentioned throughout the *Discourses*, but see especially 1.14 on God, 1.6, 1.16 and 3.17 on providence, and 1.12.25; see *Fragments* 3 and 8. For other primary sources on nature and God see: Alexander of Aphrodisias, *On Fate* 191.30–192.28 = LS 55N; Aulus Gellius, *Attic Nights* 7.2.3 = LS 55K; Calcidius, *Timaeus* 144 = LS 54U; DL 7.87–9 = LS 63C, 7.135–6 = LS 46B, 7.147 = LS 54A, 7.148–9 = LS 43A; MA 2.9, 4.23, 8.5–7/46/50, 10.6; *ND* 1.39 = LS 54B; Seneca, *Ep.* 16.4, *Natural Questions* 2.45, *On Providence*. For a pre-Stoic account of providence, see Xenophon, *Memorabilia* 1.4.3–9, 4.3.3–18. For secondary sources see: Bobzien 1998, 45–7; Lapidge 1978; Long 1986, 147–78; Long 2002, 20–7; Sandbach 1989, 31–2; Striker 1991; Xenakis 1969, 40–55.)

Chapter 27

Just as a target is not set up in order to be missed, so neither does the nature of evil exist in the world.

Commentary

Key terms

evil (*to kakon*)   **target** (noun) (*skopos*)

Epictetus may mean by this sentence that just as a **target** is not set up with the specific purpose that the archers should miss it, Zeus does not create and sustain the world with the specific purpose that **evil** should exist in it, or that anything should turn out badly. This interpretation, which we can call the weaker thesis, seems to allow that just as it is inevitable that the target be missed, at least on occasion, so too it is inevitable that sometimes something **evil** should occur, though it always remains the case that Zeus does not set out with the intention that anything **evil** should happen. This seems to be Chrysippus' view of **evil**. At *Attic Nights* 7.1 (= LS 54Q), Aulus Gellius reports that Chrysippus (third head of the Stoa, *c.* 280– *c.* 207 BC) responds in his *On Providence* to the charge that if providence rules human affairs then nothing evil would occur. Discussing disease in particular (though the argument applies more generally), Chrysippus says that disease is an inevitable consequence of the universe having the particular constitution that it happens to have. By way of illustrating his point, Chrysippus offers the example of the thinness of the human skull (which is liable to damage under the effect of even slight blows) which could not be otherwise if nature is to endow it with the functions she intends it to have (if the bones were any thicker, there wouldn't be enough room for all the organs). This weaker thesis, then, recognises that there are **evils** in the world, but that they are inevitable side-effects of how the world happens to be.

A stronger thesis, which I think Epictetus favours, takes the words 'the nature of **evil** does not exist in the world' at face value (see *Discourses* 2.1.4, for instance). He cannot deny the existence of illness and death, nor that property is perishable, nor that when illness strikes or when property is destroyed, people suffer distress. The whole point of Epictetus' programme in Stoic ethics constitutes the attempt to relieve people of their distress *whilst their losses and calamities carry on as usual* (this is why he regards his lecture room as a hospital – he cannot take away the calamities themselves, but he can cure the distress they produce; *Discourses* 3.23.30). This makes the nature of **evil** *internal* to everyone's experience, but not an *external* feature of the world. We create our own experience of **evil** by not making proper use of impressions and by assenting to false judgements – and if this is the case, everyone is already in possession of their own cure, if only they can see how to apply it (*Discourses* 1.6.28/37/40).

Epictetus' claim is that good and **evil** are found in the condition of one's moral character (*prohairesis*), and that one's being subject to **evil** cannot depend upon facts about anything external (*ektos*) that lies beyond one's moral character (and is therefore *aprohairetos*; see *Discourses* 1.8.16, 1.29.24, 2.1.4, 2.16.1, 3.10.18, 3.20.1).

The *prokoptôn* therefore must constantly remind themselves of the distinction between their *prohairesis* (moral character) on the one hand, the condition of which constitutes the only source of good and **evil**, and *ta ektos* (external things) on the other hand, whose continued presence and character matter as the material upon which their *prohairesis* operates. What matters is the way in which one makes use of external things to engage in one's undertakings, not the success of the undertakings themselves. Since the disposition of our own moral characters is in our power (*eph' hêmin*), and since that disposition correlates precisely with our experience of good and **evil**, it follows that our experience of good and **evil** is completely in our power. All we have to do in the face of any supposed **evil** is to remind ourselves that this cannot be an **evil** for us, though it may, of course, prove detrimental to some undertaking or other. In failing to make proper use of impressions, and in judging incorrectly that we have been harmed, we will fall prey to a *pathos* (disturbing or violent emotion) and lapse into some vicious action; and letting that happen is the only **evil** we can suffer.

In one sense, we will have to say that **evil** exists in the world, because the world is full of vicious people. But viewed from my own unique perspective, there is no **evil** in the world, for the **evil** of all those vicious people *can never be an evil for me*, and so the world external to my own *prohairesis* (moral character) is not, for me, a source of **evil** unless I decide to make it so by judging matters incorrectly. The viciousness of someone else is a matter for them, and if their actions should touch upon my affairs, then I will count myself blessed that my virtue is being tested. If through diligence the exercise of my virtue makes it stronger, then the advantage is all mine, even if the other party should mistakenly think that in stealing from me, insulting me, or what have you, the advantage is theirs (see *Discourses* 3.20).

Finally, we should relate this discussion to Stoic terminology, and say that what we have hitherto taken to be **evil** is, of course, *indifferent* (*adiaphoros*; see for instance *Discourses* 1.30.1–3 and Introduction to Epictetus, 'What is really good'.)

(See also *Discourses* 1.24.1, 2.5.5, 3.3.8–10, 3.10, 3.13.13, 3.17.8, 3.18, 3.24, 4.10.28–30. For primary sources on good and evil, the beneficial and virtue see: DL 7.94–103; *Fin.* 3.10, 3.49; Seneca, *Ep.* 71.32, 76.15–17, 85.24–32/39–40, *On the Happy Life* 16.1; Stob. 2.5a–b1/5d–m/6d/11h. For the notion that adversity trains us in perfecting virtue, see Seneca *On Providence*; for the same thought in Epictetus, see for instance *Discourses* 3.20. For secondary sources, see Algra 2003, 170–2; Inwood 1985, 115; Long 1968; Long 1986, 168–70; Motto and Clark 1993, Chapter 5; Nussbaum 1994, 115.)

Chapter 28

How angry you would be if someone handed over your body to just any person who happened to meet you! Are you not ashamed, then, when you hand over your mind to just any person you happen to meet, such that when they abuse you, you are upset and troubled?

Commentary

Key terms

body (*sôma*)   **mind** (*hê gnômê*)

Who indeed would acquiesce in the handing over of their **body** to a third party to use and abuse as they pleased? Having one's **body** handed over to the care of others happens, for example, when one is put in prison, conscripted into military service, or (in Epictetus' day) taken into slavery. People universally view anything of this sort happening as the greatest of misfortunes, which is why, of course, imprisonment in our own time is so commonly resorted to as the appropriate punishment for a wide range of crimes and misdemeanours. What we do with our **bodies**, the actions we use them to perform, what we feed them, how we dress them, where they travel, where they live and in what manner – all these things we want to have in our control. People are invariably affronted when their power over these matters is removed or compromised.

How strange then that people seem unconcerned about handing over their **minds** to other people. Though, to be more precise, what people hand over is power over their states of **mind**, their moods and emotions, and thereby their well-being. How strange that we should let the actions and opinions of 'just any person' we happen to meet upset and trouble us! The slightest insult or unfavourable comment can send some people into an angry rage or into the depths of despair. We all see examples of this general phenomenon dozens of times a day, and as often as not it is we ourselves who are guilty of handing over our **minds** to 'just any person'.

Doing so is, of course, quite incompatible with a 'good flow of life' (*euroia biou*) and undermines our progress towards happiness (*eudaimonia*). But as we know, Stoic teaching will help us to cure this fault. If our ultimate good is identical with the condition of our moral character (*prohairesis*), with the disposition of our inner selves, then what other people do or say is of no concern to us at all. They may turn people against us or disrupt our undertakings by what they do, and they may even do so deliberately. But so what? Their stupidity, their folly and their vice is a matter for them. If they will listen, the Stoic *prokoptôn* will try to teach them. But otherwise, the *prokoptôn* is concerned solely with their own actions and with their own disposition. What is an insult to a Stoic but something to which no heed should be taken? For a Stoic, an insult can only do good, for it exercises patience and forbearance. And should an insult ever contain a germ of truth, then the Stoic will be thankful that their fault has been exposed. Any attempt to ridicule, embarrass, or hurt by revealing a fault is of no consequence, and the Stoic will never respond to such an attempt – instead they will be able to reflect on their fault and correct it. This is another instance of the Stoic being thankful for everything that happens – for everything that happens serves to benefit the Stoic's progress towards virtue.

(On handing one's body over to someone else, see *Discourses* 1.12.19; see also 3.20.9.)

Chapter 29

[1] In every undertaking, consider what comes first and what comes after, then proceed to the action itself. Otherwise you will begin with a rush of enthusiasm having failed to think through the consequences, only to find that later, when difficulties appear, you will give up in disgrace. [2] Do you want to win at the Olympic Games? So do I, by the gods! For that is a fine achievement. But consider what comes first and what comes after, and only then begin the task. You must be well-disciplined, submit to a diet, abstain from sweet things, follow a training schedule at the set times, in the heat, in the cold – no longer having cold drinks or wine just when you like. In a word, you must hand yourself over to your trainer, just as you would to a doctor. And then, when the contest comes, you may strain your wrist, twist your ankle, swallow lots of sand, sometimes be whipped, and after all that, suffer defeat. [3] Think about all this, and if you still want to, then train for the games, otherwise you will behave like children, who first play at being wrestlers, then at being gladiators, then they blow trumpets, then act in a play. In the same way, you will first be an athlete, then a gladiator, then an orator, then a philosopher, but you will do none of these things wholeheartedly – but like a monkey, you will mimic whatever you see, as first one thing, then another, takes your fancy. All this because you do not undertake anything after properly considering it from all sides, but randomly and half-heartedly. [4] So it is when some people go to see a philosopher and hear someone speak such as Euphrates (and who can speak like him?) – they too want to be philosophers. [5] But first consider what sort of undertaking this is, then examine your own capacities to see if you can bear it. So you want to be a pentathlete or a wrestler? Look at your arms, your thighs, examine your back. Different people are naturally suited to different tasks. [6] Do you think that if you do these things you can still eat in the same way, drink in the same way, give way to anger and irritation, just as you do now? You must go without sleep, endure hardship, live away from home, be looked down on by a slave-boy, be laughed at by those whom you meet, and in everything get the worst of it: in honours, in status, in the law courts, and in every little affair.

[7] Consider carefully whether you are willing to pay such a price for peace of mind, freedom and serenity, for if you are not, do not approach philosophy, and do not behave like children, being first a philosopher, next a tax-collector, then an orator, and later a procurator of the Emperor. These things are not compatible. You must be one person, either good or bad. You must cultivate either your ruling principle or external things, seek to improve things inside or things outside. That is, you must play the role either of a philosopher or an uneducated person.

Commentary

Key terms

bad (*kakos*)
capacities (*phusis*, nature)
Euphrates (*Euphratês*)
external things (*ta ektos*)
freedom (*eleutheria*)
good (*agathos*)
Olympic Games (*ta Olumpia*)
pay the price (*antikatallassomai*, to exchange one thing for another)
peace of mind (*apatheia*, without passion, freedom from passion)
philosopher (*philosophos*)
ruling principle (*hêgemonikon*)

serenity (*ataraxia*, without trouble)
status (*archê*, the office that one holds)
things inside (*ta esô*)
things outside (*ta exô*)
train for the games (*erchou epi to athlein*, come to be an athlete)
undertaking (*ergon*)
uneducated person (*idiôtês*, one who suffers *idiôteia*: want of education)
well-disciplined (*eutaktos*)

Epictetus warns us that making progress as a **philosopher** is an arduous business. The training that the Stoic *prokoptôn* must submit to is comparable with that undertaken by the athlete who endeavours to win at the **Olympic Games**. The ideal of the Stoic Sage cannot be pursued on a whim, but only with unrelenting dedication on the part of the person who has mapped their course in advance and who is prepared for the tests they must endure. Those who wish to **train for the games** must fully consider the nature of their **undertaking** and the strength of their **capacities** which they will need to carry them through. So too for the **philosopher** who will have to radically change their ways.

If we make a commitment to this training, we will no longer be able to carry on as before – obviously we will no longer be able to 'give way to anger and irritation', for that is to indulge in passion (*pathos*) and lose our 'good flow' (*euroia*); we must, for instance, guard against thinking that the pleasure of eating and drinking is something good for us, for it is not, and deepening our practical grasp of this doctrine is perhaps best advanced by sticking to the plainest of diets, and drinking only water. Neither must we indulge the bad behaviour of our fellow diners, for that is to be complicit in their self-harm; and thus we run the risk of being branded by our friends as prudes or spoilsports. Making progress is going to be fraught with difficulties, some more troubling than others. For Epictetus' students, even attending his classes meant facing and overcoming obstacles since most of them, if not all, would have had to travel long distances away from home, and both travel and lodging in a strange town would likely to have been attended by hardships of all sorts (see *Discourses* 2.21.14).

We have already seen (*Handbook* 22 and commentary) that the **philosopher** must expect to be misunderstood and ridiculed (see *Discourses* 1.11.39, for instance). They are no longer interested in **status**, for one thing, and those who might have conferred it may pass over the **philosopher** in favour of others whose demeanours (including perhaps ambition and greed) more readily conform to the usual expectations. Apparently, Epictetus even thinks that the **philosopher** will face discrimination in the law courts.

The Stoic **philosopher** must do two things at once, and the first is perhaps more easily accomplished than the second: they must dedicate themselves to acquiring a thorough understanding of the principles of Stoic philosophy, and they must secondly dedicate themselves to applying those principles in practice. The principles are of no use if they are not instrumental in transforming vexation of spirit, distress and unhappiness into **peace of mind**, **freedom** and **serenity**.

> The philosophers urge us not to be content with only learning [*mathê*], but to add practice [*meletê*] as well, and then training [*askêsis*].
>
> (*Discourses* 2.9.13)

In the course of these commentaries, we have already largely mastered the principles, and at *Discourses* 4.12.7–18 Epictetus offers a fairly comprehensive summary, which may be paraphrased thus:

These general principles are the first things to which we must pay attention:

(a) No one is master of another person's moral character (*prohairesis*);
(b) in the sphere of one's moral character (*prohairesis*) and nowhere else is to be found one's good and evil;

(c) thus no one has the power to provide us with what is good nor to involve us in what is evil;

(d) and we ourselves alone have authority over ourselves in this regard.

(e) Accordingly, where we have secured for ourselves what is good, we can have no excuse for being disturbed about external things [*ta ektos*].

(f) There is one whom we must please, to whom we must submit and whom we must obey – and this is God;

(g) for God has entrusted into our care our own selves, and our moral character (*prohairesis*) is subject only to ourselves with respect to which we have been given rules for its proper use.

(h) And when we follow these rules we need pay no heed to those who say anything different.

(i) If we are annoyed by people who censure us, our distress results merely from lack of training.

(j) So practically, we must hold unswervingly to never going in pursuit of anything external [*ta ektos*], for these things are not our own, but are disposed as God ordains.

(k) Instead, we must pursue wholeheartedly only those things that lie within the sphere of our moral character (*prohairesis*), and other things only so far as they are given us.

(l) We must remember who we are, and what actions properly fulfil the requirements that our roles place upon us [see Chapter 30 and commentary].

(m) Whenever we deviate from any of these principles, our loss is immediate: not loss concerning anything external, but with respect simply to the action itself.

Such a list might profitably augment principle (k) by mentioning things indifferent, preferred and dispreferred (*adiaphoros, proêgmenos, apoproêgmenos*), and the notion of pursuing them with reservation (*hupexhairesis*) in accordance with nature in the fulfilling of our roles. The list might also supplement principle (f) by reminding us that proper submission to God results never in blaming anyone or accusing anyone, but acquiescing in good spirits in the governance of the universe, and principle (d) might have added to it the point that our authority here results from making proper use of impressions – but otherwise this list is reasonably serviceable (more condensed summaries of basic principles can be found throughout the *Discourses*: see for instance 1.4.18–21, 2.23.42).

But it is not enough simply to know philosophical principles (to know the arguments that support them, to understand the force of those arguments, and to be able to rehearse them compellingly before others); we must also develop the capacity to put them into practice. The ability to do this perfectly is what distinguishes the Sage from the **philosopher**. This way of seeing philosophy and how it functions turns it into an art or technique (*technê*) after the fashion of flute-playing, shoemaking, writing, or carpentry (see *Discourses* 1.15.2, 2.21.17–18, 3.22.19–20, 4.1.63–118). And it is not enough just to know that my happiness and 'good flow' (*euroia*) are constituted by the disposition of my moral character (*prohairesis*), and that the correct disposition is maintained by the proper use of impressions. Knowing this is of no avail *unless I can actually use impressions correctly*, by actually assenting only to what should be assented to (1.20.7).

Thus the Stoic *prokoptôn* must strive to be conscious at all times of what they are assenting to, to stand as it were between their awareness of mere facts, of how things stand, and their evaluations of those facts. One may literally maintain a dialogue with oneself such that as things happen one says to oneself, 'Now, what has happened here?' 'Ah yes, this is not in my power and is nothing to me.' 'How then should I respond?' 'In my role as such-and-such, I shall be acting virtuously in accordance with nature if I do *this*.' Or sometimes a dialogue might go like this: 'Now, I appear to be experiencing a *pathos*.' 'Yes, stop everything and think: this is because I have assented wrongly to an impression.' 'The best course then is to go back to the offending impression and judge it correctly.' 'Does it concern something **external**?' 'Yes.' 'Then it is nothing to me.' And so forth.

The choice before Epictetus' student, which is of course the same choice we have ourselves, is that of either taking up the profession of **philosopher**, or of remaining an '**uneducated person**' by ignoring or forgetting Stoic principles, and of course by not putting those principles to practical work. If we choose the first option, our task will be to modify and perfect our '**ruling principle**', our own selves, the **things inside**, our desires and aversions, impulses, opinions, judgements and intentions; alternatively we must apply ourselves to **external things**, to **things outside**, and give up all hope for lasting and unshakable **peace of mind**, **freedom** and **serenity**. This is the difference between succeeding and failing as a human being, between being **good** or **bad**.

In holding to **well-disciplined** practices, in the manner of an athlete, the Stoic *prokoptôn* will **pay the price** of 'getting the worst in everything', being ridiculed and passed over. In the early stages, **paying this price** may prove a daunting challenge; but paying it is *only temporary* whilst the *prokoptôn's* practice is unperfected, whilst external things still seem important, and whilst it still matters to them how others judge them. The *prokoptôn,* of course, allows for the possibility that even an **'uneducated person'** may sometimes point out faults that need correcting – but otherwise, what others think or say or do is of no more consequence than an unexpected shower, a broken window, or any other trifling incident amongst the things that happen that provide the material upon which the *prokoptôn's* moral character (*prohairesis*) exercises its capacities. Instead of judging, for instance, 'This person has insulted me,' the *prokoptôn* making progress will be able to say, 'This person, to be sure, did attempt to insult me, and from a malicious disposition at that! But their disposition and the actions that issue from it are nothing to me. My "good flow" (*euroia*) is assured, and my serenity (*ataraxia*) is secure.'

Euphrates, at 29.4, was an eminent Stoic lecturer, praised by Pliny, who knew him personally (*Letters* 1.10); Epictetus offers a substantial quotation from Euphrates at *Discourses* 4.8.17–20.

(The reference to being whipped in 29.2 probably refers to the punishment meted out to sprinters caught committing false starts. For more references to the athlete as a metaphor for the Stoic *prokoptôn*, see *Discourses* 1.4.13, 1.18.21–3, 1.24.1–2, 1.29.33–8, 2.5.15–17, 2.17.29, 2.18.22, 3.10.6–8, 3.20.9, 3.21.3, 3.22.5–8, 3.23.1–2, 3.25.1–5, 4.4.30, 4.9.14–15; *Handbook* 51.2. See Long 2002, 120–1. For more on philosophy as an art of living or a way of life, see Hadot 2002, Striker 1986, and especially Sellars 2003.)

Chapter 30

The actions that are appropriate for us can generally be determined by our relationships. He is your father. This tells you to take care of him, to yield to him in all things, to put up with him when he abuses you or beats you.

'But he is a bad father.'

Nature did not provide for you a good father, but a father. Your brother wrongs you? Well then, maintain your relationship to him. Do not think about what he is doing, but about what you will have to do if you want to keep your moral character in accordance with nature. For no one can harm you unless you wish it. You will be harmed only when you think you are harmed. If you get into the habit of looking at the relationships implied by 'neighbour', 'citizen', 'commander', you will discover what is proper to expect from each.

Commentary

Key terms

appropriate actions (duties) (*ta kathêkonta*)	**in accordance with nature** (*kata phusin*)
bad (*kakos*)	**nature** (*phusis*)
harm (verb) (*blaptô*)	**moral character** (*prohairesis*)
	relationship (*schesis*)

To live **in accordance with nature** one must act in ways that are **appropriate**, proper, or fitting for the specific kind of creature that one happens to be. In the natural world, plants and animals flourish as they should quite spontaneously, from moment to moment responding to circumstances quite automatically. For plants and animals, which lack self-consciousness and any capacity for free will, questions regarding what should be undertaken, and how, simply make no sense. But for human beings, the situation is of course altogether different, for human beings are rational and self-conscious. Over and above sharing with other creatures a wide range of natural instincts and impulses, we have an awareness of ourselves and the situations in which we are acting: we can choose to act one way rather than another, and we can give reasons for what we do (see DL 7.108 and Stob. 2.7.8 = LS 59B, where we are told that an **appropriate action** is one that, 'when done, has a reasonable defence'.) And unlike animals, who can do no more than respond moment by moment to what is happening, although of course we must also respond to what happens, we have the capacity to plan ahead, to choose our undertakings for reasons that we can articulate, and make ourselves into the sorts of people we want to be (see Annas 1993a, 27–46).

The task of understanding and committing ourselves to the doing of what is **appropriate** (*kathêkon*) for us is the second of Epictetus' three 'topics' (*topoi*), and concerns how we can properly maintain our 'natural and acquired relations' (*Discourses* 3.2.4). Our 'natural relations' are those we have in virtue of to whom and when we were born, and depending upon our circumstances will include son/daughter, brother/sister, nephew/niece, and so forth: we have these **relationships** in virtue of what other people do. Other **relationships** are acquired as a result of what we do ourselves, and may include teacher, lover, spouse, student, friend, and so forth. Becoming a parent, however, appears to fall into both types of **relation**; *having a child* and caring for it is something natural, but *becoming a parent* is something that one chooses to do, or not, and once one *is* a parent one cannot stop being one, in contrast to being a student, say, which one ceases to be simply by quitting college. Indulging in a philosophical analysis of the different types of **relation** is not required, however, for understanding Epictetus' point here: which is that the *name* of the **relation** we have, or acquire, tells us what we need to know to carry on our profession always doing (or aiming to do) what is **appropriate** (see *Discourses* 2.10.1–11, for instance). For example, the name 'teacher' tells us – in a fairly obvious way simply by bringing to mind the notion of what teaching is – what one must do to be a good teacher (that is, what is **appropriate** for a teacher): one must have a mastery of one's subject and a proficiency in conveying knowledge and techniques to one's students; one must be patient, yet strict when strictness is called for; one must show dedication and enthusiasm, not least as a model for the student to emulate, and so on. (It is perhaps important to point out that Epictetus chooses to couch his teaching not in terms merely of *acquiring* a profession – of simply being a teacher, for example – but in terms of *maintaining our **relationships** to other people*; see *Discourses* 4.12.16–18: for one is what one is, and one does what one does, with reference to other people, and ultimately to serving one's community and contributing to God's plan for the world.)

An **appropriate action** is something I am required to do on the basis of how **nature** has constituted the world, including my own **nature** as a human being (both personal and general) and the specific circumstances and **relationships** in which I am located or which I choose for myself in pursuit of my undertakings. To follow up Epictetus' example in this chapter, how my father behaves *towards me* has no bearing on how I, as a son, should behave *towards him*: indeed, **nature** is under no obligation to provide me with what I would most prefer, but whether or not it does, it is the **relationship** itself that instructs me how to act. The manner in which my father undertakes his **duties** as a father is a matter for him, so even if he is a **bad** father, the very worst in the world, hard to get along with or even cruel, I will all the same strive to be a good son by doing what is **appropriate** for a son who cares for his father. In doing this – because I understand what I am doing and why – I will be able to keep my **moral character** (*prohairesis*) **in accordance with nature**; that is, I will remain free from the violent or disturbing emotions (*pathê*). As we know, my father's bad behaviour can **harm** me only when I judge that I have been **harmed** (see *Handbook* 1.3, 5 and 16), and to return briefly to the terminology of Chapter 29.7, the price I must pay for peace of mind, freedom and serenity (*apatheia, eleutheria, ataraxia*) is holding to those actions that are **appropriate** for a son. I look for no reward or any particular outcome in all this (that my father might mend his bad ways, for instance; though he might) – I already have my reward in keeping my **moral character** (*prohairesis*) **in accordance with nature**.

And so with all our **relationships**. In doing what is proper (*kathêkon*) with respect to each one, and accepting willingly the obligations that fate bestows on us, and taking up in good spirits the obligations we acquire through our choice of undertakings, we will provide for ourselves a 'good flow of life' (*euroia biou*).

It is worth remarking that the *Discourses* do not make any mention of the Stoic doctrine of *right actions* (*katorthômata*). This appears to be an omission on Epictetus' part, and it is hard to believe that his students would complete their studies in his school without being taught it. An understanding of this doctrine may well not be required for practical training in Stoic living, but it seems hard to accept that in the more formal parts of Epictetus' syllabus it would not have appeared at all. This gives further weight to the possibility that the *Discourses* once constituted a larger text, and that it is in the lost parts that the *katorthômata* made their appearance.

The performance of an **appropriate action** does not distinguish a virtuous person from a vicious person: just to stay alive, the vicious person must do many things that are **according to nature** (they must eat and drink, and take care of their health to a certain standard), and they will often also do what is **appropriate** in their **relationships**, such as caring for children, honouring debts, and helping friends. But the vicious person does these things from the wrong motives, usually focusing on their own (non-moral) advantages: they may, for example, repay a debt in the hope of gaining some further favour, not because it is the right thing to do. An **appropriate action** (*kathêkon*) is **in accordance with nature**, but when it is *also in accordance with virtue*, it becomes a right action (*katorthôma*). A right action (*katorthôma*) is thus defined as an **appropriate action** (*kathêkon*) that is 'complete' or 'perfect' (*teleios*; Stob. 2.7.8/8a/11a/11e) – it is completed or made perfect by the agent acting for the right reasons in the fulfilling of what virtue requires. (The virtues are 'complete' because once you have them nothing further is required for living well; Stob. 2.7.5b/11g: so right actions, actions performed virtuously, are said to be 'complete' also; see Pomeroy 1999, 116 nn. 113–15.)

It is possible, of course, that Epictetus deliberately avoided employing the *katorthômata* in his exposition. His doctrine of **moral character** (*prohairesis*) and how the *prokoptôn* can maintain it in the proper condition seems to avoid the need for making an account of the *katorthômata* (because an **appropriate action** when performed by an agent whose *prohairesis* is maintained in the proper condition – by only ever assenting to correct impressions – will thereby be a virtuous action). Also, the doctrine of *prohairesis* focuses the moral worth of any action immediately and exclusively on the agent, whereas the concept of right action (*katorthôma*), if not thoroughly understood, runs the risk of giving the impression that moral worth can attach to actions in their own right, a notion which the Stoics reject.

(See *Discourses* 3.1.25/27, 3.10.19–20, 3.11.4–6, 3.23.1–5. See also *Discourses* 1.11 where Epictetus discusses family affection and what is appropriate for a father – with a man who was so upset when his daughter was ill that he couldn't bear to be in the house with her, so stayed away until news of her recovery came – not in terms of what is *kathêkon*, but in terms of what is rational (*eulogistos*), right and good (*orthos kai agathos*), and in accordance with nature (*kata phusin*). See *kathêkon* in Glossary A for further references to the *Discourses*, and to DL and Stob. For general accounts of the Stoic notion of appropriate actions, see Annas 1993a, 96–8, 168–9; Cooper 1999b; Inwood 1985, 200–5, 211–14; Inwood and Donini 1999, 697–9, 727–31; Kidd 1978; Long 1986, 190–2; LS 59; Rist 1969, 97–111; Sandbach 1989, 45–8. For accounts directed specifically at Epictetus, see Bonhöffer 1996, 244–89; Dobbin 1998, 72–3, 133, 158; Hijmans 1959, 65, 83; Inwood 1985, 116–18; Long 2002, 231–44; and especially Sellars 2003, 139–41 including footnotes.)

Chapter 31

[1] Know that the most important thing regarding devotion to the gods is to have the right opinions about them – that they exist and administer the universe well and justly – to stand ready to obey them, to submit to everything that happens, and to follow it willingly as something being accomplished by the most perfect intelligence. Do this and you will never blame the gods nor accuse them of neglecting you. [2] But you will not be able to do this unless you remove the notions of good and bad from things that are *not* in our power, and apply them only to those things that *are* in our power. For if you believe that anything not in our power is good or bad, then when you fail to get what you want or get what you do not want, it is inevitable that you will blame and hate those responsible. [3] For every living thing naturally flees and avoids things that appear harmful (and their causes), and pursues and admires things that are beneficial (and their causes). It is impossible, then, for someone who thinks they are being harmed to take delight in what they suppose is causing the harm, just as it is impossible for

them to take delight in the harm itself. [4] This is why even a father is reproached by his son when he does not give him a share of those things the son regards as good. Thus, in thinking a king's throne to be something good, Eteocles and Polynices became enemies. This is why the farmer reproaches the gods, and so too the sailor, the merchant, and those who lose their wives and children. For people are devoted to what they find advantageous. Therefore, whoever takes proper care of their desires and aversions, at the same time also cares properly for their devotion. [5] But it is everyone's duty to offer libations, sacrifices and first-fruits according to tradition, with a pure disposition, not slovenly or carelessly, neither too meanly nor beyond our means.

Commentary

Key terms

advantageous (*sumpheron*)	**harmful** (*blaberos*)
aversion (*ekklisis*)	**in our power** (*eph' hêmin*)
bad (*kakos*)	**not in our power**
beneficial (*ôphelimos*)	(*ouk eph' hêmin*)
blame (verb) (*memphomai*)	**reproach** (verb) (*loidoreô*)
child (*teknon*)	**right opinions** (*orthai hupolêpseis*)
desire (*orexis*)	**submit** (*eikô*)
devotion (to the gods) (*eusebeia*)	**take care of** (*epimeleomai*)
gods (*theoi*)	**universe** (*to holos*)
good (*agathos*)	**wife** (*gunê*)
harm (noun) (*blabê*)	

This commentary should be read in conjunction with the entry for *theos* (**God**) in Glossary A.

Epictetus employs the plural form *gods* in this chapter, but elsewhere he also uses the terms 'God' and 'Zeus', and all three terms are essentially interchangeable in Stoic thought (see DL 7.147 = LS 54A); the Stoics also identify **God** with providence, fate, reason, nature, and the world itself (see DL 7.148, LS 54U, *ND* 1.39 = LS 54B).

How his students should understand their relationship to **God** is of key importance for Epictetus. In order to make progress towards Stoic wisdom and to acquire the capacity to keep their moral character (*prohairesis*) always in the proper condition, the *prokoptôn* has to maintain the right sort of *eusebeia* (devotion, reverence, or piety) to **God**. They have to become *eusebês* (devout, reverent, or pious), and this is accomplished by holding the **right opinions** about **God** – specifically, that **God** exists, and that He administers the **universe** 'well and justly', and then to **submit** to everything that happens, and accept it willingly.

To develop such a frame of mind, we need to maintain the outlook that we have already explored, that what is **not in our power** has no connection to and no significance for what is truly **good** and **bad** for us. To live in ignorance of this insight will make it inevitable that we will **blame** whomever we judge is responsible for depriving us of what we believe to be **beneficial**, or for **harming** our interests. Thus, as pre-Stoics, so to speak, or after progress has begun but in moments when our focus lapses, we will **blame** our neighbours or friends or family members for the **harm** we mistakenly think they have brought upon us; for although they may have inadvertently or even deliberately undermined our undertakings, they cannot, we will remember when our focus returns, harm *us*.

But such a lapse of focus, a forgetting of Stoic principles, when it comes to illness and death, to the weather and the forces of nature, will lead to our **reproaching God** when we are deprived of what we take to be **advantageous** – such as the persistence of our own good health and that of our **wives** and our **children**, our remaining alive and *their* remaining alive, and also fair winds and calm seas if we are sailors, and weather favourable to our crops if we are farmers, and weather favourable to our undertakings even when we are not sailors or farmers.

To live continually holding that nothing that happens is actually **good** or **bad**, because the only **good** is the condition of our moral character (*prohairesis*), and that **God** brings about all that happens just as it should, 'well and justly', is at one and the same time to properly **take care** of both our **desires** and **aversions**, and our **devotion** to God.

The notion of Stoic **devotion** to **God** can be expanded more fully by emphasising a number of further points. The fully pious (*eusebês*) person will believe that human beings are made by **God** (*Discourses* 1.9.7), that we are 'akin to' and 'come from' **God** (1.9.13), and that we can be regarded as being the 'sons of **God**' (1.3.1, 1.9.6). Our reason is in fact shared with **God** (1.9.5), not merely in the sense that we share the same *capacity* for reason, but that we are literally parts or fragments of **God** (1.14.6, 1.17.27, 2.8.11); thus the faculty that we have to make proper use of impressions (if we can recognise that we have it, and train ourselves in its correct use), is all we need to endure everything that happens (1.1.7, 1.6.40; see also 2.6.9, 4.1.100). This is why we should be grateful to **God** (1.4.32, 1.12.32, 2.23.5, 4.4.18), sing praises to **God** (1.16.16–21, 2.18.13, 3.26.30) and never find fault with anything that He gives to us (1.14.16, 3.5.8). Our immunity to all **harm** is complete when our progress is complete, when we fully align our will with that of **God's** will, when what comes about is always exactly what we wish for ourselves when in the role of the dog tied to the back of the cart in Hippolytus' analogy (*Refutation of Heresies* 1.21.2 = LS 62A) we can always match our movements with those of the cart (which represent the way things go, the will of **God**) so as never to be dragged along against our will, moaning and bewailing our lot, or fighting against what is inevitable (2.7.13, 2.16.42, 2.17.22, 4.7.20; Seneca, *Ep.* 107; the analogy of the dog tied to the cart is discussed towards the end of the commentary to *Handbook* 53). At *Discourses* 2.17.23–5 Epictetus suggests that we should 'offer up' our **desires** and **aversions** to 'Zeus and the other gods', that we should let **God** fulfil or frustrate our **desires** as He pleases. Through this exercise, we transfer responsibility for our **desires** being fulfilled or not to **God,** and we rightly limit our responsibilities to using our impressions correctly and maintaining our **devotion** to God by accepting, and if possible by *willing*, everything that comes to pass as what is proper and appropriate for **God's** creation. Our task as players in His drama is nothing more than doing what is fitting and expected for people assigned our specific roles, thankful for the opportunity to live as human beings, and for what we are given (but not resentful or disappointed by what we are not given).

The injunction of 31.5 is perhaps difficult to follow for Stoics in the modern world. The Pagan revival is as yet in its infancy, and most Stoics will find it difficult to locate venues where they can join with others in the worship of Zeus and the other deities of the Greco–Roman pantheon (conceived by Stoics as aspects of the one godhead). But there is nothing to prevent our making private devotions according to our inclinations. Perhaps at dawn when the warmth of the sun awakens the world and reminds us that we are all brought into being and sustained by the movements of **God's** hand arranging events and working both the small and the mighty transformations that constitute our personal histories and the history of the world – perhaps as we open ourselves to such a vision of things, we can say a word to **God**, as we might to a friend, to someone who knows us and is conscious of our plight, to confirm that all is well with us because we have all that we need to flourish and live well, and that we are thankful for being the sort of creature, self-conscious and rational, for whom such a vision and an understanding of matters is possible. Some, perhaps, may like to focus their thoughts by reciting a brief hymn to Zeus, such as the one we find in *Handbook* 53.1, or this one:

Zeus I shall sing: of the gods he is best, he is also the greatest.
Wide is his vision. He governs and brings everything to fulfillment,
Whispering words unto Themis, who sits inclining toward him.
Favor us, scion of Cronus, all-seeing, most honored, and greatest!
(To Zeus, *Homeric Hymn* 23, trans. Hine)

In Greek myth, Eteocles and Polynices were the two sons of Oedipus
who became king of Thebes (by killing his father and marrying his
mother, without realising that they were his parents). Upon Oedipus'
discovering the truth and going in shame into exile, his two sons went to
war over the throne of Thebes and died fighting each other in single
combat. (Eteocles and Polynices are mentioned elsewhere by Epictetus
at *Discourses* 2.22.13 and 4.5.29.)

(See also *Discourses* 1.6, 1.9, 1.12, 1.16, 1.17.28, 2.23.42, 4.1.89–
90/99, 4.7.6–11; DL 7.134–9/147–9; LS 54. For more on Epictetus
and God see Dobbin 1998, 86–8, 101–13, 123–8, 136–45, 148–55,
158–61, 180–1; Hijmans 1959, 13–16; Long 2002, *passim*; Rist 1985;
Xenakis 1969, 40–55. For more on the Stoics and God, see Long 1986,
147–52, 179–84; Mansfeld 1999, 464–9; Sandbach 1989, 69–82;
Sedley 1999, 382–6.)

Chapter 32

[1] When you make use of divination, remember that you do not know how events
will turn out (this is what you have come to learn from the diviner), but if you really
are a philosopher you know before you come what sort of thing it is. For if it is one
of the things that are not in our power, then necessarily what will happen will be
neither good nor bad. [2] Therefore do not bring desire and aversion to the diviner
(for, if you do, you will be fearful of what you may hear), but go with the
understanding that everything that happens will be indifferent and of no concern
to you, for whatever it may be it is in your power to make good use of it, and that
no one can hinder you in this. Go with confidence to the gods as your counsellors,
and afterwards, when some advice has been given, remember from whom you
have received it and whose counsel you will be disregarding if you disobey.
[3] Approach the diviner in the way Socrates thought appropriate, that is, only in
those cases when the whole question turns upon the outcome of events, and
when there are no means afforded by reason or any other art for discovering what
is going to happen. Therefore, when it is necessary to share a danger with a friend
or with your country, do not ask the diviner whether you should share the danger.
For even if the diviner should happen to tell you that the omens are unfavourable,
that death is foretold, or mutilation to some part of the body, or exile – even at this

risk, reason requires you to stand by your friend or share the danger with your country. Pay attention, therefore, to the greater diviner, Pythian Apollo, who threw from the temple the man who did not help his friend when he was being murdered.

Commentary

Key terms

aversion (*ekklisis*)
bad (*kakos*)
desire (*orexis*)
divination (*mantikê*)
diviner (*mantis*)
friend (*philos*)
gods (*theoi*)
good (*agathos*)

indifferent (*adiaphoros*)
in our power (*eph' hêmin*)
not in our power
  (*ouk eph' hêmin*)
philosopher (*philosophos*)
Pythian Apollo (*Puthios*)
Socrates (*Sôkratês*)

It was common practice, quite normal and usual, in Epictetus' time (as it had already been for centuries) for people to visit oracles, diviners, soothsayers and dream interpreters – either in the formal setting of a temple, or by soliciting the services of a private practitioner. Indeed, no undertaking of any importance would have been entered upon without seeking the guidance and support of the **gods**, and we should remember that Epictetus' remarks in this chapter are made against the background of **divination** being familiar to, and the common experience of, probably all his students, and note also that Epictetus' Stoic predecessors 'defended nearly every sort of divination' except, it seems, Panaetius (Cicero, *On Divination* 1.6./72; see 1.82–7; Book 1 of this work is probably based on Posidonius' *On Soothsaying*; see MacKendrick 1989, 197; see also DL 7.149; *ND* 2.12/162–4; *NQ* 2.32).

The topic of omens and portents was briefly touched on in *Handbook* 18. Epictetus now returns to the subject of **divination** to remind his students that, for Stoics who have recourse to a **diviner**, two important distinctions should always be brought to bear. The first (which underpins the remarks of *Handbook* 32.1 and 32.2), with which we are of course already well acquainted, is the distinction between what is **in our power** and what is not. If the **diviner** tells us about how events will turn out with reference only to what will actually happen and not to our own judgements, **desires**, **aversions**, and intentions, then what we hear concerns only external things that are **not in our power**, that are **indifferent** with respect to being **good** or **bad**, and are of no concern to us. Epictetus reminds us that it is the **gods**, through the medium of the **diviner**, who have counselled us about the future, and that no matter what happens, our task, because this is what is **in our power** and where what is **good** for us is to be found, is to 'make good use of it', which generally means using our impressions properly (and not assenting to any false judgements and lapsing into a passion), and dealing appropriately with every contingency, striving to treat other people fairly and justly, to exercise self-restraint, and to face calamity and unpleasantness with courage.

The second distinction, taken up in *Handbook* 32.3, is between what we are told will happen, and how we should act in response. When there is no way of finding out what will happen, seeking the services of a **diviner** is legitimate, but what we should *not* do as Stoic **philosophers** is look for any advice as to how we should act in the matter, for this is something we already know in advance. If danger is to come, or is foretold by the **diviner**, we already know that our task is to stand by our **friend** and share the danger with them, or if our child is ill (see *Discourses* 1.11), we already know that our duty (what is appropriate for one who wishes to live in accordance with nature) is to stay with her, comfort and care for her in her distress, for that is what duty and virtue require. Our **good** lies in doing such things, irrespective of what actually happens and what the **diviner** may or may not recommend. (Bizarre though it may seem to many readers, I ought perhaps to note my personal experience with **divination**. For several years I worked as a **diviner** using the Tarot, and clients invariably wanted to know – after the matter in hand had been mapped out and its future development sketched – *what they should do*. They were frequently quite insistent that I should tell them how to proceed, wholly reluctant to immerse themselves in their own responsibilities, but no matter how persistent their protestations, I refused to guide them beyond stating, as I saw it, what seemed likely in consequence of their following the various alternatives open to them. The most I ever did was to reveal those alternatives which they could not see for themselves, but I refused to make their decisions for them.)

I am not aware of any references in the ancient literature to **Socrates** visiting a **diviner** (though Epictetus refers only to **Socrates**' attitude to what counts as 'approaching the diviner appropriately', and not to any actual instances of **Socrates** going to a **diviner**). **Socrates** appears to stand in for the fully wise person who knows what is appropriate for someone visiting a **diviner**.

The story of the **friend** who was ejected from the temple by **Pythian Apollo** can be found in Aelian's *Historical Miscellany* (3.44) and in Simplicius' commentary to this chapter of the *Handbook*.

Aelian recounts that a delegation of three **friends** sent by their fellow townspeople to consult the Delphic oracle of Apollo were set upon by bandits just as they arrived at Delphi. One of the three men simply abandoned his **friends** and ran away. The other two fought off the robbers; some they killed, and the others fled. Finally, when one was wrestling with the last remaining robber, his companion, intending to come to his aid, killed his **friend** instead of the robber with an ill-aimed blow of his sword. Later, in the presence of the **Pythian** priestess, the man who had run away was denied an oracle and told to leave the temple because when his **friend** was dying he had refused to help. But to the man who tried to help, but failed, was rendered the following oracle: *You killed your friend while defending him; blood has not polluted you, and your hands are cleaner than before* (trans. Wilson 1997, 175–7).

Simplicius offers this story as two separate incidents, both involving separate sets of only *two* **friends**. In the first account, the pair is set upon by the bandits, and while the first **friend** runs away to save himself, the second is killed. The surviving **friend** appears before the priestess to be ejected by **Apollo** from the temple with these words: *Though present at the side of a friend who was dying, you did not defend him. You approach impure. Depart from our beauteous shrine* (trans. Brennan and Brittain 2002b, 86). The second story tells of two other men who similarly fell among bandits. One tried to help his **friend** by hurling his spear at a bandit, but missed and killed his **friend**. This man did not dare to enter the temple because he thought that in killing his **friend** he had made himself impure. But **Apollo**, through his oracle, told him: *You killed your companion, defending him. The blood of slaying does not pollute you. You are more pure than you were before* (trans. Brennan and Brittain 2002b, 87).

Epictetus' students, we must presume, were familiar with this story, or at least with some version of it, and Epictetus uses it to point out that what matters is not how events actually turn out, but the quality of character we bring to those events in our efforts to live as Stoic **philosophers**, conscious of what our reason (which is also God's reason) requires. And whatever the **diviner** may say is neither here nor there with respect to *that*.

(See also *Discourses* 2.7, 2.16.16–17; Stob. 2.7.5b12/11s. For a discussion on Socrates and divination, see Brickhouse and Smith 1994, 189–201. For more on Roman religion and divination, see for instance Scheid 2003, 111–26, and Shelton 1998, 375–77. Socrates appears in the *Handbook* five times, in this chapter and at 5, 33.12, 46.1, and 51.3; he is quoted twice, in 53.3 and 53.4. For the numerous references to Socrates in the *Discourses*, see the very end of the commentary to *Handbook* 51.)

Chapter 33

[1] From the outset, establish for yourself a certain character and disposition that you will maintain both when you are by yourself and with other people.

[2] For the most part, keep silent, or say only what is required in few words. On rare occasions, when circumstances call for it, we will speak, but not about ordinary things: not about gladiators, nor horse-racing, not about athletes, nor about food and drink (which are the usual topics); and especially do not talk about people, blaming or praising or comparing them. [3] If at all possible, turn the conversation of the company by what you say to more suitable topics; and if you happen to be alone amidst strangers, keep silent. [4] Do not laugh a great deal, nor at many things, nor without restraint.

[5] Avoid swearing oaths altogether, if possible; otherwise refuse to do so as far as circumstances allow.

[6] Avoid banquets given by strangers and uneducated people. But if there is ever an occasion to join in them, take every care never to slip into the ways of the uneducated; be assured that if your companion is dirty it is inevitable that in their company you will become dirty yourself, even if you happen to start out clean.

[7] As to things concerning the body, take only what bare necessity requires with respect to such things as food, drink, clothing, shelter and household slaves: exclude everything that is for outward show or luxury.

[8] As for sex, you should stay pure before marriage as far as you can, but if you have to indulge, do only what is lawful. However, do not be angry with those who do indulge, or criticise them, and do not boast of the fact that you do not yourself indulge.

[9] If you are told that someone is saying bad things about you, do not defend yourself against what is said, but answer, 'Obviously this person is ignorant of my other faults, otherwise they would not have mentioned only these ones.'

[10] It is not necessary for the most part to go to public games; but if it is ever appropriate for you to go, show that your first concern is for no one other than yourself – that is, wish only to happen what does happen, and wish only those to win who do win, and in this way you will meet with no hindrance. Refrain entirely from shouting or laughing at anyone, or getting greatly excited. And after you have left, do not talk a great deal about what happened (except in so far as it contributes to your own improvement), for doing so would make it clear that you have been impressed by the spectacle.

[11] Do not go randomly or thoughtlessly to public readings; but when you do go, maintain your own dignity and equanimity, and guard against offending anyone.

[12] When you are about to meet someone, especially someone who enjoys high esteem, ask yourself what Socrates or Zeno would have done in such circumstances, and you will have no difficulty in making proper use of the occasion.

[13] When you go to see someone who has great power, propose to yourself that you will not find them at home, that you will be shut out, that the doors will be slammed in your face, that this person will pay no attention to you. And if in spite of all this it is your duty to go, then go, and bear what happens, and never say to yourself, 'It wasn't worth the trouble!' For that is the way of the uneducated person, someone who is bewildered by external things.

[14] In conversations, avoid talking at great length or excessively about your own affairs and adventures; however pleasant it may be for you to talk about the risks you have run, it is not equally pleasant for other people to hear about your adventures. [15] Avoid also trying to excite laughter, for this is the sort of behaviour that slips easily into vulgarity and at the same time is liable to diminish the respect your neighbours have for you.

[16] There is danger also in lapsing into foul language. So whenever anything like this happens, if the opportunity arises, go so far as to rebuke those who behave in this way; otherwise, by keeping silent and blushing and frowning, make it clear that you disapprove of such language.

Commentary

Key terms

angry (*epachthês*)
bad (*kakos*)
banquet (*hestiasis*)
blame (verb) (*psegô*)
body (*to sôma*)
character (*charaktêr*)
compare (*sunkrinô*)
critical (*elenktikos*)
dignity (*semnos*)
disposition (*tupos*)
equanimity (*eustathês*)
external things (*ta ektos*)
improvement (*epanorthôsis*)
keep silent (*aposiôpaô*)

keep silent (*siôpaô*)
oath (*horkos*)
praise (verb) (*epaineô*)
public games (*to theatron*)
rebuke (verb) (*epiplêssô*)
respect (noun) (*aidôs*)
sex (*aphrodisia*)
Socrates (*Sôkratês*)
uneducated (*idiôtikos*)
way of the uneducated, vulgar
     (*idiôtismos*)
without offence (*anepachthês*)
Zeno (*Zênôn*)

Epictetus exemplifies the sort of **disposition** of **character** that the Stoic *prokoptôn* is trying to develop with reference to a number of activities and social situations which are clearly intended to be illustrative rather than exhaustive. His general drift is to exhort his students to pretty much steer clear of social contact, but especially to be wary of interacting with '**uneducated**' people (that is, people ignorant of philosophy; see for instance *Discourses* 3.16.16); they should certainly avoid **banquets** given by such people. And when such events cannot be avoided, they must guard against lapsing into the '**ways of the uneducated**', for that would be to return to how they were before their Stoic training commenced, valuing **external things**, falling prey to the passions, and **blaming** other people and the gods for their misfortunes. The general rule appears to be that of **keeping silent**, so as to avoid discussing other people, **praising** or **comparing** them, for what other people do has absolutely no bearing on the *prokoptôn's* progress (except only that bad behaviour in others can often test one's patience and exercise the restraint of **anger**); the primary concern of the Stoic is their own **improvement**, and this endeavour cannot be furthered by **criticising** the behaviour of others.

Epictetus does not condemn **sex** out and out. It is better not to indulge, and to confine sexual activity to one's marriage. Again, **criticising** others who indulge, when one does not, serves no purpose, and tends to remove the spotlight from one's own progress by shining it fruitlessly upon the faults of others.

Talking about 'the usual things' encourages us to value them, to find them important when, in themselves, they have no importance. Our moral progress is not affected by this athlete rather than that one winning the race; the world is not somehow better, and we ourselves are certainly not better off, if this gladiator prevails over that one. So **public games** are out, except only when we are obliged to accompany someone else; and while we are there, we will remain detached from events. What happens at such spectacles is of no importance to what really matters; we should be merely witnesses to what happens without becoming engaged in the proceedings.

Perhaps the injunction not to **offend** anyone at public readings attaches to the possibility that the *prokoptôn* might upset the speaker by **criticising** their oratory, or of simply not **praising** it with sufficient enthusiasm.

One place, however, where **criticism** and **rebuke** are merited it seems is in response to the use of bad language (*Handbook* 33.16) – a fault that the *prokoptôn* will assiduously avoid, but a misdemeanour so awful it seems that the Stoic will disapprove of it even if all they can do is frown and blush.

In any social contact, we all run the risk of being **criticised** by others. This, the *prokoptôn* does not resist or worry about; they are aware of their faults, and their Stoic training, they know, is at least in part an endeavour to correct such faults. Our faults cannot be made worse by people saying **bad** things about us – not unless we respond inappropriately by getting **angry** or by **criticising** the person who has just **criticised** us. Faults cannot be defended, they can only be mended or revisited. It is the wish not to revisit them, and an understanding of why this is important, that in part separates the *prokoptôn* from the 'uneducated'. A smooth flow of life (*euroia biou*) is promoted by preserving one's **dignity** and **equanimity**, and in the face of difficulties and troubles one can maintain these qualities of **character** by keeping in mind what **Socrates** or **Zeno** would do. They were perfect Sages, or very nearly so, and if we know how they would behave, and why, there is nothing to stop us doing exactly the same. When our **disposition** is tested perhaps, like method actors, we can 'be' **Socrates** or **Zeno** – untroubled, courteous, courageous, self-reliant, temperate and mindful of being in service to God. Our focus on being this way can only be disrupted by valuing things inappropriately, by finding things to be important when they are not, and consequently falling prey to the passions, and thus having our 'good flow' (*euroia*) ruined not by circumstances or by the actions of other people, but by *ourselves*.

All the topics discussed above concern how we should interact with others. Although Epictetus opens this chapter making references to maintaining the correct **disposition** both with regard to *being alone* and *being with other people*, it appears that the issue of how to conduct ourselves when alone is addressed only in *Handbook* 33.7, which discusses how we should behave with **respect** to caring for our **bodies** – and the message here is a simple one, that we should hold to a strict simplicity. Why we should do this seems obvious enough. If, for example, we are worried about whether our clothes are sufficiently fine and fashionable, or whether our food is suitably sophisticated, or our houses agreeably lavish and luxurious, then we are worrying about the wrong things, and the quality of our 'good flow' (*euroia*) will depend upon whether or not we have these things. That, of course, is to follow the '**ways of the uneducated**' and to fall into **vulgarity**.

I do not know why in section 33.5, Epictetus counsels against swearing **oaths**. The Stoic will maintain their integrity, telling the truth, honouring debts, keeping promises and such like (or at least endeavouring to do so), regardless of whether they have sworn an oath or not. Despite counselling against swearing oaths here, at *Discourses* 1.14.15–17 Epictetus says that we ought to swear an allegiance to God – conceived as the guardian *daimon* that God has assigned to everyone – never to find fault with anything that He gives us. This oath is a private matter concerning the way the Stoic understands their relationship to God. And this relationship, and how the Stoic conducts themselves generally, is surely untouched by being required by someone else to swear an oath. The Stoic will not on their own account initiate the swearing of oaths, since to do so, as already suggested, is of no consequence and makes no difference as to whether they will try to carry out some action. If, in the view of someone else, some transaction is placed on a firmer foundation by the swearing of an oath, I do not see why the Stoic would have any objection. The Stoic's whole life is really the endless fulfilling of an oath to live as well as they may, always content with their lot, mindful that being in service to God they are in virtue of that commitment also in service to everyone in their community, to benefit and never harm, to behave nobly and honestly both as an example to others, and as the only means by which their humanity can be fully realised.

(Socrates appears in the *Handbook* five times, in this chapter and at 5, 32.3, 46.1, and 51.3; he is quoted twice, in 53.3 and 53.4. For the numerous references to Socrates in the *Discourses*, see the very end of the commentary to *Handbook* 51. Zeno in 33.12 is Zeno of Citium the founder of the Stoic school, who at the beginning of the third century BC after having studied with a variety of teachers – including Crates the Cynic – began teaching in the *poikilê stoa* – painted porch or colonnade – in the agora at Athens. His followers were first known as Zenonians after their teacher, but were soon enough called Stoics after the place where they met. Diogenes Laertius devotes Book 7 of his *Lives of Eminent Philosophers* to Zeno of Citium and a general exposition of Stoic philosophy. Zeno appears in the *Discourses* at 1.17.11, 1.20.14, 2.13.14–15, 3.21.19, 3.23.32, 3.24.38, 4.8.12, and 4.9.6.)

Chapter 34

When you get an impression of some pleasure, as in the case of other impressions, guard against being carried away by it, but let the matter wait for you, and delay a little. Now consider these two periods of time, that during which you will enjoy the pleasure, and that when the pleasure has passed during which you will regret it and reproach yourself. Next set against these how pleased you will be if you refrain, and how you will commend yourself. When, however, the time comes to act, take care that the attraction, allure and seductiveness of the pleasure do not overcome you, but set against all this the thought of how much better it is to be conscious of having won this victory over it.

Commentary

Key terms

guard against (*phulassô*)   **regret** (verb) (*metanoeô*)
impression (*phantasia*)   **reproach** (verb) (*loidoreô*)
pleasure (*hêdonê*)   **victory** (*nikê*)

The work that the Stoic *prokoptôn* is trying to further, that of securing for themselves a 'good flow of life' (*euroia biou*), is ruined by falling prey to the *pathê*, the disturbing or violent emotions. For the Stoics, all passions fall under four generic types: with respect to things anticipated in the future, someone may suffer the fear (*phobos*) of some expected evil, or the desire (*epithumia*) of some expected good; and with respect to present events, someone may suffer the distress (*lupê*) of something judged evil, or the **pleasure** (*hêdonê*) of something judged good. The Stoic's 'good flow' (*euroia*) is spoiled directly by experiencing the disagreeable passions of fear and distress, but is also undermined by experiencing what might be taken to be the agreeable passions of desire and pleasure (though a desire unfulfilled soon enough becomes distressing). Even the *pathos* of **pleasure** is detrimental to the Stoic, because the judgement that occasions it, that something present is good, is false, and holding to this judgement is irrational, simply because it is always irrational to hold to what is false. Holding to what is false makes it likely, if not inevitable, that someone will pursue the wrong objectives, viewing them as more important than what is actually important, putting aside perhaps their duties to others, treating people unkindly in the pursuit of pleasures and those things that produce pleasures, and thereby living contrary to nature and viciously – all of which puts happiness and well-being (*eudaimonia*) beyond their grasp.

The Stoic must stand **guard against** the allure of **pleasures**. Here, in part, is what the Stoic's progress consists in – a moving from old ways in which **pleasures** are judged good and desirable, to a new way of understanding that **pleasure** is to be avoided: no **pleasure** is good (for only the virtues and actions motivated by virtue are good; see DL 7.94, and Stob. 7.5a/6e, for instance), and judging that any **pleasure** is good is false, and holding to that judgement is irrational simply because it is indeed false.

In this chapter of the *Handbook*, Epictetus gives us advice as to how we can resist the attraction of **pleasures**. This advice seems to be applicable to **pleasures** themselves, and to securing those things that are instrumental in producing **pleasures** (such as food, drink, possessions, the company of 'uneducated' people, and many other things), and is probably not going to help the person who has already started enjoying their **pleasure**, since by this time the error of judging the **pleasure** to be good and desirable has already been made. Thus, when we are told to **guard against** being carried away by an **impression** of some **pleasure**, the **impression** we are being warned against cannot be that of a **pleasure** actually present, but that of a **pleasure** anticipated or expected. 'Impression', for the Stoics, is not confined only to the case of sense perception (though this is the type of impression usually referred to), but may also denote any mental item that comes into awareness, including hopes, intentions, plans, expectations, wishes, memories, imaginings and even dreams, but also generalisations (such as 'money is good', 'centaurs do not exist') and conceptualisations ('two is the square root of four'). (For *phantasia* denoting non-sensory items of awareness, see Annas 1992, 72; Long 1999, 575–6; Long 2002, 130, 214; Sandbach 1996, 10–11.)

The Stoic can gain **victory** over an **impression** that some specific **pleasure** ought to be pursued, and that, if immanent, should be indulged in, by withholding their assent. The exercise by means of which this can be done, offered here, requires the *prokoptôn* to step out of time, as it were, and hold up alternative and opposing **impressions** in order, hopefully, to be convinced that the original **impression** that urged the pursuit of **pleasure** should *not* command assent. First, the *prokoptôn* should picture themselves enjoying the **pleasure**, and second they should picture the time after the **pleasure** has passed during which they will recognise their error (for their Stoic training has already shown them why this is indeed an error), **regretting** what they have done and **reproaching** themselves for their folly. And third, they should picture to themselves the alternative future in which they refrain from indulging in the **pleasure** and commend themselves for doing so: this is the alternative in which their progress is furthered. The other alternative is the one in which their progress is undone.

The *prokoptôn* recognises that in being tempted by a **pleasure**, they are actually being offered the choice of selecting something even more agreeable (that is, the rejection of the **pleasure**, for this is what adds to

progress, as opposed to what subtracts from it). This is, of course, the
choice between ruining their 'good flow' (*euroia*) and preserving it.

(At *Discourses* 2.11.19–25, Epictetus offers a proof for pleasure not
being the good; at 2.17.12 he points out that some people take the good
to be pleasure, but others take it to be wealth, and yet others take it to be
health; the Stoic view that pleasure numbers amongst the indifferent
things is found at 2.19.13. At 2.22.7 we learn that the foolish person,
amongst other things, sometimes regards wealth and pleasure as good,
sometimes an evil. In *Fragment* 14, Epictetus informs us that it is his
sense of self-respect (*aidôs*) that prevents him from regarding pleasure as
'the good and end of life', '*agathou kai telos tou biou*'.)

Chapter 35

When you do something from a clear judgement that it ought to be done, never
try to avoid being seen doing it, even if you expect most people to disapprove. If,
however, it would not be right to do it, avoid the deed itself. But if it *is* right, why be
afraid of anyone who wrongly disapproves?

Commentary

Key terms

disapprove (*epiplêssô*)   **right** (*orthos*)

How the Stoic *prokoptôn* should regard the approval and **disapproval** of
other people has been touched upon in *Handbook* 13, 23, and 33.9, and
has been treated more fully in *Handbook* 22 and 24; the topic will be
addressed again in Chapter 42 (see especially commentaries to Chapters
22, 23, and 24). The Stoic *prokoptôn* will, of course, take the greatest
care to respond appropriately to criticism of their conduct rendered by
their teacher and fellow students, and will remain alert to the possibility
that remarks from even 'uneducated' people may reveal faults that need
to be corrected, but otherwise they will remain untouched and unmoved
by the **disapproval** of other people. For what do other people know?
They do not know in what good and bad reside, they know only dimly
what is in accordance with nature and what is not, and they do not know
how to follow God or even what that means. The only thing that matters
when deciding how to act is doing what is **right**, and that is determined
by doing what virtue and duty require for the specific role that one has
and the precise circumstances in response to which one acts. That other
people may criticise and **disapprove** of what we do is, of course, not in

our power, and is something indifferent that has no bearing on our 'good flow of life' (*euroia biou*): 'our good flow' (*euroia*) is not added to when someone praises us, neither is it diminished when someone **disapproves**.

There is perhaps an exercise that can add to our training here, for when someone criticises us we are alerted to re-evaluate our decision and to affirm – if this is where wisdom lies – that our business is not to care about what this person thinks, but to care about how God will judge us, and about the condition in which we are maintaining our moral character (*prohairesis*). Our wish as Stoics is to be free of the disturbing or violent emotions (*apathês*), free of troubles (*atarachos*), and fearless (*aphobos*) of whatever fate may bring our way, including the condemnation of others. The Stoic never fears the **disapproval** of others who may see them doing what is **right**.

(See *Discourses* 3.12.16, 3.23, 3.24.50–1, 4.4.44.)

Chapter 36

Just as the propositions 'It is day' and 'It is night' can be used meaningfully in a disjunctive proposition, but make no sense in a conjunctive proposition, so at a banquet, to choose the largest share may make sense with respect to nourishing the body, but makes no sense for maintaining the proper kind of social feeling. Therefore, when you are eating with someone else, bear in mind not merely the value to your body of what is set before you, but also the value of maintaining the proper respect for your host.

Commentary

Key terms

banquet (*hestiasis*)   **social feeling** (*koinônikos*)

The disjunctive (compound) proposition that Epictetus refers to here is made by joining the disjuncts 'It is day' and 'It is night' with the logical connective 'or': 'Either it is day or it is night' – and this compound proposition always states something true, because one disjunct or the other is true at any one time. But if we use the two simple propositions as *conjuncts* to make a conjunctive proposition using the logical connective 'and', we produce a proposition that is always false, whatever the facts may be about the time of day: 'It is the case both that it is day and that it is night' – because one of the conjuncts must always be false, and conjunctions are true only when *both* conjuncts are true.

In practical terms, if one wishes to convey meaningful information, this conjunction has no value – the proposition makes no sense, because there are no circumstances that make it true. Similarly, in the practical context of relating to other people, honouring one's host at a **banquet**, and 'maintaining the proper kind of **social feeling**', it makes no sense to take the largest share for oneself. Taking the largest share may satisfy one's interest to nourish the body, but undermines one's interest to promote the right kind of **social feeling**. One does not attend a **banquet** with the primary intention of nourishing the body (though, of course, it is likely to be nourished to some, perhaps even complete, degree). The purpose of attending the **banquet** is to maintain one's social relations and to behave respectfully towards one's host and the other guests. The fate of the largest share will be determined by the host, we may presume, or else by another guest less concerned with proper **social feeling**.

Chapter 37

If you undertake a role that is beyond your capacities, you both disgrace yourself in that one and also fail in the role that you might have filled successfully.

Commentary

Key terms

capacity (*dunamis*)   **role** (*prosôpon*)

This chapter underlines the warning already given in Chapter 29, that before entering upon our undertakings we should make sure that we possess the necessary **capacities** in a state of preparedness appropriate for the demands that will be placed upon them. In Chapter 29, it is clear that Epictetus is referring to the specific undertaking of Stoic training, and it seems clear enough that in the present chapter, he means the term 'role' to refer to that of Stoic philosopher. However, the advice offered here seems applicable generally, since our **capacities** may fail us with respect to succeeding in *any* **role**, not just that of Stoic philosopher; and if at all possible, it makes sense to avoid **roles** in which we can anticipate failure, and to pursue those in which we expect to succeed. And of course, if we expend our efforts upon undertakings that fail, we have wasted the energy that we could have otherwise devoted to something else.

Even if our **capacities** are too weak to secure real and enduring progress as Stoic philosophers, that does not mean that we should abandon the pursuit of all **roles** as pointless and contributing nothing whatever to the life of a person who wishes to flourish as well as their **capacities** will allow, even if such a life falls a long way short of the Stoic ideal in terms of making progress, emulating the Sage, or securing a permanent and enduring 'good flow of life' (*euroia biou*). Living according to nature is something that can be done to a lesser or greater degree, and in matching our **roles** to the **capacities** we actually have, our preference should always be that of choosing **roles** that promote living in accordance with nature as opposed to impairing it; the former objective is pursued by striving to be a good parent, for example, in contrast with adopting, say, the **role** of criminal mastermind. One may flourish as a criminal mastermind, to be sure, but one cannot in so doing flourish as a human being, and even 'uneducated' people have some potential to grasp that fact.

(The importance of bringing to bear the right capacity has already been discussed in *Handbook* 10 and commentary; Epictetus treats making progress in strengthening one's capacities at *Discourses* 2.18.)

Chapter 38

Just as in walking about you take care not to step on a nail or twist your ankle, so also you should take care not to harm your ruling principle. If we guard against this in every action, we will engage in affairs with greater security.

Commentary

Key terms

ruling principle (*to hêgemonikon*)

'**Ruling principle**' translates *to hêgemonikon*, and in Stoic psychology this is a power or capacity of a person's soul (*psuchê*), the other capacities being the five senses of sight, hearing, smell, taste and touch, along with reproduction and speech (see LS 53H). One's **ruling principle** is the capacity that employs and makes use of all the other capacities (*Discourses* 4.7.40; LS 53G7).

Hêgemonikon and *prohairesis* for Epictetus are essentially synonymous (Inwood 1985, 240; Long 2002, 211; Rist 1969, 229) – though he favours the term *prohairesis* over *hêgemonikon* more than twice as often in the *Discourses* (see Rist 1969, 231) – thus, both *hêgemonikon* and *prohairesis* make use of the other capacities (*Discourses* 2.23.5–29, 4.7.40); the philosopher's progress is secured by watching over (*têreô*) their *hêgemonikon* and caring for (*epimeleomai*) their *prohairesis* (3.10.16, 3.5.7), and by cultivating (*exergazomai*, *ekponeô*) their *hêgemonikon* and *prohairesis* (1.4.18, 3.6.3); both *hêgemonikon* and *prohairesis* should be kept in accordance with nature (*kata phusin*; 1.15.4, 3.4.9, 3.9.11, 3.10.11, 4.4.43; *Handbook* 14, 30); the philosopher's good lies in preserving both their *hêgemonikon* and *prohairesis* by making proper use of impressions (1.29.1–3, 2.18.27–30); and no one is master (*kurios*) over someone else's *hêgemonikon* (4.5.4) nor over someone else's *prohairesis* (4.12.7–8).

In favouring the term *prohairesis* over *hêgemonikon*, Epictetus makes frequent mention of things that are outside one's *prohairesis* (*ta aprohaireta*; 2.1.4–6/12, 2.13.10, for instance) – namely, that they are neither good nor bad, 'not in our power', and 'nothing to us' – but he does not couch this thought in terms of one's *hêgemonikon*.

'Personality is in many ways the most convincing modern equivalent for the Stoic term *hêgemonikon* ... the *hêgemonikon* is something of what we might call the "true self" or personality of each individual human being' (Rist 1969, 24–5). What Epictetus denotes by both *hêgemonikon* and *prohairesis* coincides with our notion of 'self', of that which is conscious of its own content, the external world, and of assenting, or not assenting, to impressions. Human beings are aware of their own experiences *of* the world and therefore are aware of being separate *from* the world, of holding the world in view as an *object* of awareness and judgement. This is why human beings are able to assent to impressions and to be aware of their assenting.

Everyone takes care not to step on nails or turn their ankle, and takes care to avoid injury to the body, generally. But it is not nails or injuries that threaten our well-being, for this depends upon the condition of what is internal, not what is external. The task of the *prokoptôn* is to take care of their *hêgemonikon*, of themselves, of their very essence as self-conscious, rational agents. Here is found the potential for every person to secure well-being or a 'good flow of life' (*euroia biou*). But the 'uneducated' person believes that their well-being derives from external things (*ta ektos*), from their bodies, and from their possessions and status. Certainly, these things should be cared for, in the right way, adopting the right sort of regard for them, for it is in making use of these things that we exercise virtue and fulfil our duties; but we must always remember that these things are merely on temporary loan, they are fickle and ephemeral, dependent upon forces of nature and the whims of fortune, the workings of which are only dimly comprehended and over which our powers are severely limited and never complete.

The Stoic *prokoptôn* knows that their **ruling principle** is harmed by falling prey to the passions (*pathê*), by allowing themselves to be the source of vicious actions, by doing what is contrary to nature, and by losing sight of their understanding that their rationality is a fragment of God's rationality whose proper exercise is to fulfil the role of human being by willing what actually happens as the will of God.

(For references to *hêgemonikon* and *prohairesis* in the *Discourses*, see the entries in Glossary A. For more on *hêgemonikon*, see Annas 1992, 61–70; Long 1986, 171–2, 175–7; Rist 1969, 24–44; Sandbach 1989, 83–4. For *prohairesis*, see Dobbin 1991, and 1998, 76–7; Inwood 1985, 240–2; Long 2002, 210–20; Rist 1969, 228–32.)

Chapter 39

Everyone's body is the measure for their possessions, as the foot is a measure for the shoe. If then you hold to this principle you will maintain the proper measure, but if you go beyond it, you will inevitably be carried over a cliff. Thus, in the case of the shoe, if you go beyond the foot, first you will get a gilded shoe, then a purple one, and then an embroidered one. For once you have gone beyond the measure, there is no limit.

Commentary

Key terms

measure or **standard** (*to metron*)   **property/possessions** (*ktêsis*)

Our **possessions**, we must remember, are not really ours, but are on loan from God who will take them back when He so chooses (see *Handbook* 11 and commentary, and *Discourses* 3.24.84–8). We can have no claim over our **possessions** (nor over our bodies, status, and reputations; 4.3.10), for **property** is 'not our own' (3.24.68, 4.1.130), and not in our power (*Handbook* 1.1). Epictetus tells us to 'give up' our **possessions** (and other things) that are not in our power as 'alien to us' (*allotrios*; *Discourses* 4.1.87), for we are not our bodies nor our **possessions** (nor our reputations; 4.6.34). These things number amongst the *aprohaireta*, things that are external (*ektos*) to our *prohairesis* (moral character). Our good does not lie in having **possessions**, nor having **possessions** of a particular sort in this or that condition, but in maintaining our *prohairesis* in the right condition or, what amounts to the same thing, in adopting the right disposition of character, the nature of which we have been investigating in these pages (see 1.29.1, 2.16.1, and also 3.1.40 where Epictetus makes the specific claim that we *are* our *prohairesis*).

Doing that is both necessary and sufficient for securing happiness (*eudaimonia*) and a 'good flow of life' (*euroia biou*). Having fancy shoes will not contribute to this end, nor will having *anything*: **possessions** simply do not contribute to someone's well-being (even if, along with the vast bulk of humankind, they are deluded into thinking that they do; see 3.22.26–7). But whilst we are alive and living in this world, we will have things to do, people to care for, ends to pursue, and undertakings of all sorts to engage in – and the doing of these things will be mediated through our **possessions**. But we must never make the error of identifying ourselves with our **possessions**, or in any way linking our material prosperity to what has true value. It is obvious enough that some people who enjoy great riches are nevertheless possessed of the meanest characters, and their doom is sealed regardless of how successful they may be in accumulating **property** and wealth.

This leaves the Stoic *prokoptôn* needing to know in what way they should stand towards their **property**, and what sort of **possessions** it is appropriate to have. We have already seen, at *Handbook* 33.7, that Epictetus advocates adopting an austere simplicity (the theme reappears in *Handbook* 47). And here in *Handbook* 39, we learn that this simplicity is to be determined in strictly practical terms of what the body actually requires. What the foot needs as a matter of fact should be the '*measure*' of the shoe; the foot needs to be protected, and this protection ought to be of such a character that the foot is maintained in reasonable comfort throughout the day as it serves its function of supporting the leg, walking about, and such. In this fashion we can carry on our duties and undertakings, making proper use of impressions, without giving our foot a second thought.

To feel that it matters that we show off our feet in fancy shoes, or worry over what other people will think about the way we dress, or, heaven forbid, succumb to anxieties about how we should show off our wealth (if we have any), is to fall into passion, lose our way, fail in our progress, and ruin our 'good flow' (*euroia*). To think that one's happiness (*eudaimonia*) depends even to the slightest degree upon someone else admiring one's fancy shoes is the height of folly. But once this mistake has been made, what will we *not* want? Fashionable clothes, an opulent house, luxurious possessions of all sorts? Such will be the cravings, and perhaps even the reality, attended by, of course, the passions of fear and jealousy and frustration, of those who do not know how to measure their own foot.

(For more on Epictetus' stance on property, see *Discourses* 3.6.5–7 and 4.1.100; see 2.14.23–4 for Epictetus' comparing possessions to fodder; see also 4.1.80 and *Fragment* 18. For a similar sentiment to that expressed in this chapter, see Seneca's remarks at *Ep.* 8.5 where he recommends simple living, saying: 'Indulge the body just so far as suffices for good health. ... Your house [should] be a protection against inclement weather. It makes no difference whether it is built of turf or of variegated marble ... What you have to understand is that thatch makes a person just as good a roof as gold does' (trans. Campbell). This outlook is, of course, not the preserve of Stoicism, and we find an admirable echo of it in Henry David Thoreau where he says in the first chapter, Economy, of *Walden* (1854): 'Most of the luxuries, and many of the so called comforts of life, are not only not indispensable, but positive hinderances to the elevation of mankind. With respect to luxuries and comforts, the wisest have ever lived a more simple and meager life than the poor. The ancient philosophers, Chinese, Hindoo, Persian, and Greek, were a class than which none has been poorer in outward riches, none so rich in inward. ... There are nowadays professors of philosophy, but not philosophers. ... To be a philosopher is not merely to have subtle thoughts, nor even to found a school, but so to love wisdom as to live according to its dictates, a life of simplicity, independence, magnanimity, and trust.')

Chapter 40

Once they reach the age of fourteen years, women are addressed by men as 'madam'. Accordingly, when they see that there is nothing else but pleasing men with sex, they begin to use cosmetics and dress up, and to place all their hopes in that. It is worth our while, then, to make sure they understand that they are valued for nothing other than their good behaviour and self-respect.

Commentary

Key terms

have sex with someone (*sunkoimaomai*)
having value (*axios*)
'madam' (*kuria*)

self-respecting (*aidêmôn*)
well-behaved (*kosmios*)
woman (*gunê*)

The term translated as **'madam'** is *hê kuria*, meaning 'mistress', or 'lady' (as in the expression 'lady of the house'); the masculine form, *ho kurios*, can be translated 'master' or 'lord', and identifies someone who is head of a family, master of a house, or someone in authority.

It is important that the people around us, and in particular our children, should have it impressed upon them why they are **valued**, and that being **well-behaved** and having **self-respect** are of the utmost importance. How can anyone hope to convince teenaged girls (most of them, anyway, if not all of them) that in aspiring to be **women**, placing all their hopes in pleasing men by **having sex** with them, is not the best way to carry on? Fate has spared me the burden of being a parent (and therefore being a parent to teenaged girls), and I will not say I wish that things had been different for me on that score – so in truth, I have no personal qualifications and no personal insights to bring to bear on this topic.

Most teenagers will have no interest in philosophy, and of those that do, how many will want to learn about Stoic ethics, let alone live as Stoics? The Stoic is concerned with their own conduct, and not with the conduct of others. But as Stoics we must care for others as our roles and duties dictate, and this means doing in practical terms what is required of us, and the way we do those things will set an example for those who notice us and have an interest in how they should themselves behave and what they should value. We may feel under an obligation, at least sometimes, to explain why having this interest matters, but it is not in our power to make others heed our words, even when those to whom we speak them are our own children (see *Discourses* 1.11 which, incidentally, offers us the one surviving example in Epictetus' corpus of a sustained and complete Socratic *elenchus*; see also 3.7.25–8).

Chapter 41

It is a sign of foolishness to spend a lot of time on things that concern the body, such as exercising a great deal, eating and drinking a lot, defecating and having sex. These are things that should be done in passing. Instead, you should turn your whole attention to the care of your mind.

Commentary

Key terms

body (*sôma*)   mind (*gnômê*)
foolishness (*aphuia*)

Epictetus counsels against indulgence and excess in matters concerning the **body**. As we know, he teaches that our 'good flow' (*euroia*) and happiness (*eudaimonia*) are not to be found in external things (*ta ektos*), and therefore are not to be found in the **body** (*Discourses* 3.22.26–7). The **body**, along with everything else that is external to our *prohairesis* (*aprohaireta*), is 'not in our power' (*ouk eph' hêmin*; 1.22.10, 4.1.66/ 100/130; *Handbook* 1.1) and is 'nothing to us' (1.29.24, 1.30.3). Our **body** is not our good (4.3.10), and numbers amongst all the other external things that we should 'give up' (4.4.33). Even in those cases where the focusing of attention upon the **body** is not appropriately described as indulgent or excessive in the questionable and disagreeable sense that Epictetus means (as appears to be the case respecting athletic training, martial arts training, and perhaps a number of other pursuits), the *prokoptôn* must still be absolutely clear that success in training one's **body** is not at all the same thing as success in taking care of one's **mind** by mastering the proper use of impressions.

Thus, it is **foolish** to focus our attention upon our **body** as our primary aim, for doing so, no matter how laudably, cannot in itself promote our securing what is of true value, which is the capacity to make proper use of impressions and thereby maintain our moral character (*prohairesis*) in the proper condition. The Stoic who is making good progress may, of course, devote themselves to the life of the athlete, say, and become accomplished in this endeavour; in which case their striving to make proper use of impressions will be exercised from within a life that is devoted to this end. But they do not make proper use of impressions, if they do, *because* they succeed as an athlete; they make proper use of impressions merely *at the same time* as they succeed as an athlete, and how they look after their **body** is incidental to their true work as a Stoic. And this is so generally: our progress as Stoics must be secured against the background of whatever sort of life we adopt or have thrust upon us by circumstance.

However, even though how we look after our **bodies** is incidental, something we do 'in passing' as Epictetus says, to our real work of caring for our **minds**, we should all the same take proper care of our **bodies**, because this is the charge that Zeus has laid upon us, to take proper care of the things that are given to us and to be thankful for the time we are permitted their use (*Discourses* 2.16.27–8, 4.11.17; *Handbook* 11). To take proper care of one's **body** means never lapsing into indulgence and excess, and it certainly means not lapsing into indulgence and excess under the guise of caring properly for one's **body**. And no matter how commendable someone's care of their **body** may be (striving for athletic excellence, for example), if they do not also take proper care of their **mind**, they have accomplished nothing of value as a Stoic.

(See also *Discourses* 4.1.78–81/111, 4.4.39–40, 4.11.13–18/25/32–3; *Fragment* 23.)

Chapter 42

When someone treats you badly or says bad things about you, remember that they do or say these things because they think it is appropriate. This is because it is not possible for someone to act on how things appear *to you*, but on how things appear *to them*. Accordingly, if someone holds a false opinion, because *this* is the person who has been deceived, it is *they* who suffer the harm. In the same way, if someone supposes that a true conjunction is false, it is not the conjunction that is harmed, but the person who has been deceived. If you proceed, then, from these principles, you will be gentle with the person who abuses you, saying on all such occasions, 'To them, this is how it seemed.'

Commentary

Key terms

appropriate (*kathêkon*)
bad (*kakos*)
badly (*kakôs*)
deceive (*exapataô*)

falsely appear (*kakôs phainomai*)
['if someone holds a false
opinion...' '*ei kakôs phainetai...*']
gentle (*praôs*)
harm (verb) (*blaptô*)

How we should respond when people treat us **badly** has already been remarked upon in Chapter 4 (with reference to being abused at the public baths) and in Chapter 20 from the point of view that the harm produced by insults comes not from the person who tries to abuse us, but from our own judgement that we are being insulted (and the remedy for the Stoic is found in learning the correct use of impressions). Here, in Chapter 42, Epictetus extends his discussion by pointing out that first, the person who treats others **badly** or says **bad** things about them thinks that doing so is **appropriate**, and second, that their actions in fact cause **harm** to themselves and not to their intended victim.

Epictetus' point is surely sound, that people act on how things appear to *them*, and on their beliefs regarding what they think is **appropriate** and advantageous (see *Discourses* 1.22.13 and 1.28.6, for instance). How else can anyone act? The Stoic *prokoptôn* does the very same thing, aiming to secure what they believe is most advantageous, their peace of mind (*ataraxia*), equanimity (*euroia*), and fearlessness (*aphobia*) – and that, in this particular situation, is accomplished by resisting the impression that being treated **badly** or having **bad** things said of them constitutes a real **harm**. The Stoic who is the victim of abuse knows that they are neither disadvantaged nor harmed by such abuse, because the only good is virtue and action motivated by virtue, and the only evil is vice and action motivated by vice – and amongst these evils are the passions (*pathê*), violent or disturbing emotions that are contrary to reason, that arise from making false evaluative judgements about what is good and bad, one source being the erroneous belief that being the victim of other people's abuse is something harmful.

It is not something harmful – and the Stoic's *euroia* ('good flow') and *eudaimonia* remain theirs, unaffected and undiminished. As we know, Epictetus teaches his students that their *prohairesis* is maintained in the right condition, and their *euroia* kept safe, by always being alert to their dismissing as 'nothing to them' whatever is not in their power (*Handbook* 1.5). The **bad** things said of us are 'nothing to us' because they are *aprohairetos*, external to our *prohairesis*, the actions of other people that cannot impinge upon our virtue and therefore cannot do us harm. But further, on the understanding that the **bad** things said of us are indeed false, it is the person who **holds these false opinions** who is **deceived** and thereby harmed, for they are disadvantaged by these false beliefs (that someone is due criticism for which justification is lacking, or that there is something to gain in abusing others), making themselves spiteful, vindictive, anti-social and contemptible; in a word, they make themselves vicious, and bring upon themselves the only sort of evil that a human being can truly suffer. Towards such a person, Epictetus urges his students to be **gentle**, for how things seemed to them has hurt them, and they are in consequence less human than they might have been. They may never learn, and they will in all probability end their days as someone 'uneducated' (*apaideutos* or *idiôtikos*). But the *prokoptôn* should not let this tragedy, which is not their own, interfere with, much less arrest, their progress.

(See *Discourses* 1.28.10/23, 4.4.7/39–40.)

Chapter 43

Every circumstance has two handles. Use one, and it may be carried; but use the other, and it cannot be carried. Therefore, whenever your brother treats you unjustly, do not take hold of the matter by the handle that he has wronged you (for this is the handle by which the matter cannot be carried), but rather by the other handle, that he is your brother, that you were raised up together, and you will take hold of it using the handle by which it may be carried.

Commentary

Key terms

handle (*labê*)	**to do wrong, to act unjustly** (*adikeô*)

'Handle', of course, is a metaphor for one way of seeing something. This strategy, of distinguishing different ways in which a situation can be interpreted, has already been outlined in *Handbook* 36 where we can view the aim of partaking in a banquet to be either that of nourishing the body or that of maintaining the proper kind of social feeling. It is in pursuing the latter aim that the Stoic conducts themselves in a befitting manner.

In the present case, that of being **treated unjustly** by one's brother, the Stoic *prokoptôn* can adopt one of two interpretations and say, either (1) 'My brother has **wronged** me. He has abused and hurt me, and in consequence I am affronted and aggrieved, I am put out and angry; and, of course, my "good flow" (*euroia*) has been jeopardised,' or (2) 'My brother has **treated me unfairly**, and in doing so he has caused harm to himself, for he has failed as a brother and a human being. But he has not harmed *me*, even if he has harmed my property, my status, or some other external thing, over which I always knew I had no absolute power. But what will always remain in my power is how to conduct myself in the face of how others conduct themselves, so I will be a brother to my brother always, and treat him well and kindly, no matter the depths of his folly, no matter how strongly his **unjust deeds** provoke me, and no matter how deliberate and cruel his actions towards me may become. This I do to keep my own humanity safe.'

Why does Epictetus refer to *two* **handles**? Are there not sometimes many different ways to understand a situation – or at least three or four? Well, yes indeed. But only one of them will disclose the correct Stoic response, the *Stoic **handle***: and in choosing this one to the exclusion of the others, the *prokoptôn* demonstrates the correct use of impressions and maintains their moral character (*prohairesis*) in the proper condition, free of the disturbing or violent emotions (*apathês*), happy (*eudaimôn*), serene (*atarachos*) and magnanimous (*megalopsuchos*). All the other '**handles**', if used to 'pick up' the situation that one faces, will lead to failure, disappointment, and the ruin of one's 'good flow' (*euroia*). Thus, we must be careful to take hold of that **handle** by which circumstances may be carried.

Chapter 44

These inferences are invalid: 'I am richer than you, therefore I am better than you';
'I am more eloquent than you, therefore I am better than you.' But these are better
argued: 'I am richer than you, therefore my property is greater than yours;' 'I am
more eloquent than you, therefore my speech is superior to yours.' For *you*, of
course, are neither property nor speech.

Commentary

Key terms

better (*kreissôn*)   **property/possessions** (*ktêsis*)
invalid (adjective) (*asunaktos*)

Do we not all recall, at one time or another, being judged by others
according to our wealth, or **possessions**, or status? Is this not how
'uneducated' (*apaideutos* or *idiôtikos*) people generally carry on? The
Stoic knows, of course, that people are properly judged not by such
extraneous and transitory qualities that come when fortune beckons
them and go again at her behest, but by the permanent dispositions of
character (the qualities of one's *prohairesis*, no less) that the *prokoptôn*
has come to realise constitute their true good. And it is preferred, to be
sure, that one can explain one's philosophy for the benefit of others in an
eloquent manner, but one is not a worse person for lacking a talent that
is possessed by only a few. What counts is the wish to be of service, and
taking what steps one may in the effort to fulfil this endeavour.

For indeed, the only valid conclusion that can be drawn from 'Person
A is richer than Person B', is that Person A possesses greater wealth, and
nothing more. It is **invalid** to say that ownership of **property** or riches
makes someone **better** as a human being, not, that is, without further
premises that establish a logical link between the value of someone's
possessions and their value as a person. (The Stoics, of course, contend
that no such link exists.)

We are neither our **possessions** nor our eloquence, though if fortune
grants us these things, we are duty bound to make every effort to make
use of them wisely for the benefit of all. It is not the things we may use
that make us better people, but the fact that we attempt to use them well.
Goodness lies in the intention to act wisely, not in possessing the
material resources that are employed to fulfil the intention.

Chapter 45

Does someone bathe hastily? Do not say that they do so badly, but hastily. Does someone drink a great deal of wine? Do not say that they do this badly, but that they drink a great deal. For until you understand their motives, how do you know that what they do is bad? Understand this and you will never receive convincing impressions but assent to quite different ones.

Commentary

Key terms

assent (verb) (*sunkatatithemai*)   **convincing, or cognitive,**
badly (*kakôs*)   **impression** (*phantasia katalêptikê*)

This chapter expands on the idea expressed in the previous chapter, that external signs, what we see of someone, be that their wealth or their eloquence – and in this chapter, their bathing or their drinking habits – provides insufficient evidence for our drawing conclusions about their moral character.

Seeing people in a hurry at the public baths must have been a common experience for Epictetus and his students. (The public baths, we may recall, have already appeared in Chapter 4.) But what shall we say of someone who bathes hastily? That they bathe **badly**, and that this makes them a bad person? Sometimes, inevitably, such a judgement must be right. But it would not be right with respect to the person who bathes quickly in order to attend to some important duty; settling for a fair compromise between bathing adequately and attending to such a duty does not mean that someone is doing anything **badly**. Keeping an appointment after having to bathe hurriedly is surely better than arriving late but in a state of unequalled cleanliness.

We cannot know whether someone does something **badly** unless we know their motives for acting as they do. And there is, of course, the wider question as to why the Stoic would be judging other people in the first place. Clearly the *eudaimôn* (happy) life does not draw nearer to us if we can but notice it drawing further away from someone else! Our 'good flow' (*euroia*) is not secured by drawing attention to how much it is dammed up in other people! The business of the Stoic is to find and mend their own faults regardless of their awareness of faults in others – and anyway, as Epictetus points out, something like bathing hastily may not even be a fault if the motive behind the action is morally sound.

The '**convincing impression**' in the final sentence is *phantasia katalêptikê*, and is often translated by '**cognitive impression**' (see especially LS 40).

> Of impressions, one kind is cognitive, the other incognitive. The cognitive, which they [the Stoics] say is the criterion of things, is that which arises from what is and is stamped and impressed exactly in accordance with what is.
>
> (DL 7.46, trans. Long and Sedley 1987 = LS 40C1–2)

A **cognitive impression**, then, by its very nature, convinces us of what is the case. But in the present situation, what *is* the impression that we find 'convincing'? Well, the impression that someone is bathing hastily: for that is what we actually witness. We have the impression of someone disrobing in a hurry, carelessly tossing their clothes onto the shelf in haphazard fashion, then rushing off to the hot bath where they jump in, and in only a moment, without the courtesy to acknowledge or converse with their fellow bathers, they jump out again and rush off to plunge into the cold pool from where they rush back to their clothes, speedily putting them on after a half-hearted attempt to rub themselves down – then but a moment later they have gone out into the street again, and the bathhouse is just as it was before they came in. That is what we saw, and that is all we are entitled to be convinced by. If we **assent** to anything more than 'There goes someone whom we saw bathing in a really hurried way' then we risk **assenting** to something false. Without knowing further facts, we just do not know whether this somewhat bizarre behaviour is the product of vice or of virtue.

And thus we should always be ready to hold steady with what is truly convincing, and not go any further into mere conjecture. We make proper use of impressions by **assenting** only to what is convincing, but we use them ill if we **assent** to anything that originates in our own fancy.

(Epictetus refers to *phantasia katalêptikê* in the *Discourses* at 3.8.4 and 4.4.13. For more on the *phantasia katalêptikê*, see LS 40–1 for primary sources and commentary. See also Frede 1999a; Long 1986, 123–31; Rist 1969, 133–51; Sandbach 1989, 85–9; Sandbach 1996; Striker 1996c and 1996e.)

Chapter 46

[1] On no occasion call yourself a philosopher, and do not talk a great deal amongst uneducated people about philosophical principles, but do what follows

from those principles. For example, at a banquet do not talk about how people ought to eat, but eat as someone should. Remember how Socrates had so completely eliminated ostentation that people would come to him wanting him to introduce them to philosophers, and he would take them off to other philosophers: so little did he care about being overlooked. [2] And if a discussion about philosophical principles should arise in uneducated people, keep silent for the most part, for there is great danger that you will immediately vomit up what you have not yet digested. And when someone says to you that you know nothing, and you are not offended, then know that you have begun your work. For sheep do not show the shepherd how much they have eaten by vomiting up their fodder, but they digest their food within to produce wool and milk on the outside. So do not display your philosophical principles to uneducated people, but show them the actions that result from the principles when you digest them.

Commentary

Key terms

actions (*erga*)
banquet (*sumposion*)
offended (*daknô*)
ostentatious (*epideiktikos*)
philosopher (*philosophos*)

philosophical principles
    (*theôrêmata*)
Socrates (*Sôkratês*)
uneducated person (*idiôtês*)
work (*ergon*)

This chapter expands further on the theme introduced in Chapters 13, 22 and 23, that of how the Stoic *prokoptôn* should act in the company of **uneducated** people. Here, the general thrust of the chapter is that **philosophical principles** should be applied to the production of **actions**, and not be put on display for general discussion. The *prokoptôn*, we are told, is not barred from talking about **philosophical principles** *at all*, rather they must not talk about them 'a great deal', *and in particular* the *prokoptôn* must not talk about them in the context of revealing themselves to be a **philosopher** (46.1). To do that invites ridicule (*Handbook* 22), and risks appearing foolish and stupid (*Handbook* 13). So at the **banquet**, the perennial example of the gathering where the *prokoptôn* must conduct themselves properly (not that on other occasions the *prokoptôn* can ever lapse into *improper* conduct), the *prokoptôn* will eat as they should, and not assail their fellow diners with explanations of the **principles** which govern their actions: they set an example without the need for drawing attention to what they are and what they are doing; the progress of the *prokoptôn* is not furthered by other people knowing that they are a **philosopher**. Their model is **Socrates**, and they avoid the **ostentatious** absurdity of wanting to be seen to be a **philosopher** by not referring to themselves as such, and thus recognise progress in their **work** when what little they do mention of **principles** is rejected and they are not **offended**. **Principles** have value only when they are put to **work**, and one instance of their being put to **work** occurs when the *prokoptôn* is told that they know nothing, when their **principles** are rejected and ridiculed, and through it all they remain dispassionate (*apathês*), caring nothing for the disapproval or even contempt of others.

The **principles** in question are, of course, all those Stoic doctrines that we have been discussing in this book, that only virtue is good and vice is bad whilst all else is indifferent; that happiness (*eudaimonia*) and a 'smooth flow of life' (*euroia biou*) are secured by living in accordance with nature (*kata phusin*) by mastering the correct use of impressions and following God, accomplished when one's moral character (*prohairesis*) is maintained in the right condition free of the violent or disturbing emotions (*apathês*); and so forth with respect to unpacking these ideas in fine detail including, for instance, the notion that the Stoic accepts everything that happens as the will of God and endeavours to fulfil their duties in ways appropriate for someone trying to satisfy the profession of human being to the highest excellence.

In voicing the metaphor of *digesting* **principles** which result in **actions** befitting a Stoic and comparing it to sheep digesting fodder which results in the production of wool and milk, Epictetus suggests that the *prokoptôn* should embrace these **principles** in a way that goes beyond mere intellectual assent to let them penetrate their very being, to change their constitution in the most profound way. The *prokoptôn* does more than simply act on these **principles**: they embody them. They do not act as they do because the **principles** guide them to do so, but because they have transformed their very essence as a rational consciousness, and now they engage with the world permanently mindful of being a fragment of Zeus and doing and thinking and judging *precisely* in accordance with His will – for now their actions and thoughts are also His actions and thoughts.

(The digestion metaphor appears at *Discourses* 2.9.18 and 3.21.1–3, and we find it again in Seneca, *Ep.* 2.2–4. Epictetus uses another metaphor for mastering and acting on principles, that of fruit growing and ripening, at 1.15.6–8 and 4.8.36. See Sellars 2003, 121–3. For difficulties in persuading 'uneducated' people, see *Discourses* 2.12; and for relating to them generally, see *Discourses* 3.16. Socrates appears in the *Handbook* five times, in this chapter and at 5, 32.3, 33.12, and 51.3; he is quoted twice, in 53.3 and 53.4. For the numerous references to

Socrates in the *Discourses*, see the very end of the commentary to *Handbook* 51.)

Chapter 47

Once you have adapted your body to plain simple living, do not make a show of it. When you drink water, do not declare on every occasion that you are drinking water. If you want to train yourself to endure hardships, do it by yourself, away from other people. Do not embrace statues, but if you are ever thirsty, take a mouthful of cold water and spit it out without telling anyone.

Commentary

Key terms

body (*sôma*)   show off, make a display
hardship (*ponos*)   (*kallôpizô*)
plain simple living (*euteleia*)   train (verb) (*askeô*)

Following on from the point made at *Handbook* 46.1, Epictetus again reminds his students that their practice is a private matter, and their capacity to **train** their **bodies** in **simple living** is not something that should be **displayed** on purpose. Of course, one's **living simply** is going to be noticed, at least sometimes, by other people; but the *prokoptôn's* intention is not that their way of life should be noticed, let alone praised, but that their way of life should itself be their practice, the direct manifestation of their making progress in the correct use of impressions, in following God and accepting everything that comes about, mindful of the sort of participation in the world's unfolding that they hope to master. And that participation in practical terms means honouring their service to God as a parent, spouse, friend, teacher, student, or what have you, and always being happy in the doing of what is appropriate for their roles, whether those roles were deliberately assumed, or whether they fell to them through the workings of circumstance.

The Stoic **lives simply** because luxury, extravagance and ostentation contribute nothing to their 'good flow' (*euroia*), and indeed may detract from it. If someone were to think that wealth, for instance, was good, something worthy of desire and worthy of efforts to obtain it, then they are travelling in the opposite direction to that of the Stoic trying to make progress. Wealth may be a preferred indifferent, to be sure, because *if used wisely* it can promote for one's friends and family, and for the wider community, life that is more in accordance with nature rather than less in accordance with nature. But the Stoic themselves certainly does not need wealth, and some Stoics, we may be sure, will have positively avoided it – leaning more to the Cynic point of view – as a potential impediment to their progress.

The ability to live untroubled by **hardships** is of no little importance to the Stoic. The quality of one's moral character (*prohairesis*) is, or should be, wholly independent of one's happening upon **hardships**, because one's happiness (*eudaimonia*) is dependent upon the way in which one engages with life, and not upon one's life being free of troubles. It would appear from what Epictetus says here that it would have been normal for his students to deliberately **train** their resilience by seeking out **hardships** similar to the way in which an athlete **trains** their **body** for the rigours of their sport; but this must be done in private, away from public gaze. For should the *prokoptôn* ever become aware of that gaze and become confused as to whether it is something they want, or whether their efforts really have the purpose of attracting that gaze and being admired for their hardiness, then they have missed the path and mistaken their hardiness as a **display** for soliciting approval instead of a means by which they can permanently throw off **hardship** and remain oblivious to it. Someone suffering this confusion is essentially saying, 'Look at me, and admire me for my suffering,' whereas the true Stoic endures all that fate brings without any subjective experience of suffering at all. (That is, they will experience the *sensation* of numbing cold, say, or the burning of a scald, but they will have no experience of *suffering*; they will have the sensation of pain, of course, but that will not be attended by any mental distress. They will not curse their ill-fortune for they do not assent to the impression that anything bad has befallen them. They will follow the advice of *Handbook* 10, and look to see what capacity they have for dealing with what has happened.)

The example of embracing statues is in all probability a reference to Diogenes of Sinope, the Cynic:

> In summer he used to roll [the tub he took for his abode] over hot sand, while in winter he used to embrace statues covered with snow, using every means of inuring himself to hardship.
>
> (DL 6.23, trans. Hicks)

This practice, says Epictetus, is too extreme, and at *Discourses* 3.12.1–4 he includes it with others that are 'unnatural and fantastic' (*para phusin* and *paradoxos*); and at 4.5.14 he remarks that nature has not given to human beings the faculty required for embracing statues (nor that required for strangling lions, either). Instead of embracing statues and the like, we should focus our attention on the faculties that we actually have – our self-respect (*aidos*), our trustworthiness (*pistis*), and our capacity to make the correct use of impressions – and learn to use them properly. However, the notion of embracing statues can have, it seems, a metaphorical value: at 3.12.10 Epictetus tells his students that anyone wishing to control their quick tempers should, when they are insulted and restraining their anger, **train** their patience by *imagining* that they are embracing a statue.

Chapter 48

[1] The condition and character of the uneducated person is this: they never look for benefit or harm to come from themselves, but from external things. The condition and character of the philosopher is this: they look for every benefit and harm to come from themselves. [2] The signs that someone is making progress are these: they blame no one, they praise no one, they find fault with no one, they accuse no one, they never say anything of themselves as though they amount to something or know anything. When they are impeded or hindered, they blame themselves. If someone praises them, they laugh inwardly at the person who praises them, and if anyone censures them, they make no defence. They go about as if they were sick, cautious not to disturb what is healing before they are fully recovered. [3] They have rid themselves of all desires, and have transferred their aversion to only those things contrary to nature that are in our power. They have no strong preferences in regard to anything. If they appear foolish or ignorant, they do not care. In a word, they keep guard over themselves as though they are their own enemy lying in wait.

Commentary

Key terms

accuse (*enkaleô*)
aversion (*ekklisis*)
benefit (noun) (*ôpheleia*)
blame (*psegô*)
character (*charaktêr*)
condition (*stasis*)
desire (*orexis*)
enemy (*ho echthros*)
external things (*ta ektos*)
find fault with (*memphomai*)
foolish (*hêlithios*)

harm (noun) (*blabê*)
hinder (*kôluô*)
ignorant (*amathês*)
impede (*empodizô*)
keep guard over (*paraphulassô*)
make progress (*prokoptô*)
philosopher (*philosophos*)
praise (verb) (*epaineô*)
preference (*hormê*)
sick (*arrôstos*)
uneducated person (*idiôtês*)

This chapter revisits the distinctions introduced in *Handbook* 5, between (1) the **uneducated person** (the *idiôtês* who is *idiôtikos* and *apaideutos*), (2) the person whose instruction has begun (*prokoptôn*) and who is therefore **making progress** (*prokopê*), and (3) the person whose learning is complete, the Stoic Sage (*sophos*), who is wise (*phronimos*) and good (*spoudaios*), and also 'fine and excellent' (*kalos kai agathos*). Epictetus uses the term '**philosopher**' (*philosophos*) for people in category (2), including himself, his students and interlocutors who have embarked upon philosophical training, and also for those people to whom the trainee **philosopher** would go, teachers and authors, for instruction. The **philosopher**, after all, is the person who loves wisdom and endeavours to acquire it, but who does not necessarily possess it. Thus it is the **character** and **condition** of the person in category (2) that Epictetus wishes to contrast with the person in category (1).

The **condition** of the **uneducated person** is **characterised** by their making the mistake of thinking that the **benefits** and **harms** that come to them have their source in **external things**: they think that they are **benefited** by being in receipt of wealth, say, or by enjoying good health (or any of the other preferred indifferent things) – and they think that they are **harmed** by being denied or deprived of such things. Their capacity to experience good things and avoid bad things is thus dependent upon the whims of fortune and upon their actions producing the outcomes they want. When fortune brings what they had hoped to avoid, and when their actions fail to result in the desired outcomes, then they will bewail their bad fortune and be subject to the frustration occasioned by the failure of their actions; they will be angry with those people whom they can **blame** for contributing to their failures, and they will be envious of those who are in receipt of what they wanted for themselves. As we know, such a person is permanently cut off from happiness (*eudaimonia*) and a 'good flow of life' (*euroia biou*), even if they occasionally, or even quite frequently, enjoy the sorts of pleasures taken to be desirable and valuable by '**uneducated people**'.

The **philosopher** intent upon understanding the true nature of what is good, and upon **making progress** towards an enduring and consistent happiness (*eudaimonia*), does not want to be like that. If they can apply the Stoic principles we have been investigating, they will live in a completely different way. They will know that **benefit** and **harm** depend not at all upon the condition of **external things**, but solely upon the condition of their own moral character (*prohairesis*), and over that, with training, they can have complete control. Since no one can really **benefit** them or **harm** them there will never be any reason to **blame** or **praise** anyone; they will not **find fault** with anyone, nor have occasion to **accuse** anyone. If they find that they are **impeded** or **hindered** in anything, they know that they have failed to make proper use of impressions and have judged something **external** to be good or bad when it is really indifferent – and this is why they can **blame** themselves (but not in a spirit of chastisement, but with the intention of correcting their error). They take no notice when someone **praises** them, for this is not a **benefit**, and they make no response when they are censured, for this does not **harm** them (though, as we have remarked before, the *prokoptôn* is always wise to consider the possibility that a censure may reveal a fault that needs attention). Similarly, they have no concerns about appearing **foolish** or **ignorant**.

They have stopped having **desires** for things, for the way things go is in the hands of fate and will accord with the plans that Zeus has for the world. Thus their **preferences** are always for only and exactly what actually comes about, and they endeavour always to contribute to the world's unfolding by doing what is appropriate (*kathêkon*) and right (*katorthos*).

Similarly, the *prokoptôn* has no **aversion** to anything that happens, but only to those things that are 'contrary to nature that are in our power', and these are the passions and the vices that arise when we fail to make proper use of impressions and assent to false judgements about what is good and bad (for a discussion of 'things contrary to nature that are in our power', see the first half of the commentary to *Handbook* 2), and whose presence makes happiness (*eudaimonia*) impossible.

The medical model of philosophy which appears in the final sentence of 48.2 (and which was mentioned briefly at the opening to the commentary to *Handbook* 2), in which philosophy is conceived as a therapy for the cure of sickness in the soul analogously to the way in which standard medicine applies remedies to illness in the body, was prevalent in ancient Greek and Hellenistic philosophy. We find it in Plato and Aristotle; and later, Epicurus said this:

> Empty is that philosopher's argument by which no human suffering is therapeutically treated. For just as there is no use in a medical art that does not cast out the sicknesses of bodies, so too there is no use in philosophy, unless it casts out the suffering of the soul.
>
> (Epicurus, in Porphyry, *To Marcella* 31,
> trans. Nussbaum 1994, 13; also at LS 25C.)

Later still, Seneca wrote this in one of his letters to Lucilius:

Just as the sick man, who has been weak for a long time, is in such a condition that he cannot be taken out of the house without suffering a relapse, so we ourselves are affected when our souls are recovering from a lingering disease.

(Seneca, *Ep.* 7.1, trans. Gummere)

Much later, Stobaeus in his *Epitome of Stoic Ethics* (drawing on the first-century BC work of Arius Didymus), wrote:

For just as the health of the body is a correct mixture of the hot, cold, dry, and wet elements of the body, so too the health [*hugieia*] of the soul [*psuchê*] is a correct mixture of the beliefs [*dogmata*] of the soul.

(Stob. 2.7.5b4, trans. Pomeroy)

And writing 150 years before Arrian went to study with Epictetus, Cicero wrote:

A medical science for the mind does exist: it is philosophy. And unlike medicine for the body, the help of philosophy is something we need not look to others to gain. Instead, we should make every possible effort to become capable physicians for ourselves. ... Of this one thing you must be assured: unless the mind is healed – which cannot happen without philosophy – there will be no end to our unhappiness.

(Cicero, *TD* 3.6/13, trans. Graver)

The prevalence of the medical model appears to have annoyed Cicero who, at *TD* 4.23, berates the Stoics, and especially Chrysippus, for placing so much emphasis on the analogy between diseases of the soul and diseases of the body. So as heir to the Stoic tradition, it is not surprising to find that Epictetus mentions or alludes to the analogy a handful of times. At *Discourses* 3.23.30 he refers to the philosopher's classroom as a treatment room or hospital (*iatreion*); at 2.18.8–9 he employs the term *arrôstêmata* (ailments) to refer specifically to infirmities of the soul, and explains the need to quieten the desire (*epithumia*) of one's governing principle (*hêgemonikon*) and restore it to its proper condition by applying the right sort of therapy (*therapeia*). At 3.13.8 he explains how we should devote ourselves to, amongst other topics, the study of the things that still distress (*thlibô*) us and how they can be treated (*therapeuô*); and at 4.8.31 he imagines the Cynic philosopher asking his audience to judge whether he is free of troubles (*atarachos*), and if so to hear him explain the remedies (*pharmaka*) by which he cured (*therapeuô*) himself. (See *Discourses* 2.18.10–11 for comparing the cure of 'affections of the mind', *tês psuchês pathôn*, with recovering from a fever; and 2.21.15 for the idea of being cured, *therapeuô*, by purifying, *ekkathairô*, one's judgements, *dogmata*. See also 2.21.22 and 3.23.27.)

So now in *Handbook* 48.2, Epictetus makes an explicit reference to the medical model of philosophy. He conceives of the *prokoptôn* as someone who is **sick**, who has discovered that philosophy (Stoic philosophy in particular) can explain the nature and source of their **sickness**, and can provide a remedy which through dedication on the part of the philosopher/patient may eventually effect a cure. One is **sick** because one's moral character (*prohairesis*) falls prey to the passions (*pathê*), which disturb or even destroy one's 'good flow' (*euroia*), and which propel one to act viciously in pursuit of objectives that are mistaken for being good when they are really indifferent (*aidiaphoros*). Everyone in category (1) is in this condition; their passions and vices ravage them like painful diseases which disable and debilitate and make happiness (*eudaimonia*) impossible. The philosopher in category (2) is, of course, also in a very bad way, but their joy flows from their understanding of what is wrong and their knowledge regarding what is required for a transformation to a better state. So they go about like an invalid whose sickness is liable to be made worse by any little thing; it takes but a moment for an impression to slip by unchallenged, whereupon one is in an instant in the grip of a passion, dangerously close to committing a vicious action, or actually engaging in one.

In the final sentence of *Handbook* 48, Epictetus slips abruptly from the medical model to a military analogy, in which the *prokoptôn's* mission is to **keep guard over** themselves. The Stoic has no **enemy** but themselves; if things go wrong, or if they are **hindered** or **impeded** in anything, they know that they are themselves to **blame**, for they have judged something to be good or bad when really it is indifferent. This is what it means to **make progress**, to watch oneself unceasingly, and to let pass only those impressions that have been properly tested (*Discourses* 1.20.7; see 4.3.7/11).

(See especially Seneca, *Ep.* 75.7–18. Marcus Aurelius uses the verb *therapeuô* in the sense of 'cure' at MA 5.28 and 12.16. For more on the distinction between the uneducated person and the philosopher, see *Discourses* 3.19. For more on the analogy between philosophy and medicine, and for citations to primary sources, see Moes 2000; Nussbaum 1986 and 1994; and Sellars 2003, 41–2, 64–8. See also

Sellars 2003, 59–64 for more on the distinction between the *sophos*, the philosopher, and the uneducated person.)

Chapter 49

When someone prides themselves on being able to understand and explain Chrysippus, say to yourself, 'If Chrysippus had not written obscurely, this person would have nothing on which to pride themselves.' But what do I want? To understand nature, and to follow her. Therefore I seek someone who can explain this to me, and when I hear that Chrysippus can do so, I go to him. But I do not understand his writings; so I seek someone who can explain them to me. Now, up to this point there is nothing to be proud of. When I find someone to explain them, what remains is my putting his principles into practice; this is the only thing to be proud of. But if I am impressed merely by the act of explaining, what else have I accomplished but become a philologist instead of a philosopher, except only that I can explain Chrysippus instead of Homer? No, when someone says to me, 'Explain Chrysippus to me,' rather than feel proud, I would blush when I am unable to manifest actions that agree and harmonise with Chrysippus' teaching.

Commentary

Key terms

actions (*erga*)   philologist or grammarian or
Chrysippus (*Chrusippos*)   critic (*grammatikos*)
follow (*hepomai*)   philosopher (*philosophos*)
nature (*phusis*)

Chrysippus, mentioned only here in the *Handbook* and more than a dozen times in the *Discourses*, is Chrysippus of Soli (*c*. 280–*c*. 207 BC), the third head of the Stoic school, whose writings are now lost, excepting only fragments quoted and paraphrased by later writers, and to whom Diogenes Laertius devotes a section of his work, *Lives of Eminent Philosophers* (DL 7.179–202). There, we learn that he was a pupil of Cleanthes (the second head of the Stoic school), and that he achieved exceptional eminence as a philosopher (DL 7.179), of whom it was said, 'If it wasn't for Chrysippus, there would have been no Stoa' (DL 7.183). His writings, apparently, numbered in excess of 700 titles, and Diogenes lists 150 of them – such a copious output maintained by writing 500 lines per day (DL 7.181), a task not so amazing if Diogenes is right in recording that Chrysippus wrote repeatedly on the same topics, and filled his works with quotations from other writers to such a degree that, according to his detractor Apollodorus of Athens, if one were to take out all the extraneous quoted matter there would be nothing left (DL 7.180–1). Diogenes reports that Chrysippus' style of writing 'was not successful' (DL 7.180), and this remark accords with Epictetus' comment in this chapter of the *Handbook*, that Chrysippus wrote obscurely, and with *Discourses* 1.17.15–18 where he mentions seeking for the person who can properly interpret Chrysippus.

We have already noted, in the Introduction to Epictetus, 'Epictetus' Stoicism', that Aulus Gellius informs his readers that the *Discourses* 'undoubtedly agree with the writings of Zeno and Chrysippus' (*Attic Nights* 19.1.14), and that Epictetus praises Chrysippus as the 'great benefactor' who will show us the way to attaining serenity (*euroia*) and peace of mind (*apatheia*) by living in harmony (*sumphônos*) with nature (*Discourses* 1.4.29). And it would be odd if Epictetus were to refer to Chrysippus as often as he does, but at the same time depart in any marked way from his teaching. It is likely, therefore, that Epictetus presents his Stoic philosophy in terms – of tenets and content at least, if not of style – that conform closely, or even very closely, to Chrysippus' earlier formulations of Stoic doctrine. And we may note that there is nothing in the fragments of Chrysippus that hint at any significant departures on Epictetus' part. The fact that Chrysippus' writings came to be viewed as Stoic orthodoxy is at least partly attested to by Epictetus' decision, 300 years after they were first in circulation, to include them in the curricula for his own students (see Gould 1970, 12–13).

But making progress as a Stoic is, of course, more than making progress in one's understanding of **Chrysippus** (see *Discourses* 1.4.7, and also 2.17.34/40 and 2.23.44). There is no merit, and indeed no point, in being able to understand Chrysippus (a task that, to be sure, requires dedication and effort) if what is learned is not manifested in one's **actions**. The task of the Stoic philosopher is to **follow nature**, and Chrysippus will explain what that means and how it is to be accomplished. Acquiring this knowledge will make one merely a **philologist**, someone who stops at the point of being able to explain Chrysippus and, from the standpoint of what the Stoic is trying to achieve, this is nothing to be proud of. It is merely the first stage that has value only to the extent that it supports the essential step of putting into practice the principles that one learns from Chrysippus, and in doing that one makes of oneself a **philosopher**.

(Chrysippus appears in the *Discourses* at 1.4.6–7/9/28–9, 1.10.10, 1.17.11/13/15–18, 2.6.9–10, 2.16.34, 2.17.34/40, 2.19.5/9/14,

2.23.44, 3.2.13, 3.24.81, and 4.9.6. For more on Chrysippus, see especially Gould 1970.)

Chapter 50

Hold fast to the things herein proposed as if they were laws, as if it would be sacrilegious to transgress them. Pay no attention to what people say about you, for this is no longer yours.

Commentary

Key terms

commit sacrilege (*asebeô*)	**pay attention** (*epistrephô*)
hold fast to (*emmenô*)	**propose** (*protithêmi*)
laws (*nomoi*)	**transgress** (*parabainô*)

This short chapter revisits and re-emphasises the two key ideas already presented in *Handbook* 22, where we are told that (1) we should hold to what is best (which is, as we know, following God and living in accordance with nature) as a task we have been assigned by God, and (2) we must be prepared to be criticised and ridiculed by other people who are ignorant of what philosophy professes and what, as philosophers, we are trying to do. Here, in Chapter 50, Epictetus adds that we must **hold fast** to 'the things herein **proposed**' (the Stoic teachings of which we have been learning), and that to abandon this undertaking would be to **commit sacrilege**. The doctrines we have been shown stand as **laws**, the **transgression** of which would offend against God: looking at *Discourses* 1.12.7, for instance, we see Epictetus remarking that the person who is 'good and excellent' (*kalos kai agathos*) submits willingly to 'him who administers the universe' just as the good citizen submits to the laws of the state. For Epictetus, then, to follow God and **'hold fast'** to Stoic principles means obeying Him, and to fail in that endeavour means disobeying Him, and that of course is **sacrilege**. Should we fail in our **holding fast** to Stoic principles, then we also offend against ourselves, for we will hand ourselves over to fear and grief, anger and distress, frustration and unhappiness, and live as the authors of our own misery until God releases us by sooner or later taking us away from the shore of this world (see *Handbook* 7).

In their ignorance of what provides for happiness (*eudaimonia*) and a 'good flow of life' (*euroia biou*), those who are 'uneducated' (*apaideutos* or *idiôtikos*) in philosophy (or in any of the spiritual paths that strike out in the same direction as the Stoic's course) will misunderstand our practice, and perhaps be jealous of the equanimity that our progress secures, and will simply respond to some spiteful impulse to criticise and ridicule anyone who is different. Well, none of that matters to the Stoic. We should not **pay attention** to what such people say of us; what they say, no less than the ignorance that underlies it, are things indifferent, and not in our power. We do not strive to make progress in living in accordance with nature in order to have people ignorant of philosophy say nice things about us! Such people must find their own way. If in their want of understanding they should crave for teachers, teachers will be found by those who seek them.

(On relating to other people, see especially *Handbook* 22 and commentary. See also, with their commentaries, Chapters 13, 23, 24, 29, 33.9, 35, and 42. For more on 'law', *nomos*, see *Discourses* 1.12.7, 3.11.1, 3.24.42–3, 4.1.152–8, 4.3.12, 4.7.32–6; and see also 3.17.6 for the expression 'law of nature'. Epictetus refers to the 'law of God' at 2.16.28, and to plural 'laws' at 1.13.5; see also 1.29.4/19.)

Chapter 51

[1] For how long will you put off demanding of yourself the best, and never to transgress the dictates of reason? You have received the philosophical principles to which you ought to agree, and you have accepted them. What sort of teacher are you waiting for, that you put off improving yourself until they come? You are no longer a child, but a grown adult. If you remain negligent and lazy, always piling up delay upon delay, fixing first one day then another after which you will attend to yourself, you will fail to make progress without even realising, but will continue to live as someone uneducated until you die. [2] From this moment commit yourself to living as an adult, as someone who is making progress, and let everything that appears best to you be a law that you cannot transgress. And if you are presented with anything laborious, or something pleasant, with anything reputable or disreputable, remember that the contest is *now*, that the Olympic Games are *now*, that it is no longer possible to put them off, and that progress is won or lost as the result of just once giving in. [3] This is how Socrates attained perfection, by paying attention to nothing but reason in everything that he encountered. But even if you are not yet Socrates, you should live as someone who wishes to be Socrates.

Commentary

Key terms

adult (*anêr*, man)
best (*beltistos*)
child (*meirakion*, boy)
improvement (*epanorthôsis*)
law (*nomos*)
make progress (*prokoptô*)
Olympic Games (*ta Olumpia*)

pay attention (*prosechô*)
philosophical principles
  (*theôrêmata*)
Socrates (*Sôkratês*)
teacher (*didaskalos*)
transgress (*parabainô*)
uneducated person (*idiôtês*)

Once we have been shown the **philosophical principles** of the Stoics, and once we have understood and accepted them, what remains is for us to put those **principles** to work, to become examples of excellence (*aretê*), to secure for ourselves the sort of **improvement** that will make us Stoics who manifest the **principles** in all the actions which jointly constitute our lives – the doing of which, if done properly in an enduring fashion, *is* a life whose flow is smooth (*euroia biou*). We are no longer **children** in the care of **adults**, but **adults** ourselves, for whom putting off this commitment to **make progress** does not make any sense, and in prevaricating we run the risk of never starting out, of remaining '**uneducated**' until it is too late and our time is all used up. We already have to hand the **teachers** that we need, in the form of Epictetus' writings, and in the writings of others (especially Seneca and Marcus Aurelius), but also in other people whom we may find who have also taken up Stoic teaching as a philosophy to live by.

Epictetus reminds us again (see Chapter 50) that once we know what is **best** (following God and living in accordance with nature) and once we accept the truth of where happiness and where human flourishing lie, our failure to **make progress** is tantamount to **transgressing** a **law**. Our training is of course incomplete, and is the work of a lifetime, but when the very next thing happens to us, it will be as if we have been thrust into the arena at the **Olympic Games**, and here is our chance to win **progress**. Will we win victory, or will we humiliate ourselves by giving in to a bit of irritation, or by getting angry at someone, or at the person who breaks our cup – as if our well-being really is dependent on such petty little things?

Our model is again **Socrates**, and like him we must use reason (*logos*) in all our encounters, which means making only correct evaluative judgements, and never thinking that something is bad for us when it is really indifferent; that is, we must make proper use of impressions. That is all we have to do to **make progress**. Sometimes, the realisation of this truth can strike home and become stunningly obvious, and when such insights come our way we should try to hold on to the quality of consciousness that at such moments we enjoy – for this is the transformation of the soul that Epictetus endeavours to teach.

The notion that our **progress** is lost by giving in only once is found again at *Discourses* 4.3.4–6, where Epictetus offers the analogy of the helmsman who can lose his ship as the result of even one small error (see also 2.18.31). But in other places he adopts a different stance, saying that even when we falter there is nothing to stop us trying again, that once we achieve victory, it is as if we never faltered (3.25.1–5); and he gives the example of the wrestling-master who tells the boy who has fallen to get up and wrestle again (4.9.14–16). This latter outlook, contrary to that in *Handbook* 51.2, seems to make the most sense and to offer the most hope, for as Epictetus remarks at 4.12.19, it is not possible to be completely without fault (that surely, is the destination at which **progress** aims), but it is possible to always be intent upon avoiding faults. It is to this that we should **pay attention**.

(Socrates appears in the *Handbook* five times, in this chapter and at 5, 32.3, 33.12, and 46.1; he is quoted twice, in 53.3 and 53.4. Socrates appears in the *Discourses* in excess of 50 times, at 1.2.33/36, 1.9.1/22, 1.12.3/23, 1.17.12, 1.19.6, 1.25.31, 1.26.18, 1.29.16–17/29/65, 2.1.15/32, 2.2.8/15/18, 2.4.8, 2.5.18, 2.6.26, 2.12.5/14, 2.13.24, 2.16.35, 2.18.22, 2.26.6, 3.1.19–21/42, 3.5.14–17, 3.7.34, 3.12.15, 3.14.9, 3.16.5, 3.18.4, 3.21.19, 3.22.26, 3.23.22–5/32, 3.24.38/40/60/99, 3.26.23, 4.1.41/123/159–64/169, 4.4.21–2, 4.5.2/33, 4.7.29, 4.8.22–6, 4.9.6, 4.11.19–21.)

Chapter 52

[1] The first and most necessary topic in philosophy concerns putting principles to practical use, such as, 'We ought not to lie.' The second is concerned with demonstrations, such as, 'Why is it that we ought not to lie?' And the third is concerned with confirming and articulating the first two: for example, 'Why is this a demonstration?' For what is a demonstration, what is entailment, what is contradiction, what is truth, and what is falsehood? [2] Thus the third topic of study is necessary for the second, and the second is necessary for the first. But the most necessary, the one where we ought to rest, is the first. But we do the opposite – we spend our time on the third topic, upon this we expend all our efforts, whilst entirely neglecting the first topic. Thus, whilst at the same time as lying, we are more than ready to explain why it is wrong to lie.

Commentary

Key terms

principles (*dogmata*)   **the use to which something is put** (*chrêsis*)

The 'topics of philosophy' that Epictetus lists here are *not* the topics he introduces elsewhere, and which constitute an important feature of his exposition of Stoic ethics (see *topoi* in Glossary A, and 'The three *topoi*' in the Introduction to Epictetus). The second topic here, in *Handbook* 52, would appear to correlate with our modern notion of metaethics, which is where, today, we would place Epictetus' example of the enquiry he means to identify, that of establishing the reasons for maintaining the truth of moral imperatives such as 'We ought not lie,' and this topic is presumably meant to scope over all such questions regarding the foundations of ethics. As we know, the sort of answer that Epictetus would make to this particular question, and others, will make reference to the concepts we have been discussing – what is truly good, the virtues, the vices and the passions, freedom, serenity and fearlessness, and how these and others can be fitted together to form an understanding of what happiness and flourishing consist in, and how maintaining one's moral character (*prohairesis*) in the right condition by paying attention only to what is in our power results in a 'smooth flow of life' (*euroia biou*). All this we know.

The third topic mentioned here, about demonstration, entailment, contradiction and truth, appears to correlate with our modern notion of philosophical logic. Ability in this third topic is required for proficiency in the second topic, which in turn is required for identifying the **principles** whose application promotes the progress that as Stoic philosophers we are trying to secure.

Epictetus laments the fact that his students expend their efforts on the third topic to the detriment of the first – and end up failing to make **practical use** of the **principles** that they can prove they are obliged to live by! Being skilled in logic is of no use at all unless one's study promotes one's progress towards *eudaimonia* (see for instance, *Discourses* 1.7, 1.8, 1.26.9, 3.23.41, and 3.24.78–9).

Chapter 53

[1] We must always have these thoughts at hand:

'Lead me, Zeus, and you too, Destiny,

Wherever you have assigned me to go,
and I'll follow without hesitating; but if am not willing,
because I am bad, I'll follow all the same.'
[2] 'Whosoever properly with necessity complies
we say is wise, and understands things divine.'
[3] 'Well, Crito, if this pleases the gods, let it happen this way.'
[4] 'Certainly, Anytus and Meletus may put me to death, but they cannot harm
me.'

Commentary

Key terms

at hand (*procheiros*)
bad (*kakos*)
Destiny (*Peprômenê*)
follow (*hepomai*)
necessity or fate or destiny
    (*anankê*)

things divine (*ta theia*, the acts
    of the gods, the course of
    providence)
Zeus (*Zeus*)

The first line of 53.1 appears in the *Discourses* at 2.23.42, 3.22.95, and
also at 4.4.34 where Epictetus attributes the text to Cleanthes; the first
two lines of the text are repeated at 4.1.131. Seneca presents the same
verse (which he also attributes to Cleanthes) rendered by him in Latin,
but includes extra lines, thus:

> [... I'll follow all the same,] and suffer,
> In sin and sorrow what I might have done
> In noble virtue. Aye, the willing soul
> Fate leads on, but the unwilling drags along.
> (Seneca, *Ep.* 107.11, trans. Gummere)

In the second line of 53.1, **Zeus** is of course the supreme being,
whom we have been discussing on and off in this book; He is the divine
intelligence that blends with undifferentiated matter to create and
sustain the world, and in whose rationality all human beings share, with
respect to whom the Stoic *prokoptôn* endeavours to maintain the right
sort of relationship, referred to by Epictetus as 'following God' (see *theos*
in Glossary A, along with *Handbook* 31 and commentary; see also
especially Long 2002, 142–206). *Peprômenê*, '**Destiny**' (derived from
the verb *porô*, meaning to give, offer, furnish) is the personification of
that power by which we are allotted, **fated** or **destined** to have what

comes to us in life. The short hymn that Epictetus quotes should be read in conjunction with a much larger *Hymn to Zeus* by Cleanthes (translated in LS 54I; Inwood and Gerson 1997, 139–41; and in Blakeney 1921). Epictetus' hymn is not quoted from the longer text, and neither does it appear to be a paraphrase of a section from it. Cleanthes is Cleanthes of Assos (331–232 BC), student of Zeno, and second head of the Stoic school, succeeded in turn by Chrysippus. Diogenes Laertius (7.168–76) offers a brief biography of Cleanthes, but does not list in specific terms any hymn to Zeus. (For other fragments, and further references to Cleanthes, see LS Index of Philosophers.)

The lines in 53.2 are from Euripides (fragment 956 in the Nauck edition).

The final words of the *Handbook* are from Socrates, being paraphrases from Plato. The line in 53.3 occurs at *Crito* 43d, where Socrates has just awoken in prison to find that Crito has come to see him, and what it is that Socrates is happy to let 'happen this way', should its doing so please the gods, is of course his own execution (this paraphrase appears again at *Discourses* 1.4.24, 1.29.18, 3.22.96, and 4.4.21).

The line in 53.4 is from the *Apology* (30c–d), and Anytus and Meletus are Socrates' accusers, charging him with impiety and corrupting the youth of Athens. Their case will prove successful, and Socrates will be sentenced to death by poison. (This line also appears in the *Discourses* at 1.29.18, 2.2.15, 3.23.21.)

These thoughts we must always have **at hand** because they remind us of how the world is, and how we should stand to the world and to God; the Stoic seeks to 'attach themselves to God' because in doing so they may 'travel safely [through life]' (4.1.98). The hymn in 53.1 summarises the pledge that the Stoic *prokoptôn* makes to attach (*proskatatassô*) themselves to God. Epictetus continues, after answering this question put to him by his interlocutor:

'What do you mean by "attach" themselves?'
  That what God wills, they too may will, and what God does not will, they may not will either.
'How then is this to be done?'
  How else but by examining the purposes of God and his governance of the world. What has He given me to be my own, and independent, what has He reserved for himself? He has given me all that lies within the sphere of my moral character [*prohairesis*], and has put it in my hands, unfettered, unhindered.
      (*Discourses* 4.1.99–100, trans. Matheson, modified)

The end to which our Stoic training takes us is that of becoming the person 'who wishes to be at one with God, and to blame God and man no longer, to fail in nothing, to feel no misfortune, to be free from anger, envy, and jealousy' (*Discourses* 2.19.26, trans. Matheson). And this we do by not just passively accepting what God ordains for the world, though we do that happily (2.23.42), but by *sharing in* the governance (*archê*) of the world with God, as a 'friend [*philos*] and servant [*hupêretês*] to the gods' (3.22.95), and this we accomplish by setting about our tasks and fulfilling the roles we have been assigned in ways appropriate for someone intent upon making progress. An act of kindness, for instance, *is* of itself one small way in which God's touch fashions the history of the world, and that brief moment in time will be lodged there in the world's history forever, part of the structure of the universe, indelibly recorded because we chose to act that way, because it was fitting for us to do that. From such small actions is the history of our planet made, and perhaps there are people more or less like us, perhaps with philosophies more or less like the Stoicism we are investigating, elsewhere in the universe on their own planets, similarly contributing to and constructing their own histories: this in part is how God's rationality is manifest in the world – how it makes real things, and how it rests in the very things that happen.

Epictetus talks of willing (*ethelô*) what God wills, of aligning his wishes (*sunethelô*) with those of God, and collaborating (*sunormaô*) with God, and thus attaching (*proskeimai*) himself to God as servant and follower (*diakonos kai akolouthos*; *Discourses* 4.7.20). When Cleanthes wrote these lines about '**following** without hesitation', and of having to **follow** even when one is **bad** and not willing, he may have been aware of the dog and cart analogy later to be quoted by Hippolytus (d. AD 235), employed by Zeno and Chrysippus – though some scholars doubt whether Hippolytus' attributing of this text to Zeno and Chrysippus is correct, and Bobzien (1998, 357) conjectures that the analogy really belongs to Epictetus, invented by him for the purpose of elucidating Cleanthes' *Hymn*, and that it originally featured in those sections of the *Discourses* that have been lost. The text in question, already alluded to in the commentary to *Handbook* 31, reads:

They too [Zeno and Chrysippus] affirmed that everything is fated, with the following model. When a dog is tied to a cart, if it wants to follow it is pulled and follows [*hepomai*], making its spontaneous act coincide with necessity [*anankê*], but if it does not want to follow it will be compelled in any case. So it is with men too: even if they do not want to, they will be compelled in any case to follow what is destined.

(Hippolytus, *Refutation of All Heresies* 1.21.2,
trans. Long and Sedley 1987 = LS 62A)

Whether or not this analogy originated with Epictetus and, if it did, whether or not he made use of it in his schoolroom, it is perhaps instructive to think about how the example of the dog tied to the cart illustrates Epictetus ethical teaching – for I think that it does, and I think it does so in quite subtle ways. The dog, of course, represents us, and the cart to which we are tied represents the forces and influences that work upon us to give to our lives those qualities and characteristics that they have, including such features as our parents, our gender, the culture into which we are born, our intelligence and our creativity, our dispositions and our proclivities – but also specific events that we will encounter, such as storms at sea, illnesses, and so forth. All these things represented by the cart constitute the constraints and limits within which our lives will take their shape. These are the things that of **necessity** feature in our personal **destinies**, and make them what they are.

On the face of it, this picture of the dog being pulled along seems rather bleak, yet Epictetus would wish to reject any tendency towards pessimism and resignation, because the dog has a choice. It can trot along willingly, making every effort to take that path which otherwise the cart will pull it along anyway, or it can resist, getting pulled and dragged against its will along the very same path. It is in doing the former, of willingly going along with one's own **fate**, that one may enjoy the only sort of freedom that, say the Stoics, is available to human beings – and in doing so, with the understanding that one is travelling through the world that is unfolding just as Zeus decrees it, one demonstrates one's 'understanding of **things divine**'. We are free to do what we want, within the limits imposed by our **fate**, and in this sense we are free agents, not entitled to complain; and what we do try to do, as Stoics, we do 'with reservation' (see *Handbook* 2.2 and commentary, and especially Inwood 1985, 119–26) because we do not know for certain which of our actions will succeed and which will fail; and we place our hopes not in succeeding, but trying as befits us. But if our actions fail, then like the dog that does not wish to be pulled along, we must quickly change our course and once again work within the restraints that foiled our first efforts. This assessment, I am inclined to say, appears to be incorporated in the analogy in this way: although the dog is tied to the cart, the tether may be fairly loose or fairly tight, and a degree of looseness will permit the dog to veer just a little to left or right as it pleases whilst the cart in front sticks unwaveringly to its course. This aspect of the analogy I feel is intended, because only the very shortest of tethers permits no deviation whatever, and if the possibility of deviation is meant to be denied, then the creator of the analogy would have chosen a different image – something like a puppet on strings, perhaps.

The freedom that interests Epictetus, and the freedom we may all enjoy, if only we can exercise the capacities that Zeus has given us, is the freedom to be *free from* things – to be free of fear (*aphobos*), free from distress (*alupos*), free of the passions (*apathês*), and free from troubles generally (*atarachos*; see for instance *Discourses* 4.1.83–4, 4.3.7). And this sort of freedom is ours as soon as we start to follow the cart willingly, careful not to let the tether get too tight so that it pulls us, accepting willingly what happens, happy to work within the restraints that events impose, happy to contribute to Zeus' plans for the world by doing what circumstances require of us.

We did not choose how **fate** would constrain and circumscribe our lives: it is not up to us which physical laws should order the world, and it is not in our power to control absolutely the actions of other people, nor the weather, nor which party wins an election, nor whether our children will be beautiful or win acclaim; we cannot will to be rich, nor to be healthy, nor to be young again, as we cannot through merely wishing make others love us no matter how much we want them to. But we can choose how we will respond to the things that happen, and as Stoics we will respond virtuously – bravely when faced with dangers or hardships, temperately when faced with opportunities to indulge, justly and fairly in our dealings with other people, and wisely with respect to all our choices. And whatever does happen, no matter how severely we might have been provoked before, now we know that we must use our impressions correctly, and never think that anything bad has happened, for we are immune to harm, and we can ride out the most dismal of **destinies**, if we must, worthy of taking the strain when others might have failed, rising to meet any challenge as a friend of Zeus.

Here is how I have come to think of **fate**, and what it means to be bound to one's **fate**, and this I feel is at least consistent with the Stoic outlook even if the ancient Stoics did not think in these precise terms. There is a body of truth that describes the whole world and everything that happens in its history, comprised of all those statements that are true, and excluding all that are false. This body of truth *is* the **fate** of the world. Everything described therein that has happened could not have happened other than how it did – for if it did happen otherwise, statements so describing those events would be part of the body of truth instead; and everything that is yet to happen will happen just as described, for only what actually will happen is recorded in the body of truth. And within this body of truth will be found, for each of us, that set of statements that describes down to the very last detail our own lives; everything about us that is true, past and future, is recorded there, and this is our **fate**, fixed and woven, like a pattern in a carpet, into the fabric of time by all those things that constrain and circumscribe our lives, and by all those events that causally impinge on us and what we try to do. If we resist our **fate**, and like the dog pull uselessly on the tether, then our doing so will be part of our **fate**. But some of the statements listed in those parts of the body of truth that describe our lives are there because of what we decide to do. I may for instance be **fated** to care for a friend, but that may be because I willingly set about doing so; and because the restraints upon me allow for the success of my trying, I am like the dog who tries stepping a bit to one side to find that the tether is not so taut as to prevent its doing so.

If we are not **fated** to have the sorts of dispositions that are needed for succeeding as Stoics, then we will not make any decent progress and, say the Stoics, we will be doomed to misery and disappointment because we will keep on desiring indifferent external things believing them to be good. So in the end, I suppose it all comes down to having faith that Zeus is doing what is best for the world, and our participation in His creation is just as it is meant to be, even if we are miserable. If so, we may as well make the attempt to hold to the conviction that *we have after all* been blessed with the disposition to succeed as Stoics. We may be right, and we will find out in the trying.

(Epictetus makes frequent mention of God in the *Discourses*: see the entry for *theos* in Glossary A for references but, with respect to the discussion in hand, see especially *Discourses* 1.9.24, 1.12.15–17/25, 2.10.5, 2.17.29, 3.7.36, 3.11.1–2, 3.24.95, and Fragment 8. We can find another short hymn to God at *Discourses* 1.16.16–18; see also 3.26.29–30. See MA 3.10, 4.9–10, 4.23/25–6/33/40/45, 5.8, 6.38, 7.9, 7.57, 9.6, 10.5–6/14/20–1/25/28, 12.11; and see Seneca, *NQ* 2.36; *On Providence* 2.4, 5.6–9; *Ep.* 76.23, 96.1–2, 107. For more on Socrates' accusors, Anytus and Meletus, see Brickhouse and Smith 2000, 27–8. For Plato's treatment of Socrates' trial and execution, see his dialogues *Apology*, *Crito*, and *Phaedo*; for recent scholarship, see the essays in Brickhouse and Smith 2002; for book-length treatments, see Brickhouse and Smith 1989, and Reeve 1989. Epictetus does not discuss the problem of fate, determinism, and free will, holding as we know to the doctrine that one's moral character, *prohairesis*, is always free to desire, intend, judge and assent as it pleases, so I have decided not to discuss the topic in any real depth here, though I attempt this elsewhere, in Seddon 1999; see also Taylor's chapter on fate in Taylor 1992, 54–67. Stoicism's detractors, as we might imagine, objected to the notion of fate, saying that if everything is fated, then one must be fated to assent and judge, or perform any 'voluntary' action, just as one does, and that free will and therefore moral responsibility are illusory. The Stoics, of course, felt they could meet these objections: see LS 55 and 62. For more on the Stoics on fate and determinism, see Bobzien 1997, 1998 especially 330–57, 1999; Frede 2003; Hankinson 1999; Long 1996d; Reesor 1965, 1978; Rist 1969, 112–32; Sandbach 1989, 79–82, 101–8; Seddon 1999; Sharples 1996, 49–53, 74–6. For more on fate and the metaphysics of time, see Seddon 1987, especially 105–33; see also the relevant chapters in Taylor 1992.)

Part II

The *Tablet of Cebes*

The journey to happiness

Introduction to the *Tablet of Cebes*

Overview

Probably written some time in the first or early second centuries AD, the *Tablet of Cebes* is a moralising allegory of human life depicted by a fictitious tablet or plaque (*pinax*) chanced upon in the Temple of Cronus by the narrator and his friends. Despite the wording of the title identifying the author as Cebes, we do not know who this person was. It was not the Cebes of Socrates' circle (see 'Authorship and Date' below), and it is doubtful that he was the Cebes of Cyzicus mentioned by Athenaeus. The work must have already been attributed to someone with the name Cebes by Lucian's time, because he clearly refers to this work as having been written by a Cebes. We simply do not know whether the work was falsely ascribed to Socrates' Cebes, innocently or through a deliberate act of misattribution, or whether it was correctly assigned to a different Cebes. But obviously the work had an author, so we have to conclude either that (1) this was another Cebes who – apart from bequeathing us his *Tablet* – has left no other trace (as far as we know) in the historical record, or (2) Cebes was a pseudonym, or (3) his true name has been lost (FW 5–7). We will therefore refer to Cebes as the author of the *Tablet*, meaning to accord him no other attribute.

The *Tablet's* device of describing an object (in this case a work of art) places it in the genre of *ekphrasis*, meaning 'description', a type of literature (that can be either fiction or non-fiction) that describes some object, actually existing or fictitious. Other examples include, for instance, Homer's *Iliad* (end of Book 18) where Hephaestus makes Achilles' shield, forging into it cities, fields, vineyards, herds of cattle, armies in battle, and people going about their business in a riotous panorama, and in the manner that Cebes will adopt centuries later, Homer includes figures that personify Strife, Havoc, and Death. The genre remained popular right through to Cebes' time and beyond (see

Elsner 1995 and Bartsch 1989, especially the first chapters of both books), and was employed, for instance, by the satirist Lucian, who lived in the generation that followed Cebes, and whom we will meet again in 'Authorship and Date', below.

Cebes portrays a strange world in which the landscape is divided into enclosures in which may be found personifications of the Virtues and Vices, along with others, including Punishment, Repentance, and Fortune. Across this landscape wander all those who have come to be alive in the world, not knowing how best to proceed towards Happiness who sits enthroned before the citadel of the highest enclosure. We are invited to consider that the fate of those who wander the enclosures is our own fate in the real world, simplified and cut down to the key essentials. Beguiled by Fortune, the people come to be enamoured of her gifts that are dispensed and reassigned at random, and they come to believe that their happiness depends upon being in receipt of these gifts. Some find their way to False Education, where we find poets, orators, academics and professionals of all kinds who have mistaken False Education for True Education, thinking that in remaining here they possess happiness, when they do not. But it is from within False Education's enclosure that some small number of people will find the steep and stony path to True Education, where abide Happiness and the Virtues, and where the successful traveller is crowned with a power through which they become immune to the Vices, and are thenceforth able to roam freely about the enclosures in complete safety.

The *Tablet* concludes with a discussion on why it is that the things people receive from Fortune are neither good nor bad (which Stoics, of course, class as 'indifferent' things, comprising 'preferred' things and 'dispreferred' things – though these Stoic terms are not used in the text). True knowledge is thus defined as knowledge of what is truly advantageous, and the person who is welcomed by Happiness knows that only the Virtues are truly advantageous. And although the text does not identify itself as Stoic, and although it does not use the range of Stoic terminology familiar to us from Stoic writings, the *Tablet of Cebes* appears nevertheless to be fundamentally Stoic in outlook.

Authorship and date

Diogenes Laertius (probably writing in the early third century AD) includes Cebes in his *Lives of Eminent Philosophers* (2.125), recording just four facts about him – that he was a citizen of Thebes, and that three of his dialogues are extant, *The Tablet*, *The Seventh Day*, and *Phrynichus*. From the company in which he places Cebes, alongside Phaedo, Crito,

Glaucon and Simmias, this is obviously the Cebes of Socrates' circle who was present at the death of Socrates, who appears with Simmias in Plato's *Phaedo*, and who is reported in the *Crito* as being ready to provide money for Socrates' escape from prison. But we can be confident that this Cebes is not the author of the *Tablet* for a variety of reasons. First, the text refers to Peripatetics (13.2), so cannot have been written earlier than the founding of Aristotle's school, a generation after Plato's Cebes. Also, the language of the text uses late words, and classical words with later meanings, placing it much later than the time of Socrates and Plato, and this accounts for why there are no early citations to the *Tablet* in ancient literature. Indeed, the earliest certain citation occurs in the writings of Lucian of Samosata (born *c*. AD 120), of whom more in a moment. Furthermore, if the *Tablet* really is a Stoic text, as appears to be the case, then obviously the Cebes of Socrates' circle is by this fact alone out of the running, since there would not be a Stoic school with a body of literature to disseminate its doctrines until possibly a century after this Cebes' time (see FW 1–8).

In addition to the references in Diogenes Laertius and Lucian, there is another reference to a Cebes in *The Deipnosophists* by Athenaeus (*c*. AD 170–*c*. 230) where he mentions a Cebes of Cyzicus who hosts a dinner-party attended by a group of Cynics (4.156d). The courses of their meal are all dishes made from lentils, relieved only by the arrival of a smelly sea-perch which no one wants to eat (157a). Later, it is pointed out that if the only person who can do anything properly is the Stoic wise person, then only the Stoic wise person can make lentil soup properly (158a). But there are no further details about this Cebes. If he is a contemporary of the author (which is what the text suggests) then he is unlikely to be the author the *Tablet*, because Lucian, born *c*. AD 120, a generation earlier, clearly refers to a Cebes as an author in the *ekphrasis* genre, and what he writes suggests to the point of certainty that he was familiar with the text of our *Tablet*. So if our Cebes, the author of the *Tablet*, was known in Lucian's time, and sufficiently well-known as a writer of *ekphrasis* for Lucian to remark that in utilising the genre himself he is imitating Cebes, then Cebes of Cyzicus must be another, somewhat later, Cebes, and not the author of the *Tablet*. If our Cebes was an older contemporary of Lucian, or if he lived slightly earlier, that places him in the late first century or the early decades of the second century.

The way in which Lucian demonstrates his knowledge of the Cebes text is worth offering in summary. Lucian mentions Cebes' name twice in his surviving corpus. At the very end of *On Salaried Posts in Great Houses*, in which Lucian advises his young friend Timocles against taking a salaried position, he states that 'in imitation of Cebes' (42) he will paint a picture of the career he has just been discussing. In a short text of only one paragraph, Lucian asks Timocles to imagine a high, golden gateway, way up on a hill, approached by a long, steep and slippery path from which many before have slipped and fallen to their deaths. Within the gateway sits Wealth, and to him the traveller struggles to climb, led on by Hope. But the traveller is received by Deceit and Servitude, who pass him on to Toil, who in turn breaks him with hard labour and passes him ill and worn out to Old Age. Finally, the traveller is taken hold of by Insolence and Despair, at which point Hope flees and abandons him, and instead of reaching the heights of the golden gateway, the traveller is thrust out through a remote and secret door, old and pale, hiding his nakedness with his left hand and throttling himself with his right hand. At the very last, weeping Repentance can be of no aid except to help him end it all.

There is little doubt that this is a satirical inversion of the *Tablet* fable, with which Lucian must have been acquainted. No less reminiscent of the *Tablet* is Lucian's second reference to Cebes in *A Professor of Public Speaking*, in which Lucian paints a picture in words (6) for a young man who aspires to become a great public speaker. There are two roads that lead to Lady Rhetoric, whom the young man desires to marry (allegorically representing his mastery of public speaking), who sits in a high place holding the Horn of Plenty (symbolising the wealth that will accrue to a sought-after speaker), and with her are Wealth, Fame, Power, and a swarm of Compliments flying round like tiny Cupids (6–7). The first path to Lady Rhetoric is narrow and rough, the travelling upon which promises thirst and sweat; further description of this road is not required because, as Lucian points out, Hesiod has already provided us with an adequate account (in *Works and Days*, 286–92) – and this is the path that Lucian boasts he has climbed himself, successfully travelled a long time ago by only a few (8). But the second path, which Lucian had seen quite clearly from the vantage point of the first, more arduous path, is level and pleasant, having no twists and turns at all.

The young man is unsure which path is best, and at this point Lucian brings into his narrative a hardy old man, quite obviously a parallel to the old man in the *Tablet* who explains the allegory in that text, to provide the same function here. This old man will guide the young man on the first, rough path, and Lucian warns that he will talk a lot of nonsense: their journey will be demanding and difficult, taking many years to complete, requiring hard work and sacrifices of all sorts, on top of which the old man will demand a substantial fee for his services (9).

But upon the easy road, the young man will find another guide, a handsome fellow with a mincing gait and honeyed voice who styles his hair and uses perfumes (11). Go with this man upon the easy road, Lucian urges the young man, and in no time at all you will become a successful public speaker, 'king of the platform, driving the horses of eloquence four-in-hand' (trans. Harmon, 11). What the young man must take with him for the journey are ignorance, recklessness, effrontery, and shamelessness, and what he must leave behind are modesty, respectability, and self-restraint, for the latter are useless hindrances. He will also need a very loud voice, and a gait like that of his guide (15). The account continues in similar vein, detailing how the young man must make his outward appearance of primary importance, that he must learn about 15 (certainly no more than 20) Attic words with which to garnish his speeches (16); and unfamiliar words should be kept ready to toss out at the audience, who will be amazed and think the speaker's education must be far superior to their own (17). Rhetoric will heap rewards upon the person who does all this (24).

This, again, is clearly an inversion of the allegory of the *Tablet*, and the fact that Lucian mentions Cebes by name establishes beyond doubt that the text he knew is one and the same as the text we have before us now. This means that Cebes' *Tablet* must have been in circulation by about AD 150, before Lucian's satires were written.

(We may note in passing that Lucian employs *ekphrasis* elsewhere, describing in his *Heracles* a picture of Heracles; in his *Slander* (4–5) he describes a painting by Apelles of Ephesus, who depicts Slander, Ignorance, Suspicion, Envy, Treachery, Deceit, Repentance, and Truth; and in his *Toxaris* (6), Toxaris tells his interlocutor Mnesippus of a series of paintings in a temple that describe the story of Orestes and Pylades.)

On the basis of a passage in the work of Dio Chrysostom (*c.* AD 40/ 50–after 110), we may wonder whether we can be certain that the *Tablet* was in circulation perhaps 70 or 80 years earlier, in the latter half of the first century. Dio Chysostom, rhetorician, admirer and student of Musonius Rufus (the teacher of Epictetus), endured banishment, and wandered for many years across Greece, the Balkans, and Asia Minor as an itinerant teacher of Stoic–Cynic philosophy (nearly 80 of his discourses survive). At *Discourse* 1.50–84, Dio recounts that, lost in the woods one day, he met a woman who told him the tale of Heracles (58ff) who was taken by Hermes to a fantastical landscape (66ff) in which stand two mountains, Peak Royal and Peak Tyrannous. Upon Peak Royal, the highest peak, dwelt Lady Royalty, a daughter of Zeus. With her were three others as beautiful as she, Justice, Civic Order, and Peace, accompanied by Law, a grey-haired man (73–5). Hermes then took Heracles to the lower peak, Peak Tyrannous, to Tyranny, the place to which most people come (76). Tyranny was sitting upon a throne higher and more splendid than that of Lady Royalty, but as she moved, it rocked and swayed on shaky foundations (78). With her were Cruelty, Insolence, Lawlessness, Faction, and Flattery (82). When Heracles told Hermes that he liked Royalty the best, Hermes took this news to Zeus who entrusted Heracles with kingship over all humankind (83–4). Now, there is hardly a strong parallel between Dio's story and that of Cebes, though there is something of a similarity, especially in the resemblance between Tyranny's rocking throne and the round stone upon which Fortune stands in the *Tablet* (7). But to the extent that we are encouraged by this to wonder if Dio was acquainted with the Cebes text, we are no less entitled to wonder if it wasn't Cebes who was acquainted with Dio's text.

(At *Memorabilia* 2.20–34, Xenophon offers another version of the Heracles story, paraphrasing Prodicus' 'Choice of Heracles', which otherwise does not survive. After quoting Hesiod, *Works and Days* 287–94, about the road to wickness being smooth and the road to virtue being long and steep, he recounts how Heracles was pondering which road to take in life, whether to take the path to virtue or the path to vice. He is approached by two women, Virtue and Vice, and each tries to persuade him to go with her. They each describe the character of the life he will lead if he is to accompany them; the path to virtue will require toil and effort, whereas the path to vice is short and easy.)

Outline of the *Tablet*

The allegory of the *Tablet* is not told directly, but is embedded within a simple framing story told by the narrator who recounts what happened when he and his friends paid a visit to a temple of Cronus where they found many votive offerings. Amongst them was a tablet (*pinax*) on which was painted a fabulous scene showing neither a walled city nor a military camp, but depicting an enclosure surrounding two further enclosures.

They could see a crowd of people, being instructed by an old man, waiting to go through a gate into the outer enclosure, and inside they could see a large number of women. But what this all meant, they could not fathom (1).

An old man came up and offered to explain the meaning of the *Tablet*, for he had been schooled in its secrets by the philosopher who donated it to the temple many years before (2).

The old man warns them, however, that being shown the meaning of the *Tablet* is attended by a certain risk. For those who fail to understand it properly will be doomed to folly and misery, to be compared with those who fail to answer the Sphinx's riddle and get eaten by her (3).

The outer enclosure is Life, and the old man instructing the people about to enter is called Daimon. He tells them which path to take in Life (4). (But the content of his instructions is not explained until later, in sections 30–2.)

Deceit gives to all who enter, her potion of error and ignorance which causes them to forget the Daimon's instructions (5). Upon entering Life, the people are accosted by Opinions, Desires and Pleasures who lead them off in all directions, some to their doom, and some to their salvation (6). Standing close by on a round stone that symbolises her fickleness is Fortune, who dispenses, then takes back, such things as reputation, children, thrones and kingdoms (7–8). (The discussion as to whether such things are truly good is left for sections 36–43.)

Some people are tempted by Intemperance, Profligacy, Insatiability, and Flattery to enter another enclosure, that of Luxury, where for a time things will be pleasant enough. But after they have become slaves to these women, indulging in every kind of vice, they are handed over to Punishment (9). With her are Grief and Distress, along with Lamentation (the only male personification within Life) and his sister Despondency. Those who are not chosen by Repentance to escape this place are thrown into the House of Punishment to live out the rest of their days in total misery (10).

The lucky few are taken by Repentance to different Opinions and Desires, who take them either to True Education or False Education via yet further enclosures (11). The only path to True Education is to be found in False Education's enclosure, and in this enclosure are all those who are deluded into thinking that they have found True Education (12–13). But here, as outside the enclosure, Intemperance and the other Vices attempt to sway the people (14).

The path to True Education is found through a little gate that leads to a steep, rough and stony path that ascends a hill atop of which is a great rock with sheer sides (15). On the rock wait Self-Control and Endurance, and they pull up all those who have made it up the hill, and give them strength and courage before setting them upon a more easy path (16).

This is the path that leads to True Education, who sits with her daughters Truth and Persuasion outside the highest and final enclosure. They give to those whom they receive Courage and Fearlessness, which constitute the knowledge that one need never suffer anything bad in the course of one's life (17–18).

True Education gives to those she receives a purifying and curative draught that undoes the work of Deceit's potion, then takes them inside to Happiness and her daughters, the Virtues (19–21). Happiness crowns the successful travellers with flowers, bestowing a power that subdues all Vices (22–3). The Virtues then lead them back to the other enclosures where they now understand fully the plight from which they have escaped (24–6). Some people are rejected by True Education, and they also return to the other enclosures, accompanied by Distress, Pain, Despondency, Disgrace and Ignorance, eventually ending up in Luxury. Here they do not blame themselves for their failure, but True Education herself, saying bad things about her and about those who seek her (27–8).

At this point the story as portrayed in the tablet is concluded, and the rest of the text is devoted to a dialogue between the narrator and the old man concerning firstly the instructions that the Daimon gives to the people who enter Life – namely, that they should put no confidence in Fortune, that they should be impartial to her gifts, and not be surprised at anything she does, but take what she gives and depart immediately to 'the gift that is secure and safe, never to be regretted' (31). And this is the gift of True Education, knowledge of what is truly advantageous, to be granted after their journey through False Education (where they may stay to acquire what they will need for their journey), and on to True Education (32). The things they take from False Education do not in themselves make them better people, but they can help to shorten the journey (33).

The *Tablet* concludes with a somewhat laboured discussion of what Stoics regard as indifferent things (though Stoic terminology is not used in the text). Since life is enjoyed by good and bad people alike, life itself cannot be good or bad (36–8), and the same argument is applied to being healthy and being sick. Wealth is not good, because it does not help those who possess it become better people. The true advantage is possessed by those who understand how to use their wealth properly (39). The error that people make is to esteem things good and bad, thinking that things esteemed good will bring happiness, and to acquire them they will stoop to the most profane and disgraceful acts (40–1).

The final sections of the *Tablet* reiterate the points just made, and conclude with the old man instructing the narrator and his friends to practise to the point of making habitual the teaching he has just imparted (42–3).

Is the *Tablet* Stoic?

There are a number of rather striking features in the *Tablet* that
somewhat undermine its Stoic credentials. The text mentions no Stoic
philosopher, for one thing, but does mention Plato in passing (33.3),
and right at the beginning we learn that the stranger who donated the
plaque to the temple 'emulated in words and deeds the Pythagorean and
Parmenidean way of life' (2.2), suggesting to the reader new to the text
that they are about to enter upon an exposition of Pythagorean thought.
Further, the *Tablet* does not employ the Stoic terminology with which
we are familiar (see Glossary A) beyond just a few essential terms:
'happiness', 'happy', 'virtue', 'vice', 'good' and 'bad', a scattering of
specific virtues, and a few others. There are no echoes in Stoic writings of
the opening part of the fable, where the people queue up to enter Life,
first to receive instructions from the Daimon, then to be made to forget
those instructions through the effects of Deceit's potion. More than
anything, this section of the *Tablet* is likely to remind us of Plato's Story
of Er in the *Republic* (see Appendix 1).

However, if we put these anomalies aside, I am convinced that we
have in the *Tablet* a fundamentally Stoic work. Most striking of all is the
presence of Happiness, for happiness is the end (*telos*) to which the Stoic
prokoptôn (trainee) endeavours to make progress. The role that
happiness plays in Stoic ethics is symbolised in the allegory of the *Tablet*
by the figure of Happiness herself, who dwells within the highest
enclosure (which symbolises both the effort required to reach her, as well
as the value of the gift she bestows), the destination to which all travellers
aim if they are not led astray by the Vices and the appeal of Fortune's
gifts, and if they can remember the instructions given to them by the
Daimon before they enter into Life. However, the *Tablet* does not
describe the attaining of happiness in terms of living in accordance with
nature, and this is yet another puzzling omission, but instead makes it
clear that the virtues are necessary and sufficient for happiness, and this
of course is central to Stoic doctrine. Also firmly located in Stoic thought
is the point that the *Tablet* makes clear, that one suffers harm through
indulging in vice, and that the person possessed of happiness is immune
to the effects of vice and the whims of fortune.

The concept of indifferent things, those that are preferred and those
that are dispreferred, is captured by the *Tablet* in its portrayal of
Fortune, and expounded further in its account of how devotion to these
preferred things propels people into the misery of Luxury. Holding to
such devotion can only be achieved by maintaining a vicious outlook
that keeps one permanently from happiness. This, surely, characterises

the 'uneducated' person whose influence Epictetus warns us against. The story of Fortune also offers a very clear image of a key Stoic teaching that Epictetus returns to with some frequency – that of the transient nature of external things, though the *Tablet* does not extend the discussion to the length that Epictetus goes in his account of such things being on loan from God. If anything, the *Tablet* seems to be saying that material things are on temporary loan from Fortune herself. But the general thrust of the story on this point accords with Stoic doctrine, and certainly does not directly contradict it. The doctrine of indifferent things is again expounded in straightforward Stoic terms at the end of the *Tablet* (36ff), exemplified by its assertion that what is good is not wealth, but knowing how to use wealth wisely (39), and so, by implication, for all other external preferred indifferent things that people take to be advantageous.

The emphasis made by the *Tablet* that the gift one receives from Happiness is knowledge of what is truly advantageous (32) parallels Epictetus' special emphasis that happiness and a 'good flow of life' are enjoyed by people who know how to use impressions properly, which requires maintaining an awareness that nothing that happens is correctly evaluated as good or bad, but only as preferred or dispreferred with respect to furthering one's undertakings.

In the same way that we can regard Epictetus' *Handbook* as a distillation of his Stoic teaching, focusing on the key principles (and leaving out, for instance, the doctrine of the three topics), we can perhaps regard Cebes' *Tablet* as a distillation of the essential elements of Stoic ethics, cutting out everything but the most crucial parts – and doing so, at that, in a wonderfully graphic fashion which was surely intended by the author to make the account not just easy to remember, but memorable in the sense of worth remembering. Each of us may take, so to speak, a 'You are Here' sticker and place it on the *Tablet* at the spot we currently occupy, and in doing so honestly, we will perhaps have a better insight into why we have not yet found the well-being and fulfilment we hope for, and appreciate why we are going wrong, what is causing our distress, and what we must do to complete our personal journeys to Happiness.

The *Tablet of Cebes*

1. [1] We happened to be strolling around the temple of Cronus, looking at the many votive offerings dedicated there, when we saw set up in front of the shrine a tablet upon which was painted a strange scene. It depicted peculiar fables whose nature we were not able to fathom; [2] for the painting appeared to show neither a walled city nor a military camp, but presented a circular enclosure, within which were two other circular enclosures, one larger than the other. The first enclosure had a gate, and it seemed to us that a large crowd was standing near to this gate, [3] whilst within the enclosure we could see a large number of women. Beside this entrance to the first enclosure stood an old man who appeared to be giving instructions of some sort to the crowd that entered.

2. [1] We had been debating the meaning of this fable for some time when an old man, who had been standing close by, said, 'Do not be astonished, my friends, that you find yourselves baffled by this painting, for even many of those native to this place do not know the meaning of the story. [2] It was not dedicated [to the temple] by a local citizen, but by a stranger who came here long ago, someone of understanding and great wisdom, who emulated in words and deeds the Pythagorean and Parmenidean way of life. It was he who dedicated both this temple and the painting to Cronus.'

[3] 'Did you know this man personally?' I asked.

'Yes, indeed I did,' he replied. 'I was a young man, then, and I greatly admired him, for he would discuss many weighty matters. It was at that time that I also heard him often explaining the meaning of the fable.'

3. [1] 'By Zeus!' I said. 'If you have nothing else to which you must attend, please explain it to us, for we are very eager to know what the story means.'

'I will be happy to explain it, my friends,' he said, 'but first I must tell you that the explanation brings with it a certain amount of risk.'

'What sort of risk?' I asked.

'If you listen carefully,' he replied, 'and understand what I say, you will become wise and happy; but otherwise, if you fail to understand, you will become foolish, wretched, miserable and ignorant – and you will not fare well in life. [2] For the explanation is somewhat like that of the riddle by which the Sphinx used to challenge people: those who understood the riddle were spared, whilst those who failed to understand were eaten up by the Sphinx! And so it is with the explanation of the painting, because Folly, for people, is the Sphinx. [3] For these are the things wrapped in riddles: what is good, what is bad, and what in life is neither good nor bad. Thus it is that those who do not understand these things are destroyed by Folly, but not all at once in a moment like those who are eaten by the Sphinx, but rather they are brought to ruin little by little in the course of life, just like those handed over for punishment. [4] But for those who do understand these things, it is Folly who is destroyed, whilst they are saved to live their whole lives blessed and happy. Therefore listen carefully and give heed.'

4. [1] 'By Heracles! What a state of eagerness you have instilled in us, if all this is as you say!'

'Well,' he said, 'so indeed it is.'

'Be quick and explain it to us, for we will listen carefully, and will not slacken our attention when the penalty is so large.'

[2] He took his staff and pointed to the picture, saying, 'Do you see this enclosure?'

'Yes,' we said.

'Know first, then, that this place is named Life. And these people here, standing at the gate, comprise the great crowd of those about to enter into Life. [3] The old man standing above, who holds a scroll in one hand and who appears to be pointing out something with the other, is called Daimôn. To those who are going in, he is giving instructions as to what they ought to do when they have entered into Life; and he points out the path they ought to take if they are to be saved in Life.'

5. [1] 'Which path does he tell them to take, and how does he urge them to go?' I asked.

'Do you see here,' he said, 'positioned by the gate where the crowd enters, a throne on which sits a woman artificial in manner, but appearing persuasive, holding a cup in her hand?'

[2] 'Yes,' I said. 'But who is she?'

'She is named Deceit,' he replied, 'and she is the one who leads all mankind astray.'

'How does she do that?'

'She makes all those who enter Life drink of her power.'

[3] 'What is this drink?'

'It is error,' he said, 'and ignorance.'

'What then?'

'Having drunk, they enter into Life.'

'Do all of them drink of error, or not?'

6. [1] 'They all drink,' he said, 'but some drink more, some less. And do you see here, inside the gate, a crowd of women having every kind of appearance?'

'I see them.'

[2] 'They are called Opinions, Desires and Pleasures. As soon as the crowd enters, they jump up and cling to each person, and lead them off.'

'To where do they lead them?'

'Some to their salvation, but others, by deception, are led to their destruction.'

'How cruel is this drink of which you speak!'

[3] 'Indeed, all these women,' he said, 'promise that they will lead them to the best things, and to a happy and profitable life. But because of the ignorance and error of which they drank from Deceit, they do not find out which is the true way in Life; but instead they wander about aimlessly, just like those – you can see them, here – who went in first are being led astray, wherever these women direct them.'

7. [1] 'I see them,' I said. 'But who is that woman there? She appears to be blind and mad, standing on a round stone.'

'Her name,' he said, 'is Fortune. Not only is she blind and mad, but also deaf.'

[2] 'And what is her task?'

'She goes about everywhere,' he said, 'snatching from those the things they happen to have, and giving them to other people; and then immediately she takes away what she has just given them and gives it to yet others, entirely at random. Thus you might say that her symbol rightly declares her nature.'

[3] 'What symbol is that?' I asked.

'That she is standing on a round stone.'

'What does that signify?'

'That any gift from her is neither safe nor certain. For severely bitter and harsh are the disappointments that follow for those who put their trust in her.'

8. [1] 'But this huge crowd that throngs around her, what do they want and what are they called?'

'These are the people who take no thought for the morrow, and each is begging for what she throws them.'

'Why is it, then, that these people do not appear similar in appearance? Some seem to rejoice, whilst others despair, stretching out their hands to her.'

[2] 'These people here,' he said, 'rejoicing and laughing, are the ones who have received something from her. They call her Good Fortune. But those who look as though they are crying and stretching out their hands to her are the ones from whom she has taken back the things that earlier she had given them. These others call her Bad Fortune.'

[3] 'What,' I asked, 'are the things that she gives which make those who receive them so happy, whilst those who lose them weep?'

'Just those things,' he answered, 'which most people consider good.'

'But what are these things?'

[4] 'Why, wealth and reputation, high birth, children, thrones and kingdoms, and things such as these.'

'But surely these *are* good things?'

'We can discuss that another time,' he said. 'But for now let us concern ourselves with explaining the fable.'

'Very well.'

9. [1] 'Now, having passed through this gate, do you see that there is another enclosure higher up, outside which stand women dressed as courtesans usually are?'

'Certainly.'

'They are called Intemperance, Profligacy, Insatiability and Flattery.'

[2] 'Why are they standing here?'

'They watch,' he said, 'for those who receive anything from Fortune.'

'What then?'

'They jump up and embrace them, and flatter and urge them to stay with them, promising a life that will be sweet and easy and entirely free from troubles. [3] And if someone is persuaded by them to enter Luxury, for a time this will be pleasant enough, for the time, that is, he is sufficiently stimulated, but not for longer. For when he comes to his senses, he will realise that it was not he himself who has been doing the eating, but rather it was him who was being devoured and violated by her. [4] Thus, when he has squandered all those things that he was given by Fortune, he is compelled to be a slave to these women, to endure everything, acting disgracefully, and for their sakes indulging in every kind of harmful act, such as fraud, sacrilege, perjury, treason, theft and such like. After he has done all these things he is handed over to Punishment.'

10. [1] 'What is she like?'

'Do you see a bit behind them,' he asked, 'higher up, what looks like a small door, and a narrow, dark place?'

'Yes.'

'And do you see gathered together there, ugly and dirty women wearing rags?'

[2] 'Certainly.'

'This one with the whip,' he said, 'is called Punishment; that one with her head on her knees is called Grief; this one tearing out her own hair is called Distress.'

[3] 'But who is this other figure standing with them – a deformed, thin and naked man, who has with him a woman like him, ugly and thin?'

'He is Lamentation,' he said, 'and she is Despondency. She is his sister. [4] See, he is being handed over to them, and must live with them whilst being punished. After that he is thrown yet again into another place, the house of Unhappiness – here he lives out the rest of his life in total misery, unless Repentance should deliberately choose to meet with him face to face.'

11. [1] 'What happens if Repentance meets with him?'

'She releases him from his misery and introduces him to another Opinion and Desire, who lead him to True Education, but at the same time also introduces him to yet others who lead to False Education.'

[2] 'What happens then?'

'If he accepts this Opinion, who will lead him to True Education,' he said, 'then, once he is purified by her, he is saved and becomes blessed and happy his whole life long; but if not, he wanders away lost under the sway of False Opinion.'

12. [1] 'By Heracles! What another great danger there is here! But who is this False Education?' I asked.

'Do you see this other enclosure, here?'

[2] 'Certainly,' I said.

'Do you also see that standing outside the enclosure by the entrance is a woman appearing wholly pure and smartly dressed?'

'Certainly.'

[3] 'Well, most impetuous people call her Education, but she is not. She is False Education,' he said. 'But those who seek salvation by way of True Education must come here first.'

'Is there then no path that leads directly to True Education?'

'No, there is not,' he said.

13. [1] 'Who are these people walking back and forth inside this enclosure?'

'They are the devotees of False Education,' he said, 'and they are deluded into thinking that they are associating with True Education.'

'What are their names?'

[2] 'They are poets,' he said, 'orators, dialecticians, musicians, arithmeticians, geometers, astronomers, critics, hedonists, Peripatetics, and many others of the same sort.'

14. [1] 'But these women, here, who seem to be running about like the first ones, amongst whom you said was Intemperance and the others also with them – who are they?'

'They are just the same,' he said.

[2] 'Do they also enter in here?'

'Yes, by Zeus, they enter in here also, but not as often as they enter the first enclosure.'

'And the Opinions as well?' I queried.

[3] 'Yes, they too enter, for the drink the people received from Deceit is still effective in them, and those who are ignorant, by Zeus, are bound also to be foolish. For neither will opinion nor the rest of their wickedness leave them until they renounce False Education and enter upon the true path to drink of its restorative powers. [4] Thus, when they are restored and have thrown off all their wickedness – such as opinion, ignorance, and all the other bad things – then they will be saved. But the doctrines that False Education teaches to those who stay here with her will never set them free, and so they will never be able to leave these bad things behind them.'

15. [1] 'Show me the path that leads to True Education.'

'Do you see, here,' he said, 'this place higher up, inhabited by no one, appearing quite deserted?'

'I see it.'

[2] 'And do you see a little gate in front of which is a path with very few people on it? Very few pass this way, for the path is almost impassable, and appears to be rough and stony.'

'I see it,' I said.

[3] 'And there seems to be a high hill approached by a very narrow ascent having a sheer precipice on either side.'

'I see.'

'This is the path,' he said, 'that leads to True Education.'

[4] 'It certainly looks difficult.'

'And do you see high on the hill a great rock with steep cliffs on all sides?'

'I see it,' I said.

16. [1] 'Do you also see two fair and healthy women standing on the rock, eagerly stretching out their hands?'

'I see them. But what are they called?' I asked.

[2] 'One is called Self-Control,' he said, 'and the other is Endurance. They are sisters.'

'Why are they stretching out their hands so eagerly?'

[3] 'They are encouraging those who come to this place to have courage and

not flinch, telling them that they must endure a little while more, and then they will emerge upon a favourable path.'

[4] 'But when they arrive at the rock, how will they climb up? I see no path leading up.'

'The women descend the steep cliffs and pull them up to the top. And then they bid them rest. [5] Then after a while they give them strength and courage, and promise to take them to True Education. They show them that the path is agreeable, even easy, and free from evil, just as you can see.'

'So it appears, by Zeus.'

17. [1] 'Do you see,' he asked, 'in front of this grove, a place that appears to be a beautiful meadow, bathed in bright sunlight?'

'Indeed I do.'

[2] 'And can you see in the middle of the meadow another enclosure and another gate?'

'There they are: but what is this place called?'

[3] 'This is where those who are happy live,' he said. 'For here is where all the Virtues and Happiness spend their time.'

'Please continue,' I said, 'for this place is indeed as beautiful as you describe it.'

18. [1] 'Now then, do you see beside the gate,' he asked, 'a beautiful woman with a calm expression? She is mature in both years and judgement, wearing plain, unadorned clothes. She stands not upon a round stone, but upon a square one, firmly set. [2] And with her are two others who appear to be her daughters.'

'Yes, so it appears.'

'The one in the middle is Education, and the others are Truth and Persuasion.'

[3] 'But why is she standing on a square stone?'

'This is a sign,' he said, 'for those arriving here that the path leading to her is safe and secure, and that the gifts that she offers are safe for those who take them.'

[4] 'And what are these gifts?'

'Courage and fearlessness,' he said.

'What are they?'

'They are knowledge,' he said, 'that in the course of life one need never suffer anything terrible.'

19. [1] 'By Heracles! What wonderful gifts!' I said. 'But why is she standing outside the enclosure like this?'

'So that she may heal those who arrive here,' he said, 'by having them drink of her purifying powers. And thus, having purified them, she leads them to the Virtues.'

[2] 'How is this possible?' I said. 'I don't understand.'

'Ah, but you shall understand,' he said. 'Consider the case of someone who falls seriously ill. Obviously, in the first instance, they would go to a doctor, who would purge the causes of the disease, and in this way lead them back to recovery and health. [3] But if they do not obey the doctor's instructions they would no doubt deserve to suffer a relapse and succumb to the illness.'

'I understand that,' I said.

[4] 'It is just the same for those arriving here at Education,' he said. 'She takes care of them and gives them her own power to drink, so that first she may purify them and eliminate all the evils with which they came.'

'And what are they?'

[5] 'The error and ignorance of which they drank from Deceit, but also pretentiousness, desire, intemperance, anger, love of money, and all the others with which they were infected in the first enclosure.'

20. [1] 'So when they have been purified, where does she send them?'

'Inside,' he said, 'to Knowledge and the other Virtues.'

'Of what kind are they?'

[2] 'Do you not see,' he asked, 'inside the gate there is a group of women who appear attractive and modest, in plain, simple garments? They are free from affectation, in no way dressed up like the others.'

[3] 'Yes, I see,' I said. 'What are they called?'

'The first is Knowledge,' he said. 'And the others are her sisters: Courage, Justice, Goodness, Moderation, Orderliness, Freedom, Self-Control and Kindness.'

[4] 'Splendid!' I said. 'How great is our hope!'

'Indeed, if you understand,' he said, 'and if you also put into practice what you hear.'

'In that case, we will listen most carefully,' I said.

'Accordingly, you will be saved,' he said.

21. [1] 'When they are received by these women, to where are they led?'

'To their mother,' he said.

'Who is she?'

'Happiness,' he said.

'And what is she like?'

[2] 'Do you see the path there that leads to the citadel of all the enclosures, here, on this soaring height?'

'Yes.'

[3] 'Is there not seated on a high throne before the entrance, an attractive woman, nobly and simply attired, wearing a crown of exceedingly beautiful flowers?'

'So it appears.'

'She is Happiness,' he said.

22. [1] 'When someone arrives here, what does she do?'

'Happiness crowns them with her power,' he said, 'along with all the other Virtues, just like those who have won victories in the greatest contests.'

'But what kind of contests have they won?' I asked.

[2] 'The very greatest,' he said, 'for they have overcome the savage beasts that previously devoured, abused and enslaved them – they have been victorious over all of them, casting them away and winning possession of themselves, for now the beasts are *their* slaves, as they were previously slaves of the beasts.'

23. [1] 'What are these wild beasts of which you speak? I would very much like to hear.'

'To begin with,' he said, 'Ignorance and Error. Or don't you consider them to be wild beasts?'

'Indeed, wicked ones to be sure,' I said.

[2] 'Next there are Grief, Lamentation, Greed, Intemperance, and every other Vice. Over all these they are now master, no longer the slaves they were before.'

[3] 'What splendid deeds!' I said. 'And what a glorious victory! But tell me this – what is the power of the crown with which, you say, they are crowned?'

[4] 'It is the power that brings happiness, young man! For those who are crowned with this power become happy and blessed, and they place their hope for happiness not in others, but in themselves.'

24. [1] 'How noble the victory of which you speak! But once they are crowned, what do they do, and where do they go?'

[2] 'Taking them by the hand, the Virtues lead them to the place from which they first came, where they are shown those who dwell there leading wicked and wretched lives, how they are shipwrecked in life, wandering aimlessly, led captive like prisoners, some by Intemperance, some by Pretentiousness, Greed, Vanity, or the other Vices. [3] They are not capable of freeing themselves from these terrors to which they are fettered, to come here to be saved; instead, they are troubled their whole lives long. They suffer this way all because they are unable to find the path here, for they have forgotten the instructions they had from the Daimôn.'

25. [1] 'What you say seems true. But I am puzzled as to why the Virtues show them the place from where they first came.'

[2] 'This is because they did not have accurate knowledge of it,' he said, 'and did not understand what happens there. Because of their ignorance and error of which, we know, they had already drunk, they were confused, thinking that things not good are good, and that things not evil are evil. [3] Consequently, they also lived wickedly, just like the others who dwell there. But now that they possess the

knowledge of what is advantageous, they now live nobly and can see how badly the others fare.'

26. [1] 'After they have seen all this, what do they do, and where do they go next?'

'Anywhere they like,' he said. 'For all places are safe for them, just as the Corycian cave is safe for those finding sanctuary there. Wherever they come to, they will live nobly and securely. For everyone will welcome them gladly, just as sick people welcome a doctor.'

[2] 'Do they no longer fear that they can be harmed by those women you described as wild beasts?'

'No. They will not be troubled either by Distress or Grief, nor by Intemperance, Greed [3] or Poverty – nor by any other Vice. For they are master of them all, superior to everything that previously caused distress, like those who survive being bitten by a snake. For these snakes, whose venom kills everyone else, cannot harm those who possess the antidote. In the same way, nothing can cause distress to them, because they now possess the antidote.'

27. [1] 'I think what you say is true, but tell me this: who are those people who appear to be arriving here from that hill, there? Some of them are wearing crowns and appear cheerful, whilst others, without crowns, appear grief-stricken and confused, and appear to have been beaten about the legs and head, [2] and are being ordered about by certain women.'

'Those wearing crowns are the ones who have come safely to Education, and they are delighted at finding her. [3] Some without crowns, having been rejected by Education, are turning back in a miserable and wretched state; whilst others, through cowardice, fail to ascend to Endurance, and also turn back and wander where there are no paths.'

[4] 'And the women who accompany them – who are they?'

'Grief,' he said, 'Distress, Despondency, Disgrace and Ignorance.'

28. [1] 'Are you saying that all evils accompany them?'

'Yes, by Zeus!' he said. 'They all go with them. And when they arrive at the first enclosure, there to find Luxury and Intemperance, [2] they do not blame themselves, but straightaway they say bad things about Education and those who seek her out, calling them wretched, miserable and unhappy, inasmuch as having forsaken living with them, they live wickedly, they say, and do not enjoy the good things which they have themselves.'

[3] 'What things do they say are good?'

'Profligacy and intemperance, to quickly summarise. For they think that feasting like fatted beasts is the way to enjoy the greatest good.'

29. [1] 'Now, these other women, coming from over there, cheerful and laughing, what are they called?'

[2] 'Opinions,' he said. 'Having led to Education those who enter the company of the Virtues, they return to lead up others; and they bring back tidings that those they have led away are happy.'

[3] 'Do they not enter the company of the Virtues?' I asked.

'No,' he answered, 'for it is not right that Opinion enter the company of Knowledge, so they hand over their wards to Education. [4] And when Education has received them, they return again to bring others, just like ships that have unloaded their cargoes return again to be loaded anew.'

30. [1] 'You seem to explain all this very well,' I said. 'But there is one thing you have not made clear to us: namely, what are the instructions that the Daimôn gives to everyone entering into Life?'

[2] 'To be of good courage,' he said. 'Therefore you also be of good courage, for I will explain everything and leave out nothing.'

'That is well said,' I declared.

[3] Then stretching out his hand again, he said, 'Do you see that woman there, who seems to be blind, standing on a round stone, whom I told you before is called Fortune?'

'We see her.'

31. [1] 'He tells them,' he said, 'to put no confidence in her, not to regard as secure or safe anything she gives them, nor to consider it their own property. [2] For there is nothing to prevent her from taking away what she has given so as to bestow it on someone else – for this is her habit, and she does it often. For this reason he urges that they learn to be impartial towards her gifts, neither rejoicing when she gives them nor despairing when she takes them away, neither blaming her nor praising her. [3] For she does nothing rationally, but brings about everything at random and without reason, just as I told you before. Consequently, the Daimôn urges them not to be surprised at anything she may do, and not to be like bad bankers [4] who having received money from people rejoice as if it were their own, such that when it is taken back they are upset and think they have suffered something terrible, forgetting that it was on this very condition that they received the deposit, namely that nothing should prevent its repayment. [5] This is how the Daimôn bids them to regard the gifts of Fortune, and to remember that her nature is such that she takes back what she gives, only to quickly bestow it again, then again and again. Not only does she take away what she has given, but also those things that they possessed before. [6] Thus he urges them to take what she gives and at once depart towards the gift that is secure and safe.'

32. [1] 'And what is that?' I asked.

'The one that they will receive from Education, if they reach her safely.'

'And what is it?'

[2] 'True knowledge of what is advantageous,' he said, 'a gift safe and secure, never to be regretted. [3] Thus he urges them to flee immediately to her, and when they come to those women I told you about earlier – Intemperance and Luxury – he urges them never ever to trust them, but to quickly depart in order that they may come to False Education. [4] Here he bids them stay for a while and take from her whatever they will need to support their journey, and then set off immediately for True Education. [5] These are the Daimôn's instructions. Whenever anyone does anything contrary to these, or ignores them, they will perish in utter wretchedness.

33. [1] 'This is the story, my friends, that the tablet shows us. If you want to know anything more about any of these things, please ask, and I will tell you.'

[2] 'Fine words indeed!' I said. 'But what is it that the Daimôn instructs them to take from False Education?'

'Anything that appears useful.'

'And what might that be?'

[3] 'Literature,' he said, 'and all the other studies that Plato says act like bridles for the young, preventing them from being distracted by other things.'

[4] 'Must one really take these things, or not, if one's intention is to arrive at True Education?'

'Well, none of these things is actually required,' he said. 'However, they are useful for shortening the journey, though they do not help people become better.'

[5] 'Are you saying that these things are of no use at all for helping people to become better?'

'It is quite possible to become better without them – however, they are not actually useless. [6] Just as we sometimes understand what is being said through an interpreter, this does not mean that it would be pointless for us to know the language ourselves, for then we would have understood what was being said with greater accuracy. Similarly, nothing prevents one from becoming better even without such learning.'

34. [1] 'Are such scholars, then, no further advanced than anyone else with respect to being better?'

[2] 'How can we consider them further advanced, when clearly they are just as mistaken about what is good and what is bad, and remain subject to every vice? [3] For nothing prevents someone from knowing literature and mastering all the other academic studies, whilst at the same time being drunk, intemperate, greedy, unjust, treacherous, and ultimately, foolish.'

[4] 'Of course, one often sees such people.'

'In what way, then,' he asked, 'can the pursuit of academic studies promote progress towards becoming better people?'

35. [1] 'In no way, so it seems from this argument. But why do these people stay in this second enclosure,' I asked, 'as if they were drawing closer to True Education?'

[2] 'How can we think that staying here can be to their advantage,' he said, 'when we can often see people – who have arrived at True Education in the third enclosure by avoiding Intemperance and the other Vices in the first enclosure – surpass these scholars? How then can they be superior, being so stubborn and dull-witted?'

[3] 'How is that?' I queried.

'Because in the second enclosure, if nothing else, the people there claim to understand what they do not know. But as long as they have this opinion they will of necessity be unable to make progress on their journey to True Education. [4] Further, do you not also see that the Opinions from the first enclosure still have access to them? So they are no better off than those [in the first enclosure] unless they also take with them Repentance, who can persuade them that they have not found Education, but False Education, by whom they are deceived. [5] Because they have this disposition they can never be saved. You too, my friends,' he said, 'must do the same, until having pondered these words you put them into practice. You must reflect upon these things over and over, never to neglect them, and deem all the rest as secondary. Otherwise, what you now hear will be of no advantage to you.'

36. [1] 'This we will do. But explain this to us: why are the things that people receive from Fortune not good – namely, life, health, wealth, good reputation, children, success, and all the others like these? [2] Or their opposites – why are they not evil? For what you say about this seems altogether strange and unbelievable!'

'Come then,' he said, 'and try to state what appears to be the case with respect to whatever I ask you.'

[3] 'Indeed I shall,' I said.

'Tell me this,' he said. 'If someone lives wickedly, is living for this person something good?'

'I would think not; rather it seems to be something bad,' I said.

'How then can living be something good,' he said,' if for this person it is something bad?'

[4] 'Well, it appears that for those who live wickedly it is something bad, whilst for those who live nobly it is something good.'

'Are you saying, then, that living is both good and bad?'

'I am.'

37. [1] 'But that is absurd! It is impossible for the same thing to be both bad and good! You could similarly say that something can be both beneficial and harmful, or both sought after and avoided.'

[2] 'Yes – quite absurd. But how can it be that living is not really bad, when it really *is* bad for them? And if it really is bad for them, then living itself is bad.'

'But they are not the same,' he said, 'living and living wickedly. Or do you not see that?'

'Of course I don't think they're the same!'

[3] 'So living wickedly is bad, whilst living is not bad. For if it were bad, it would also be bad for those who live nobly – because their being alive would have to be bad for them as well.'

'What you say seems true.'

38. [1] 'Since life is enjoyed by both groups, by those who live nobly and by those who live wickedly, then life itself is neither good nor bad. It is just the same for those who are sick: it is not the surgery and cauterising that make you worse or make you better, but the way the surgery is done. So it is regarding the question of living: it is not living itself that is bad, but bad living.'

[2] 'Quite so.'

'This being the case, consider whether you would prefer to live wickedly or to die nobly and bravely.'

'I would prefer to die nobly.'

[3] 'Accordingly, not even dying is bad, if dying is often preferred to living.'

'That is so.'

[4] 'Indeed, the same argument applies to being healthy and being sick. For often health is not advantageous, but the opposite, depending upon the circumstances.'

'True, indeed.'

39. [1] 'Come then, let us also look into the question of wealth from the same point of view. Consider how often we can find people possessed of wealth, but living wicked and wretched lives.'

'By Zeus, there are many such people.'

[2] 'So wealth is of no help to them for living nobly?'

'Apparently not, for they themselves are bad.'

[3] 'So what makes them good is not wealth, but Education.'

'Most probably.'

'So on this view, then, wealth is not good because it does not help those who possess it to become better.'

'Apparently.'

[4] 'Being wealthy, then, is of no advantage for those who do not understand how to use their wealth.'

'So it seems.'

'How can anyone judge that something is good if there is often no advantage in possessing it?'

[5] 'Impossible!'

'Therefore, if someone understands how to use their wealth properly and skilfully, they will live well – if not, they will live wickedly.'

'What you say seems entirely true.'

40. [1] 'So this is what we have: we can esteem some things as good and reject others as bad. This is what disturbs and hurts people, that in esteeming these things and supposing that they alone bring happiness, they will undertake anything to get them, not avoiding even the most profane and disgraceful acts. [2] They are reduced to this by ignorance of what is good – for in their ignorance they fail to see that nothing good comes from evil. [3] We can see many people who have acquired their wealth through evil and shameful deeds, that is to say, through treachery, theft, murder, slander, fraud, and through many other depravities.'

'So it is.'

41. [1] 'If, as seems likely, nothing good comes from evil, and wealth comes from evil deeds, then necessarily wealth is not something good.'

'This is the conclusion to be drawn from the argument.'

[2] 'Neither wisdom nor honesty can be acquired through evil deeds, any more than dishonesty and folly can be acquired through good deeds – neither can they be found together in the same person. [3] Nothing prevents someone enjoying wealth, reputation, success, and such like, whilst at the same time being hugely wicked. Therefore, these things are neither good nor bad, since wisdom alone is good, whilst folly is bad.'

[4] 'Most adequately explained, I think!' was my reply.

[The Greek text breaks off at this point. Although the narrative does seem to have reached a satisfactory conclusion, it is possible that there was once a longer ending in the original Greek to account for the existence of an Arabic paraphrase that extends the work. The standard text of the *Tablet*, therefore, concludes with the following brief section, translated from J. Elichmann's Latin rendering of the Arabic, first published posthumously in 1640, printed by Karl Praechter in his 1893 edition, and included in the 1983 edition by Fitzgerald and White. See FW 27–8, 167 n. 120.]

'And thus we reject that opinion that these things [wealth, reputation, success, and so forth] result only from evil deeds.'

42. [1] The old man continued, saying, 'Now, this is a very important point, the same one that we arrived at before, that such things are neither good nor bad; indeed, if these things only ever resulted from evil deeds they would be altogether bad. [2] But all such things result from both types of action, and that is why we said that they are neither good nor bad, just as being asleep or being awake are neither good nor bad. [3] And it seems to me that this applies similarly to other things, such as walking, sitting, and such like, since these things are done by everyone, by educated and ignorant people alike. However, there are some things that are appropriate for one type or the other, because some things are good whilst others are bad – such as tyranny and justice, which belong only to one type, and the other to the other type. This is the case because justice always manifests in those possessed of understanding, whereas tyranny is found in those who are ignorant. [4] For, as we have said, it is not possible at any one time for such contrary qualities to be found in the same person – just as it is not possible for any one person at any one moment of time to be both asleep and awake, wise and ignorant, and so forth with respect to other qualities that we pair with their opposites.

'Well,' I said, 'I think this whole discussion has reached a most satisfactory conclusion.'

43. [1] 'Furthermore,' he said, 'I hold that all these things proceed from a divine principle.'

'Which principle do you mean?' I asked.

[2] He replied, 'Life and death, health and sickness, wealth and poverty, and all the other things which you held to be both good and bad, happen to most people through nothing evil.'

'Well, I must say that our discussion urges the conclusion that such things are indeed neither good nor bad; even so, I am not at all confident that my judgement of these things is sound.'

'This is so,' he said to us, 'because none of you possess that habit through which you may acquire this way of thinking. Therefore, throughout the whole course of your lives hold to the practice of those things I have just now explained to you, such that those things of which I have spoken will become imprinted in your minds and become a habit for you. But if you are still uncertain about anything, come back to me so that my explanations may dispel your doubts.'

Appendix 1
The story of Er

[Translation by Benjamin Jowett, from Book 10, 614b–621d, of *The Republic of Plato*, third edition, Clarendon Press, 1888.]

I will tell you a tale [continues Socrates, speaking to Glaucon]; not one of the tales which Odysseus tells to the hero Alcinous, yet this too is a tale of a hero, Er the son of Armenius, a Pamphylian by birth. He was slain in battle, and ten days afterwards, when the bodies of the dead were taken up already in a state of corruption, his body was found unaffected by decay, and carried away home to be buried. And on the twelfth day, as he was lying on the funeral pile, he returned to life and told them what he had seen in the other world. He said that when his soul left the body he went on a journey with a great company, and that they came to a mysterious place at which there were two openings in the earth; they were near together, and over against them were two other openings in the heaven above. In the intermediate space there were judges seated, who commanded the just, after they had given judgement on them and had bound their sentences in front of them, to ascend by the heavenly way on the right hand; and in like manner the unjust were bidden by them to descend by the lower way on the left hand; these also bore the symbols of their deeds, but fastened on their backs. He drew near, and they told him that he was to be the messenger who would carry the report of the other world to men, and they bade him hear and see all that was to be heard and seen in that place. Then he beheld and saw on one side the souls departing at either opening of heaven and earth when sentence had been given on them; and at the two other openings other souls, some ascending out of the earth dusty and worn with travel, some descending out of heaven clean and bright. And arriving ever and anon they seemed to have come from a long journey, and they went forth with gladness into the meadow, where they encamped as at a festival; and those who knew one another embraced and conversed, the souls which came from earth curiously enquiring about the things above, and the souls which came from heaven about the things beneath. And they told one another of what had happened by the way, those from below weeping and sorrowing at the remembrance of the things which they had endured and seen in their journey beneath the earth (now the journey lasted a thousand years), while those from above were describing heavenly delights and visions of inconceivable beauty. The story, Glaucon, would take too long to tell; but the sum was this: – He said that for every wrong which they had done to any one they suffered tenfold; or once in a hundred years – such being reckoned to be the length of man's life, and the penalty being thus paid ten times in a thousand years. If, for example, there were any who had been the cause of many deaths, or had betrayed or enslaved cities or armies, or been guilty of any other evil behaviour, for each and all of their offences they received punishment ten times over, and the rewards of beneficence and justice and holiness were in the same proportion. I need hardly repeat what he said concerning young children dying almost as soon as they were born. Of piety and impiety to gods and parents, and of murderers, there were retributions other and greater far which he described. He mentioned that he was present when one of the spirits asked another, 'Where is Ardiaeus the Great?' (Now this Ardiaeus lived a thousand years before the time of Er: he had been the tyrant of some city of Pamphylia, and had murdered his aged father and his elder brother, and was said to have committed many other abominable crimes.) The answer of the other spirit was: 'He comes not hither, and will never come. And this,' said he, 'was one of the dreadful sights which we ourselves witnessed. We were at the mouth of the cavern, and, having completed all our experiences, were about to reascend, when of a sudden Ardiaeus appeared and several others, most of whom were tyrants; and there were also besides the tyrants private individuals who had been great criminals: they were just, as they fancied, about to return into the upper world, but the mouth, instead of admitting them, gave a roar, whenever any of these incurable sinners or some one who had not been sufficiently punished tried to ascend; and then wild men of fiery aspect, who were standing by and heard the sound, seized and carried them off; and Ardiaeus and others they bound head and foot and hand, and threw them down and flayed them with scourges, and dragged them along the road at the side, carding them on thorns like wool, and declaring to the passers-by what were their crimes, and that they were being taken away to be cast into hell.' And of all the many terrors which they had endured, he said that there was none like the terror which each of them felt at that moment, lest they should hear the voice; and when there was silence, one by one they ascended with exceeding joy. These, said Er, were the penalties and retributions, and there were blessings as great.

Now when the spirits which were in the meadow had tarried seven days, on the eighth they were obliged to proceed on their journey, and, on the fourth day after, he said that they came to a place where they could see from above a line of light, straight as a column, extending right through the whole heaven and through the earth, in colour resembling the rainbow, only brighter and purer; another day's journey brought them to the place, and there, in the midst of the light, they saw the ends of the chains of heaven let down from above: for this light is the belt of heaven, and holds together the circle of the universe, like the undergirders of a trireme. From these ends is extended the spindle of Necessity, on which all the revolutions turn. The shaft and hook of this spindle are made of steel, and the whorl is made partly of steel and also partly of other materials. Now the whorl is in form like the whorl used on earth; and the description of it implied that there is one large hollow whorl which is quite scooped out, and into this is fitted another lesser one, and another, and another, and four others, making eight in all, like vessels which fit into one another; the whorls show their edges on the upper side, and on their lower side all together form one continuous whorl. This is pierced by the spindle, which is driven home through the centre of the eighth. The first and outermost whorl has the rim broadest, and the seven inner whorls are narrower, in the following proportions – the sixth is next to the first in size, the fourth next to the sixth; then comes the eighth; the seventh is fifth, the fifth is sixth, the third is seventh, last and eighth comes the second. The largest (or fixed stars) is spangled, and the seventh (or sun) is brightest; the eighth (or moon) coloured by the reflected light of the seventh; the second and fifth (Saturn and Mercury) are in colour like one another, and yellower than the preceding; the third (Venus) has the whitest light; the fourth (Mars) is reddish; the sixth (Jupiter) is in whiteness second. Now the whole spindle has the same motion; but, as the whole revolves in one direction, the seven inner circles move slowly in the other, and of these the swiftest is the eighth; next in swiftness are the seventh, sixth, and fifth, which move together; third in swiftness appeared to move, according to the law of this reversed motion, the fourth; the third appeared fourth and the second fifth. The spindle turns on the knees of Necessity; and on the upper surface of each circle is a siren, who goes round with them, hymning a single tone or note. The eight together form one harmony; and round about, at equal intervals, there is another band, three in number, each sitting upon her throne: these are the Fates, daughters of Necessity, who are clothed in white robes and have chaplets upon their heads, Lachesis and Clotho and Atropos, who accompany with their voices the harmony of the sirens – Lachesis singing of the past, Clotho of the present, Atropos of the future; Clotho from time to time assisting with a touch of her right hand the revolution of the outer circle of the whorl or spindle, and Atropos with her left hand touching and guiding the inner ones, and Lachesis laying hold of either in turn, first with one hand and then with the other.

When Er and the spirits arrived, their duty was to go at once to Lachesis; but first of all there came a prophet who arranged them in order; then he took from the knees of Lachesis lots and samples of lives and, having mounted a high pulpit, spoke as follows: 'Hear the word of Lachesis, the daughter of Necessity. Mortal souls, behold a new cycle of life and mortality. Your genius will not be allotted to you, but you will choose your genius; and let him who draws the first lot have the first choice, and the life which he chooses shall be his destiny. Virtue is free, and as a man honours or dishonours her he will have more or less of her; the responsibility is with the chooser – God is justified.' When the Interpreter had thus spoken he scattered lots indifferently among them all, and each of them took up the lot which fell near him, all but Er himself (he was not allowed), and each as he took his lot perceived the number which he had obtained. Then the Interpreter placed on the ground before them the samples of lives; and there were many more lives than the souls present, and they were of all sorts. There were lives of every animal and of man in every condition. And there were tyrannies among them, some lasting out the tyrant's life, others which broke off in the middle and came to an end in poverty and exile and beggary; and there were lives of famous men, some who were famous for their form and beauty as well as for their strength and success in games, or, again, for their birth and the qualities of their ancestors; and some who were the reverse of famous for the opposite qualities. And of women likewise; there was not, however, any definite character in them, because the soul, when choosing a new life, must of necessity become different. But there was every other quality, and they all mingled with one another, and also with elements of wealth and poverty, and disease and health; and there were mean states also. And here, my dear Glaucon, is the supreme peril of our human state; and therefore the utmost care should be taken. Let each one of us leave every other kind of knowledge and seek and follow one thing only, if peradventure he may be able to learn and may find some one who will make him able to learn and discern between good and evil, and so to choose always and everywhere the better life as he has opportunity. He should consider the bearing of all these things which have been mentioned severally and collectively upon virtue; he should know what the effect of beauty is when combined with poverty or wealth in a particular soul, and what are the good and evil consequences of noble and humble birth, of private and public station, of strength and weakness, of cleverness and dullness, and of all the natural and acquired gifts of the soul, and the operation of them when conjoined; he will then look at the nature of the soul, and from the consideration of all these qualities he will be able to determine which is the better and which is the worse; and so he will choose, giving the name of evil to the life which will make his soul more unjust, and good to the life which will make his soul more just; all else he will disregard. For we have seen and know that this is the best choice both in life and after death. A man must take with him into the world below an adamantine faith in truth and right, that there too he may be undazzled by the desire of wealth or the other allurements of evil, lest, coming upon tyrannies and similar villanies, he do irremediable wrongs to others and suffer yet worse himself; but let him know how to choose the mean and avoid the extremes on either side, as far as possible, not only in this life but in all that which is to come. For this is the way of happiness.

And according to the report of the messenger from the other world this was what the prophet said at the time: 'Even for the last comer, if he chooses wisely and will live diligently, there is appointed a happy and not undesirable existence. Let not him who chooses first be careless, and let not the last despair.' And when he had spoken, he who had the first choice came forward and in a moment chose the greatest tyranny; his mind having been darkened by folly and sensuality, he had not thought out the whole matter before he chose, and did not at first sight perceive that he was fated, among other evils, to devour his own children. But when he had time to reflect, and saw what was in the lot, he began to beat his breast and lament over his choice, forgetting the proclamation of the prophet; for, instead of throwing the blame of his misfortune on himself, he accused chance and the gods, and everything rather than himself. Now he was one of those who came from heaven, and in a former life had dwelt in a well-ordered State, but his virtue was a matter of habit only, and he had no philosophy. And it was true of others who were similarly overtaken, that the greater number of them came from heaven and therefore they had never been schooled by trial, whereas the pilgrims who came from earth, having themselves suffered and seen others suffer, were not in a hurry to choose. And owing to this inexperience of theirs, and also because the lot was a chance, many of the souls exchanged a good destiny for an evil or an evil for a good. For if a man had always on his arrival in this world dedicated himself from the first to sound philosophy, and had been moderately fortunate in the number of the lot, he might, as the messenger reported, be happy here, and also his journey to another life and return to this, instead of being rough and underground, would be smooth and heavenly. Most curious, he said, was the spectacle – sad and laughable and strange; for the choice of the souls was in most cases based on their experience of a previous life. There he saw the soul which had once been Orpheus choosing the life of a swan out of enmity to the race of women, hating to be born of a woman because they had been his murderers; he beheld also the soul of Thamyras choosing the life of a nightingale; birds, on the other hand, like the swan and other musicians, wanting to be men. The soul which obtained the twentieth lot chose the life of a lion, and this was the soul of Ajax the son of Telamon, who would not be a man, remembering the injustice which was done him in the judgement about the arms. The next was Agamemnon, who took the life of an eagle, because, like Ajax, he hated human nature by reason of his sufferings. About the middle came the lot of Atalanta; she, seeing the great fame of an athlete, was unable to resist the temptation: and after her there followed the soul of Epeus the son of Panopeus passing into the nature of a woman cunning in the arts; and far away among the last who chose, the soul of the jester Thersites was putting on the form of a monkey. There came also the soul of Odysseus having yet to make a choice, and his lot happened to be the last of them all. Now the recollection of former toils had disenchanted him of ambition, and he went about for a considerable time in search of the life of a private man who had no cares; he had some difficulty in finding this, which was lying about and had been neglected by everybody else; and when he saw it, he said that he would have done the same had his lot been first instead of last, and that he was delighted to have it. And not only did men pass into animals, but I must also mention that there were animals tame and wild who changed into one another and into corresponding human natures – the good into the gentle and the evil into the savage, in all sorts of combinations.

All the souls had now chosen their lives, and they went in the order of their choice to Lachesis, who sent with them the genius whom they had severally chosen, to be the guardian of their lives and the fulfiller of the choice: this genius led the souls first to Clotho, and drew them within the revolution of the spindle impelled by her hand, thus ratifying the destiny of each; and then, when they were fastened to this, carried them to Atropos, who spun the threads and made them irreversible, whence without turning round they passed beneath the throne of Necessity; and when they had all passed, they marched on in a scorching heat to the plain of Forgetfulness, which was a barren waste destitute of trees and verdure; and then towards evening they encamped by the river of Unmindfulness, whose water no vessel can hold; of this they were all obliged to drink a certain quantity, and those who were not saved by wisdom drank more than was necessary; and each one as he drank forgot all things. Now after they had gone to rest, about the middle of the night there were a thunderstorm and earthquake, and then in an instant they were driven upward in all manner of ways to their birth, like stars shooting. He himself was hindered from drinking the water. But in what manner or by what means he returned to the body he could not say; only, in the morning, awaking suddenly, he found himself lying on the pyre.

And thus, Glaucon, the tale has been saved and has not perished, and will save us if we are obedient to the word spoken; and we shall pass safely over the river of Forgetfulness, and our soul will not be defiled. Wherefore my counsel is, that we hold fast ever to the heavenly way and follow after justice and virtue always, considering that the soul is immortal and able to endure every sort of good and every sort of evil. Thus shall we live dear to one another and to the gods, both while remaining here and when, like conquerors in the games who go round to gather gifts, we receive our reward. And it shall be well with us both in this life and in the pilgrimage of a thousand years which we have been describing.

Appendix 2
Tables, plans, and drawing

1 Stoic values

	IN OUR POWER	NOT IN OUR POWER
	(Things that are by nature free, unhindered and unimpeded)	External Things (Things that are weak, slavish, hindered, and belong to others)
IN ACCORDANCE WITH NATURE	Opinion, Impulse, Desire, Aversion, and 'whatever is our own doing': Things that are truly good and proper to desire: The Virtues and Virtuous Actions Good Feelings (*hai eupatheiai*)	Things usually but mistakenly taken to be good – The Preferred Indifferents: Life, Health, Wealth, Reputation, Possessions, Friends, etc.
CONTRARY TO NATURE	Other things that are also 'our own doing': Things that are truly bad to which it is proper to be averse: Vice and Vicious Actions Distrubing/Violent Emotions (*pathê*)	Things usually but mistakenly taken to be bad – The Dispreferred Indifferents: Death, Sickness, Poverty, Rejection, etc.

2 Passions and 'good feelings'

	NON-WISE PERSON		WISE PERSON	
Passion or Good Feeling	Indifferent Events or Objects	Passions (*pathê*)	Indifferent Events or Objects	GOOD FEELINGS (*eupatheiai*)
DIRECTED AT WHAT WE EXPECT TO HAPPEN	Anticipated (in error) as GOOD	Desire (*epithumia*)	Anticpated as PREFERRED	Wish (*boulêsis)*
	Anticipated (in error) as EVIL	Fear (*phobos*)	Anticipated as DISPREFERRED	Caution (*eulabeia*)
DIRECTED AT PRESENT CIRCUMSTANCES	Believed (in error) to be GOOD	Pleasure (*hêdonê*)	Experienced as PREFERRED	Joy (*chara*)
	Believed (in error) to be EVIL	Distress (*lupê*)	Experienced as DISPREFERRED	No affective response

3 Indifferent things (*ta adiaphora*)

preferred (*proêgmena*)	dispreferred (*apoproêgmena*)
in accordance with nature (*kata phusin*)	contrary to nature (*para phusin*)
have value (*axia*)	have 'disvalue'(*apaxia*)
confer advantages	confer disadvantages
'to-be-taken'(*lêpton*)	'not-to-be-taken'(*alêpton*)
rational to prefer	rational to disprefer

4 Translations of *prohairesis*

This book	moral character
Boter 1999	choice, choices
Carter, 1910	my (own) mind, faculty of choice
Dobbin 1998	moral character, moral choice, choice
Hard 1995	choice, faculty of choice, sphere of choice
Higginson 1890, 1944	will
Hijmans 1959, 10, 24, 25, 65	choice, freedom of choice, moral nature
Inwood 1995, 123	moral personality
Long, George 1890, 1991, 2003	will
Long, A. A. 1996b, 162, 275, 281	moral character
Long, A. A. 2002	volition
Matheson 1916	will
Matson 1998	will
Oldfather 1926, 1928	moral purpose, moral choice
Reale 1990, 80–3	moral choice
Rist 1969, 228;1985	moral character
Rolleston 1892	purpose, will, choice
Sorabji 2000, 331	will
White 1983	choices, faculty of choice

5 Translations of *aidôs* (n) and *aidêmôn* (adj), *pistis* (n) and *pistos* (adj) in *Handbook* 24

	aidôs / aidêmôn	*pistis / pistos*
This book	self-respect	trustworthiness, trustworthy
Boter 1999	self-respecting	faithful
Brittain and Brennan 2002a/b	respectful	trustworthy
Hard 1995	sense of shame	trustworthiness, trustworthy
Higginson 1890	honour, self-respect, honourable, self-respecting	fidelity, faithful
Long, George 1991	modesty, modest	fidelity, faithful
Matheson 1916	self-respect, modest	honour, faithful
Matson 1998	self-respect, uprightness, upright	trustworthiness, faithfulness, faithful
Oldfather 1926, 1928	self-respect, self-respecting	fidelity, faithful
Rolleston 1892	piety, pious	faith, faithful
White 1983	self-respect, self-respecting	trustworthiness, trustworthy

6 The Stoic philosophers

Early Stoa

Zeno of Citium	335–263 BC	Came to Athens 313 BC. Student of Antisthenes, Crates, Xenocrates, Polemo and others. Founded Stoa *c.* 300 BC.
Persaeus of Citium	*c.* 306–*c.* 243 BC	Brought up by Zeno. Student of Zeno.
Aristo of Chios	3rd cent. BC	Student of Zeno. Held unorthodox view of the indifferents, denying the preferred/dispreferred distinction.
Herillus of Carthage	3rd cent. BC	Student of Zeno who, like Aristo, also held that distinctions of value could not be made between the indifferents.
Cleanthes of Assos	331–232 BC	2nd head of Stoa from 263 BC. Student of Zeno. Wrote *Hymn to Zeus*.
Sphaerus of Borysthenes	3rd cent. BC	Student of Zeno and Cleanthes.
Chrysippus of Soli	*c.* 280–*c.* 207 BC	Came to Athens *c.*260 BC. 3rd head of Stoa from 232 BC. Student of Cleanthes.
Zeno of Tarsus	3rd–2nd cents BC	Student of Chrysippus. 4th head of Stoa from *c.*207 BC.
Diogenes of Babylon	*c.* 240–*c.* 152 BC	5th head of Stoa. Student of Chysippus and Zeno of Tarsus.
Antipater of Tarsus	2nd cent. BC, died *c.* 129 BC	Head of Stoa from *c.*152 BC. Student of Diogenes of Babylon.
Apollodorus of Seleucia	2nd cent. BC	Student and associate of Diogenes of Babylon. Worked with Antipater of Tarsus and Panaetius.

Middle Stoa

Panaetius of Rhodes	*c.* 185–*c.* 109 BC	Head of Stoa from *c.* 129 BC. Student of Diogenes of Babylon and Antipater of Tarsus. Moved to Rome in the 140s BC.
Posidonius of Apamea	*c.* 135–*c.* 51 BC	Student of Panaetius. Opened a school in Rhodes. Visited by Cicero *c.* 78 BC.
Hecato of Rhodes	*fl.* early 1st cent.	Student of Panaetius and associate of Posidonius.
Antipater of Tyre	1st cent. BC, died shortly before 44 BC	Taught by students of Panaetius.

Late Stoa

Seneca	*c.*4 BC–AD 65	Lawyer, author, teacher of Nero, senator and official. Many of his works are extant.
Musonius Rufus	1st cent. AD	Teacher in Rome. Epictetus was his student. Extensive fragments survive in Stobaeus.
Euphrates of Tyre	died *c.* AD 120	May have been a pupil of Musonius Rufus. Knew Epictetus.
Epictetus	*c.* AD 55–*c.* 135	Student of Musonius Rufus. Teacher, first in Rome, then from *c.*89 in Nicopolis in Greece. Teacher of Arrian.
Hierocles	*fl. c.* AD 100	Wrote an *Elements of Ethics*, of which the first part survives. Other fragments are preserved in Stobaeus.
Marcus Aurelius	AD 121–180	Emperor from 161, and author of private notes, *The Meditations*.
Cleomedes	*fl.* late 2nd cent. AD	Stoic author of astronomical treatise.

Sources: Algra 1999, Hornblower and Spawforth 1996, Long 1986 and 2002, Long and Sedley 1987, Zeyl 1997.

Plan 1   Schematic overview of Cebes' Tablet showing locations of enclosures and personifications

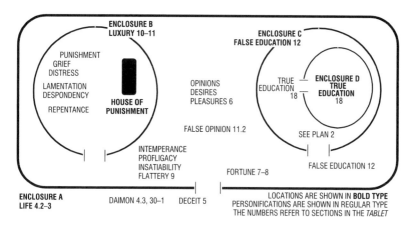

Plan 2   Enclosures C and D, False Education and True Education

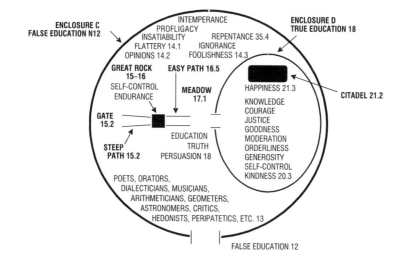

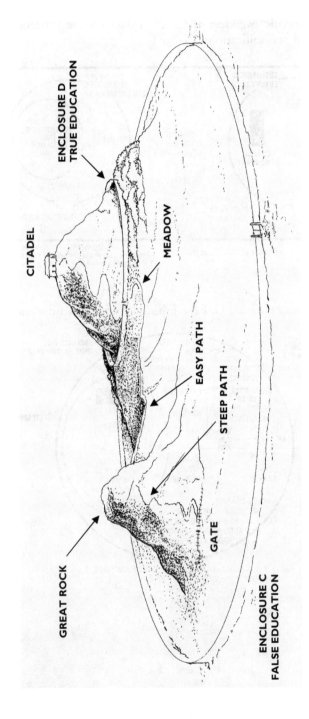

Drawing 1 The path to true education

Appendix 3

A page from the author's Stoic notebook

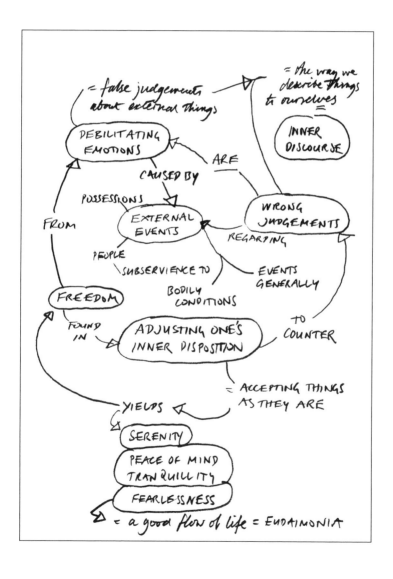

Glossary A
Epictetus

[Note: it is beyond the scope of this book to make the references in the entries below comprehensive and complete. Instead, they focus almost exclusively on Epictetus' *Discourses* and *Handbook*, on the chapter on Zeno in Diogenes Laertius' *Lives of Eminent Philosophers*, and on Stobaeus' *Epitome of Stoic Ethics*. Motto (1970) is an excellent resource for following up references in Seneca. The Loeb edition of Marcus Aurelius (Haines 1930) contains indexes and a Glossary of Greek Terms. Long and Sedley (1987) is an excellent resource with primary source extracts and commentaries arranged thematically, also containing indexes and a glossary.]

adiaphoros 'indifferent'; the *adiaphora* are any of those things that are neither good nor bad, everything, in fact, that does not fall under the headings 'virtue' or 'vice'. The indifferents are what those lacking Stoic wisdom frequently take to be good or bad, and hence taken to be desirable or undesirable. Pursuing them, or trying to avoid them, can lead to disturbing emotions that undermine one's capacity to lead a *eudaimôn* life. [See *Discourses* 1.9.12–13, 1.20.12, 1.30.3, 2.5.1–8, 2.6.1–2, 2.9.15, 2.19.13; DL 7.92/102–7; *Handbook* 32.2; LS 58; Stob. 2.7.5a/7/7a–d/7f–g.]

agathos 'good'; something *agathos* is that which truly benefits the person who possesses it, understood by the Stoics to be 'virtue', to be acquired by 'following nature', by being motivated by the right sort of impulses and keeping one's moral character (*prohairesis*) in the right condition. For Epictetus, the essence of good is the proper use of *phantasiai*, 'impressions' (*Discourses* 1.20.15), for this is what is *eph' hêmin*, 'in our power' (*Discourses* 1.22.11–12). *See also* **aretê, hormê, prohairesis, phusis.** [See *Discourses* 1.25.1, 1.27.12, 1.29.1–4, 1.30.1–7, 2.1.4, 2.2.5/8, 2.8.4, 2.16.1–2, 2.19.13, 3.3.24, 3.10.18,

3.20, 3.22.38–44, 3.24.3, 4.1.132–3, 4.5.32, 4.10.8–9, 4.12.7–9, 4.13.24; DL 7.94–5/98–103; *Handbook* 6, 19.2, 24.3, 25.1, 29.7, 30, 31.2/4, 32.1; LS 60; Stob. 2.7.5a–b/5b1/5b6/5c–m/6d–f/7g/10/ 10b/11b–d/11f/11i.]

aidêmôn 'self-respecting', of someone who possesses *aidôs*, self-respect, honour, a sense of modesty, or a sense of shame; for Epictetus, a key characteristic of the *prokoptôn's prohairesis*. Our *aidôs* is our own, and cannot be taken away, nor its use prevented (*Discourses* 1.25.4). *See also* **pistos**. [See *Discourses* 1.3.4, 1.16.7, 2.1.11, 2.2.4, 2.8.23, 2.10.15/18, 2.20.32, 2.22.20/30, 3.7.27, 3.17.5, 3.18.6, 3.22.15, 4.1.106, 4.2.8, 4.3.1–2/7–9, 4.4.6, 4.5.21–2, 4.8.33, 4.9.6/9/11, 4.12.6, 4.13.19–20; *Handbook* 33.15, 40; *Fragment* 14; for *aidêmôn* together with *pistos* see *Discourses* 1.4.18–20, 1.25.4, 1.28.20–1/23, 2.4.2, 2.8.23, 2.10.22–3/29, 2.22.20/30, 3.3.9–10, 3.7.36, 3.13.3, 3.14.13, 3.17.3, 3.23.18, 4.1.161, 4.3.7, 4.9.17, 4.13.13/15; *Handbook* 24.3–5.]

apaideutos 'uneducated'; the condition from which the Stoic *prokoptôn* tries to save themselves by learning Stoic principles and putting those principles into effect. *See* **idiôtês**. [See *Discourses* 1.8.8, 1.29.54, 3.26.28, 4.4.32; *Handbook* 5.]

apatheia 'peace of mind' (literally, 'without passion', that is, being free from passion); a constituent of the *eudaimôn* life. One who enjoys peace of mind is *apathês*. [See *Discourses* 1.4.3/28–9, 2.8.23, 2.17.31, 3.5.7, 3.13.11, 3.15.12, 3.21.9, 3.24.24, 3.26.13, 4.3.7, 4.4.9/36, 4.6.16/34, 4.8.27, 4.10.13/22/26; DL 7.117; *Handbook* 12.2, 29.7.]

aphormê 'repulsion' (the opposite of *hormê*); that which motivates our rejection of anything. See Discourses 1.1.12, 1.4.11, 3.2.2, 3.7.26/ 34, 3.12.13, 3.22.31/36/43, 4.11.6/26; DL 7.105–6; Handbook 2.2; Stob. 2.7.7c/9.]

apoproêgmenos 'dispreferred'; used of *adiaphoros* ('indifferent') things, including such things as sickness, physical impairment, death, pain, poverty, injustice, a 'bad' reputation, unpopularity, lack of practical skills, and so forth (conventionally 'bad' things, usually taken to disadvantage those who suffer them). Enduring any of the dispreferred indifferents does not detract from the *eudaimôn* life enjoyed by the Stoic *sophos*. *See also* **proêgmenos**. [See LS 58; Stob. 2.7.7b/7g.]

appropriate action *see* **kathêkon**

aprohaireta 'things independent of the moral character'. Each is *aprohairetos*. (*Discourses* 1.30.3, 2.13.10, 2.16.1; MA 6.41). *See* **prohairesis**.

aretê 'excellence' or 'virtue'; in the context of Stoic ethics the possession of 'moral excellence' will secure *eudaimonia* ('happiness' or 'flourishing'). For Epictetus, one acquires this by learning the correct use of impressions, following God, and following nature. The virtues are the only things that are good (*agathos*); they are dispositions of one's *prohairesis* (moral character) that inform actions and duties generally. Four primary virtues had been recognised since the time of Plato: *phronêsis* (prudence or wisdom), *sôphrosunê* (temperance, moderation, or self-restraint), *dikaiosunê* (justice), and *andreia* (courage or bravery). The other virtues were taken to be subordinate to these four: perseverance is a type of courage, and kindness is a sort of justice, for instance (see Stob. 5b2). The term *aretê* does not occur in the *Handbook*. The opposite of virtue, vice, is *kakia. See kalos.* [See *Discourses* 1.4.3–11, 1.12.16, 2.9.15, 2.19.13/17/21, 2.23.19, 3.3.22, 3.16.7, 3.22.59, 3.24.111, 4.1.164, 4.8.32; DL 7.89–94/ 97–8/100–2/109/125–8; Stob. 2.7.5a–b5/5b7–11/5c/5e–g/5i/5k– l/6/6d–f/8/11g–k.]

askêsis 'training', 'exercise' or 'practice' undertaken by the Stoic *prokoptôn* striving to become a Stoic *sophos*. The most important exercise for Epictetus is maintaining the correct use of impressions. (Epictetus uses the term *meletaô*, 'to practise, or train oneself in something', at *Handbook* 5.1.) *See also* **phantasia**. [See *Discourses* 2.9.13, 3.2.1, 3.10.7, 3.12; *Handbook* 14.1, 47; Stob. 2.7.5b4.]

assent *see* **sunkatathesis** and **phantasia** (impression)

ataraxia 'imperturbability'; literally 'without disturbance or trouble', translated variously as 'peace of mind', 'serenity', 'calm', 'tranquillity', or 'impassiveness'; a state of mind that is a constituent of the *eudaimôn* life. Someone possessed of this state of mind is *atarachos*. [See *Discourses* 1.4.21, 2.1.21/33, 2.2, 2.5.2/7, 3.13.13, 3.15.12, 3.21.9, 3.24.79, 4.1.84, 4.4.36, 4.6.34, 4.8.27/30–1, 4.10.22, 4.11.22; *Handbook* 12.2, 29.7.]

aversion *see* **ekklisis**

bad *see* **kakos**

boulêsis 'wish'; one of the three *eupatheiai* ('good feelings'), experienced only by the Stoic wise person. *Boulêsis* is defined as a *eulogos orexis*, a 'reasonable desire'. [See DL 7.116; Stob. 2.7.5b/9a.]

chara 'joy'; one of the three *eupatheiai* ('good feelings'), experienced only by the Stoic wise person. [See DL 7.94/98/116; *Ep.* 59; Stob. 2.7.5b/5c/5g/5k/6d.]

caution *see* **eulabeia**

desire *see* **epithumia** and **orexis**

dispreferred *see apoproêgmenos*
distress *see lupê* and *tarachê*
duty *see kathêkon*
ekklisis 'aversion' or 'avoidance'; opposite of *orexis* (desire), and along
with *orexis*, *ekklisis* should be exercised 'in accordance with nature'
(*Discourses* 1.21.2). [See *Discourses* 1.1.12, 1.4.1/11, 2.29.19, 3.2.1–
3, 3.3.2, 3.6.6, 3.12, 3.14.10, 3.22.13/31/36/43, 3.23.10, 3.24.54,
3.26.14, 4.4.28/33, 4.5.27, 4.6.18, 4.8.20, 4.10.4–5, 4.11.6/26; DL
7.104–5; *Handbook* 1.1, 2, 32.2, 48.3; Stob. 2.7.10b.]
ektos 'external'; *ta ektos*, 'the externals', are any of those things that fall
outside the preserve of one's *prohairesis*, including health, wealth,
sickness, life, death, pain – what Epictetus calls the *aprohaireta*, which
are not in our power, the 'indifferent' things. [See *Discourses* 1.15.2,
1.27.11, 2.2.10–15/25–6, 2.5.4–9/24, 2.16.11, 2.22.19, 3.3.8,
3.7.2, 3.10.16, 3.12.6, 3.15.13, 3.24.56, 4.3.1, 4.4.1–6, 4.7.10/41,
4.8.32, 4.10.1, 4.12.15; DL 7.95/106; *Handbook* 13, 23, 29.7,
33.13, 48.1; Stob. 2.7.5e/7a–b/11c.]
eleutheria 'freedom', a state of being, constitutive of the *eudaimôn* life,
enjoyed by the Stoic wise person in virtue of their capacity to
maintain their *prohairesis* in the right condition. In making the
correct use of impressions and not assenting to false judgements, the
Stoic wise person is free from disturbing emotions, and so can never
be constrained or impeded by external events or the actions of other
people. Those who are free are '*eleutheros*'. The person who is free is
said by Epictetus to be the 'friend of God' (*Discourses* 4.3.9). [See
Discourses 1.12.8–15, 2.1.21–8, 2.2.13, 2.17.29, 3.5.7, 3.7.27,
3.13.11, 3.15.12, 3.22.16/39/42–4/84, 3.24.66–7/96–8, 3.26.34–
5/39, 4.1, 4.3.7/9, 4.6.8–9/16–17, 4.7.8–9, 4.13.24; *Handbook*
1.2–4, 14.2, 19.2, 29.7; Stob. 2.7.11i/11m.]
emotion *see pathos*
end *see telos*
eph' hêmin 'in our power', 'up to us', or 'depending on us'; namely,
making the correct use of impressions, by means of which we
maintain our *prohairesis* in the right condition. This is the most
important concept in Epictetus' treatment of Stoic ethics. [See
Discourses 1.1, 1.6.40, 1.12.32–4, 1.18.12, 1.22.9–10, 1.29.8,
2.1.12, 2.2.6, 2.5.4/8, 2.13.1–2/10–11, 2.13.32, 3.3.10, 3.24.1–3/
22–3, 3.26.34, 4.1.65–83/100/128–31, 4.4.15, 4.7.8–10, 4.10.8/
28; *Handbook* 1.1–2/5, 2.1–2, 14.1–2, 18, 19.1–2, 24.1–2, 25.1,
31.2, 32.1–2, 48.3.]

epithumia 'desire', 'appetite' or 'yearning'; one of the four primary *pathê* (passions). *Epithumia* is the yearning that the non-wise person directs towards anticipated events and objects in the mistaken belief that they are of real benefit. [See DL 7.110/113; Stob. 2.7.10/10b.]

eudaimôn 'happy' or 'flourishing'; descriptive of the *sophos* (Stoic wise person). See *eudaimonia*.

eudaimonia 'happiness', 'flourishing' or 'living well' was conceived by the ancient philosophers as the *telos*, 'end' or 'goal' of life. For Epictetus, one achieves this end, of living the *eudaimôn* ('happy') life, by learning the correct use of impressions, following God, and following nature. More generally, the Stoics say that happiness consists in living virtuously (DL 7.87/89). Zeno said that happiness is 'a good flow of life' (DL 7.88, Stob. 2.7.6e) attained by 'living in agreement' (Stob. 2.7.6a). Someone who enjoys *eudaimonia* is *eudaimôn. See euroia biou; telos.* [See *Discourses* 1.4.3, 2.4.9, 3.20.15, 3.22.26–30/39/60/84, 3.23.34, 3.24.2/16–17/52/118, 3.26.18, 4.1.46, 4.4.36/48, 4.7.9, 4.8.30–1; DL 7.88/89/95/97/104/128; *Handbook* 1.4; LS 63; Stob. 2.7.5b5/5g/6c–e/7g/8a/11g.]

eulabeia 'caution'; one of the three *eupatheiai* ('good feelings'), experienced only by the Stoic wise person. [See *Discourses* 2.1, 2.2.14; DL 7.116; *Handbook* 48.1.]

eupatheia 'good feeling'; possessed by the Stoic wise person (*sophos*) who experiences these special sorts of emotions, but does not experience irrational and disturbing passions. There are three *eupatheiai* experienced by the Stoic wise person: (1) with respect to an anticipated good, whereas the non-wise person experiences *epithumia* (desire), the wise person experiences *boulêsis* (wish); (2) with respect to the presence of a supposed good, whereas the non-wise person experiences *hêdonê* (pleasure), the wise person experiences *chara* (joy); and (3) with respect to an anticipated evil, whereas the non-wise person experiences *phobos* (fear), the wise person experiences *eulabeia* (caution). There is no 'good feeling' that correlates with the non-wise person's experience of *lupê* (distress) with respect to the presence of a supposed evil. A 'good feeling' correlates with a correct judgement (and possibly *is* the affective component of such a judgement) about what is truly good (virtue, and action motivated by virtue), in contrast to a passion which correlates with a false judgement. *See pathos.* [See DL 7.116 = LS 65F.]

euroia biou 'good flow of life'; this is Zeno's definition of *eudaimonia* ('happiness'), enjoyed by the *sophos* (wise person). Epictetus usually uses the abbreviated form, *hê euroia*. In *Handbook* 8 he uses the verb *euroeô* which means 'to flow well', translated as 'all being well'. Other translators deploy a range of suitably synonymous expressions: peace of mind, peace, happiness, serenity, tranquillity, well-being, prosperity. *See also* **eudaimonia, telos.** [See *Discourses* 1.1.22, 1.4.1–5/27–8, 2.16.41/47, 2.18.28, 2.19.29, 3.10.10, 3.14.8, 3.17.9, 3.20.14, 3.22.26/39/45, 4.4.4–5/22/37/39, 4.6.35, 4.7.9, 4.12.2; MA 2.5, 5.34, 10.6; *Handbook* 8; Stob. 2.7.6e/8a.]

eusebês 'dutiful' or 'pious'; the disposition of someone who takes proper care of their devotion to the gods. [See *Discourses* 3.2.4, 4.7.9; *Handbook* 31.4; Stob. 2.7.11g.]

excellence *see* **aretê**

external thing *see* **ektos**

fate *see* **Peprômenê**

fear *see* **phobos**

free/freedom *see* **eleutheria**

God *see* **theos**

good *see* **agathos**

'good feeling' *see* **eupatheia**

'good flow of life' *see* **euroia biou**

happy *see* **eudaimonia**

hêdonê 'pleasure'; one of the four primary *pathê* (passions). *Hêdonê* is the pleasure that the non-wise person experiences when events or objects that are mistakenly believed to be of real value are present. *See pathos.* [See *Discourses* 2.11.19–22, 3.7.2–18, 3.12.7, 3.24.36–7/71–2; DL 7.85–6/93/103/110/114/117; *Ep.* 51.5–6, 59.1–2, 104.34; *Handbook* 34; Stob. 2.7.5a/10/10b–c.]

hêgemonikon 'commanding faculty', the controlling part of the soul (*psuchê*); the centre of consciousness, the seat of all mental states, thought by the Stoics (and some other ancients) to be located in the heart. It manifests four mental powers: the capacity to *receive impressions*, to *assent* to them, *form intentions* to act in response to them, and to do these things *rationally*. The *Discourses* and *Handbook* talk of keeping the *prohairesis* in the right condition, and also of keeping the *hêgemonikon* in the right condition, and for Epictetus these notions are essentially interchangeable. The *prohairesis* and the *hêgemonikon* are in the right condition when they are maintained 'in accordance with nature' or 'in harmony with nature'. [See *Discourses* 1.15.4, 1.20.11, 1.26.15, 2.1.39, 2.18.8–9/30, 2.22.25, 2.26.7, 3.3.1, 3.4.9, 3.5.3, 3.6.3, 3.9.11, 3.10.11/16,

3.15.13, 3.21.3, 3.22.19/33/93, 4.4.43, 4.5.4/6, 4.7.40, 4.10.25; *Handbook* 29.7, 38; LS 53H/K2; Stob. 2.7.5b7/10.]

hormê 'impulse to act', 'choice' or 'intention' (more appropriately translated as 'preference' at *Handbook* 48.3); that which motivates an action. 'Impulse is a motion of the soul towards something' (Stob. 2.7.9 = LS 53Q2). 'Impulse is the stimulus to action' (Cicero, *On Duties* 1.132 = LS 53J). Its opposite, repulsion, 'a motion of the soul away from something', is *aphormê*. [See *Discourses* 1.1.12, 1.4.11, 2.24.19, 3.2.2, 3.7.26/34, 3.12.4/13, 3.22.31/36/43/104, 3.24.56, 4.1.1/71–3, 4.4.16–18/28, 4.6.18, 4.7.20, 4.11.6/26; DL 7.85–6/108; *Handbook* 1.1, 2.2, 48.3; Stob. 2.7.5b3/5b5/5b13/5c/5o/7/7a/7c/7e/9/9a–b/10.]

hupexhairesis 'reservation'; the Stoic wise person undertakes all actions 'with reservation', recognising that the outcomes of all actions are not 'in their power', for only the intention to act, and to act with virtue, are in their power. Thus, in undertaking any action, the Stoic wise person understands that they will succeed in their action unless something intervenes, and if something does intervene, this is accepted as how Zeus wants the world to be, and is not an occasion for feeling upset and lapsing into passion. [See *Handbook* 2.2; MA 4.1, 5.20, 6.50, 8.41, 11.37 = *Fragment* 27; Seneca, *On Benefits* 4.34.4, *Tranquillity of Mind* 13.2–3; Stob. 2.7.11s = LS 65W.]

hupolêpsis 'opinion' or 'assumption'; the Stoic *prokoptôn* guards against holding inappropriate or false opinions – something that occurs if they do not make 'proper use of impressions'. The opinions we hold are 'in our power'; thus maintaining one's *prohairesis* in the right condition is in part accomplished by holding appropriate opinions. [See *Handbook* 1.1, 20, 31.1; Stob. 2.7.10.]

idiôtês a common, private, or uneducated person. Epictetus uses this term to denote someone who is ignorant of philosophy (in particular, Stoic ethics), and who is in this sense uneducated. An *idiôtês* is *idiôtikos* ('uneducated'). In *Handbook* 5 Epictetus also uses the term *apaideutos*, 'uneducated', and it is from this condition of being uneducated that the Stoic *philosophos* tries to save themselves (the achievement of which would be to attain *eudaimonia*), undertaken by maintaining one's *prohairesis* in the right condition, following God, following nature, and above all by making the proper use of impressions. The Stobaeus text employs the term *phaulos* ('worthless'; 'inferior' in LS) which, in this context, can be regarded as a synonym of Epictetus' *idiôtês*. [See *Discourses* 1.29.64–6, 2.12.2–4/10–11, 3.16, 3.22.87; *Fragment* 2; *Handbook* 5, 17, 29.7, 33.6/13/

55555550

4255255555555255

543555525555555552

15, 46, 48.1, 51.1; Stob. 2.7.5b10/5b12–13/5e/6c/11b/11d/11g/11i–k/11m/11s.]

idiôtismos the way or manner of the *idiôtês*, the common, private, or uneducated person (more appropriately translated as 'vulgar' at *Handbook* 33.15). [See *Handbook* 33.6/15.]

impression *see phantasia*

impulse *see hormê*

indifferent *see adiaphoros*

joy *see chara*

kakia 'vice'; characteristic of the *idiôtês*, but alien to the *sophos*. Vicious actions inevitably befall the agent who makes false judgements about what is really good and bad, and about what constitutes the *telos* and the *eudaimôn* life. Thus, from the perspective of Stoic ethics, all, or almost all people are vicious, being *phaulos* (worthless), *idiôtikos* and *apaideutos* (uneducated). The *prokoptôn* is aware of their deficiencies and turns to Stoic ethics for philosophical enlightenment and practical remedies that will require commitment to Stoic training (*askêsis*). [See DL 7.93/95–7/102/120; LS 61; Stob. 2.7.5a–b/5b1/5b8–10/5b12–13/5c/5e–g/6d/6f/7/11d/11f–g/11k–m.]

kakos 'bad', 'evil' (more appropriately 'fault' in *Handbook* 33.9); the only thing that counts as truly bad for the Stoic *philosophos* is *kakia*, 'vice' (whereas things commonly understood to be bad are regarded as *adiaphoros*, 'indifferent', by Stoics). [See *Discourses* 2.1.4, 3.3.1–4, 3.20.1–4, 3.22.23, 3.24.1–3, 4.10.8, 4.12.7–8/19–21; *Handbook* 11, 12, 16, 24, 27.7, 30, 31.2, 32.1, 33.9, 53.1; LS 60; Stob. 2.7.5a–b/5b1/5c–g/6d–e/7/10/10b–c/11g/11i.]

kalos 'fine', 'beautiful, 'honourable' (more appropriately 'proper' in *Handbook* 2.2); Epictetus describes the Stoic *sophos* as *kalos kai agathos*, 'fine and good'. *See sophos*. [See *Discourses* 1.7.2, 1.12.7, 2.10.5, 2.11.25, 2.14.10, 3.2.1/7, 3.3.1, 3.22.69/87, 3.24.18/50/95/110, 4.5.1/6, 4.8.24; DL 7.101; *Handbook* 2.2, 6, 10; Stob. 2.7.5d/6e/11g–h/11k/11s.]

kata phusin 'in accordance with nature'; the Stoic *prokoptôn* endeavours to maintain their *prohairesis* 'in accordance with nature', accomplished by making proper use of impressions, following God, and making manifest in their life the conviction that virtue is the proper *telos* ('end' or 'goal') for all rational beings. Thus to live in accordance with nature is one and the same as securing the *eudaimôn* life. That which is not in accordance with nature is contrary to nature, *para phusin*, and 'natural things' are *ta kata phusin*. (Epictetus also uses a range of essentially synonymous expressions when he urges his students to 'live in accordance with nature', talking also of 'following nature', and 'living in harmony or agreement (*sumphônos*) with nature' – though the last expression occurs in only the *Discourses* and not in the *Handbook*.) [See *Discourses* 1.11.5/8, 1.12.19, 1.15.4, 1.21.2, 1.26.2, 3.3.1, 3.4.9, 3.5.3, 3.6.3, 3.9.11/17, 3.10.11, 3.13.20, 3.16.15, 4.4.43, 4.5.5–6; DL 7.105; *Handbook* 4, 6, 13, 30.]

kathêkon any 'appropriate action', 'proper function', or 'duty' undertaken by someone aiming to do what befits them as a responsible, sociable person. The appropriate actions are the subject of the second of the three *topoi*. [See *Discourses* 1.7.1–2/21, 1.18.2, 1.22.15, 1.28.5, 2.7.1, 2.8.29, 2.10, 2.14.18, 2.17.15/31, 3.2.2/4, 3.7.24–8, 3.22.43/69/74, 4.4.16, 4.12.16; DL 7.25/93/107–10/ 118; *Handbook* 30, 33.13, 42; LS 59; Stob. 2.7.5b2–3/5b9/6a/7b/8/ 8a/9/10b/11a.]

katorthôma a 'right action' or 'complete or perfect action' undertaken by the Stoic *sophos*, constituted by an appropriate action performed virtuously. [See LS 59K–O; Stob. 2.7.8/8a/11a/11e/11l/11o.]

lupê 'distress'; one of the four primary *pathê* (passions). *Lupê* is the distress that the non-wise person experiences when events or objects that are mistakenly believed to be of real harm are present. Some translators, including Pomeroy 1999 (Stob.), use the term 'pain' for *lupê*, and it is important to stress that in Stoic philosophy of mind, *lupê* denotes *mental* pain, what someone suffers whilst in the grip of this passion (see Garrett 1999). [See *Discourses* 3.13.11, 3.22.48, 4.1.84, 4.3.7, 4.6.8; DL 7.96/110–12/118; Stob. 2.7.5b/5c/5g/10/ 10a–c/11i.]

nature *see **phusis***

opinion *see **hupolêpsis***

orexis 'desire'; properly directed only at virtue, a type of 'rational impulse' constituted by a movement of the soul towards something. Epictetus says that we should exercise desire and aversion 'in accordance with nature' (*Discourses* 1.21.1). See ***hormê***. [See *Discourses* 1.1.12, 1.4.1/11, 2.24.19, 3.2.1–3, 3.3.2, 3.6.6, 3.9.22, 3.12, 3.13.21, 3.14.10, 3.22.13/31/36/43, 3.23.9, 3.24.54, 3.26.14, 4.1.84, 4.4.28, 4.5.27, 4.6.18, 4.8.20, 4.11.6/26; *Handbook* 1.1, 2.1–2.14.1, 15, 31.4, 32.2, 48.3; Stob. 2.7.9/11f.]

passion *see **pathos***

pathos 'passion'; any of the 'disturbing or violent emotions' experienced inappropriately and sometimes excessively by those who lack Stoic wisdom and believe that externals really are good or bad, when in fact they are 'indifferent'. (The term *pathos* does not occur in the *Handbook*, and it occurs only sparsely in the *Discourses*, though terms which describe someone's experience of falling into disturbing passions abound, and these include being miserable, distressed, hindered, impeded, unfortunate, irritated, and wretched.) A *pathos*, according to the Stoics, is an excessive impulse occasioned by assenting to a false judgement based on a misunderstanding of what is truly good and bad, and can be regarded as the affective component of such a judgement, or can be identified as *the judgement itself* (DL 7.111; LS 65G3). When you have a *pathos* you are said to have an 'irrational and unnatural movement of the soul' (DL 7.110). The Stoics identified four primary *pathê*, two directed at what we expect to happen, *epithumia* (desire) and *phobos* (fear), and two directed at present circumstances, *hêdonê* (pleasure) and *lupê* (distress): thus what we first longed for, we take delight in once we have it, and what we first feared becomes the source of anguish when the time comes to suffer it. Other passions are classified under these four primary passions. Anger, sexual desire, and love of riches, for instance, are types of desire (Stob. 2.7.10b = LS 65E). The Stoic *sophos* does not experience these *pathê*, but does experience the *eupatheiai*, 'good feelings'. The Stoic *prokoptôn* endeavours to make the transition from *idiôtês*, whose life is circumscribed by the *pathê*, to *sophos*, who is entirely free from the *pathê* – and in this sense they strive to eradicate or extirpate the passions; *though*, one cannot *directly* extirpate a passion that one is already suffering any more than one can prevent sugar from tasting sweet (for instance) once the slice of cake is already in one's mouth. The Stoic *sophos simply stops experiencing* the *pathê* because they no longer make false judgements about what is good and bad, and about what constitutes the *telos* and the *eudaimôn* life. Thus, the *prokoptôn* strives not to eradicate the *pathê* directly, but to guard against making false judgements, which occurs, for Epictetus, when one fails to make proper use of impressions. *See also* **agathos, apatheia, ektos, eupatheia**. [See *Discourses* 1.27.10; 3.2.3, 4.1.115, 4.3.7, 4.6.16; DL 7.110–16; LS 65; Stob. 2.7.6d/10/10a–10e.]

peace of mind *see **apatheia**; **euroia biou***

Peprômenê 'fate' or 'destiny', conceived of as one's appointed lot in life. The key feature of fate is its *anankê* (necessity or compulsion). The training that the Stoic *prokoptôn* engages in, if successful, will result in their embracing their own fate, and that of the world generally, as wholly acceptable and even desirable, no matter what its character may be. [See *Discourses* 2.23.42, 3.22.95, 4.1.128–31, 4.4.34, 4.7.20; DL 7.149; *Handbook* 53.]

phantasia 'impression'; *phantasiai* are what we are aware of in virtue of having experiences. They are not limited only to what is sensed in perception, but include as well what we are aware of when thinking abstractly, having memories, imagining things, and so forth. An impression is an 'imprint on the soul: the name having been appropriately borrowed from the imprint made by the seal upon the wax' (DL 7.45, trans. Hicks), and this notion of what an impression is, we must suppose, derives from Plato's account in the *Theaetetus* (191c–e) of the mind being compared to a block of wax that, when impressed by perceptions or ideas, retains and remembers them for as long as the impression lasts. Whereas non-rational animals respond to their impressions automatically (thus 'using' them), over and above using our impressions, human beings, being rational, can 'understand their use' (*Discourses* 1.6.13, 2.14.15) and, with practice, assent or not assent to them as we deem appropriate. 'The use of impressions' (*hê chrêsis tôn phantasiôn*) in this wider sense is an essential component of making progress, and it is this capacity that Epictetus strives to teach his students. *See also prokopê, sunkatathesis.* [See *Discourses* 1.1.7/12, 1.3.4, 1.6.13, 1.12.34, 1.20.5/7/15, 1.27.1–2, 1.28.10–12/30–3, 1.30.4, 2.1.4, 2.8.4/6, 2.14.15–16, 2.18.8–29, 2.19.32, 2.22.5–6, 2.23.7/40/42, 3.2.5/8, 3.3.1/17/20, 3.8, 3.12.6–15, 3.16.15, 3.22.25/43/103, 3.24.69/88/108, 3.25.6, 3.26.13–14, 4.1.74, 4.3.7, 4.4.13–14, 4.5.23, 4.6.25/34, 4.7.32, 4.10.26; DL 7.45–6/49–51, 7.118; *Handbook* 1.5, 6, 10, 16, 18, 19, 20, 34, 45; LS 39A (= DL 7.49–51), 62K (= *Discourses* 1.1.7–12); Stob. 2.7.5l/7a–b/9/10c.]

philosophia 'philosophy'; literally, the 'love of wisdom', the discipline in which, as a Stoic, one immerses oneself in the pursuit of *eudaimonia*. [See *Discourses* 1.15.1–4, 1.26.15, 2.11.1, 3.10.6–7, 3.12.12, 3.13.23, 3.14.10, 3.15.12, 3.24.81, 3.26.13, 4.1.113, 4.8.9/18/34–6, 4.11.22–5; *Handbook* 22, 52.1; Stob. 2.7.11k/11m.]

philosophos 'philosopher'; literally, one who 'loves wisdom', in Stoicism the person for whom Stoic philosophy is a way of life, a way of engaging in affairs in which one aims to flourish as fully as one may in the pursuit of *eudaimonia*. The Stobaeus text employs the term *spoudaios* ('worthwhile'; 'virtuous' in LS) which, in this context can be regarded as a synonym of Epictetus' *philosophos*. [See *Discourses* 1.1.25, 1.2.26/29, 1.4.1, 1.8.11–14, 1.9.1, 1.11.28, 1.18.1–2, 1.20.7, 2.9.13, 2.14.7–9/11, 2.17.1–3/30–1, 2.24.29, 3.7.1, 3.8.7,

3.9.11, 3.13.11, 3.15.10, 3.19.1, 3.24.31, 3.26.7/35–6, 4.1.83/
132–43, 4.4.18, 4.6.12/33, 4.7.24/32, 4.8.4–23, 4.8.9/17–20;
Handbook 22, 23, 29.3–4/7, 32.1, 46.1, 48.1, 49; Stob. 2.7.5b8/
5b11/5k–l/6c/11b/11d/11g/11i–k/11m/11p–q/11s.]

phobos 'fear'; one of the four primary *pathê* (passions). *Phobos* is the fear
that the non-wise person directs towards anticipated events or objects
in the mistaken belief that they are of real harm. [See DL 7.110/112;
Stob. 2,7.5b–c/5g/10/10b–c.]

phusis 'nature'; literally 'growth', the totality of everything, including
the cosmic forces and principles that create and sustain all things.
Depending upon our point of view and the emphasis we wish to
make, *phusis* is also God, providence, fate; and also *logos*, for the
world is wholly rational because God brings about events according
to His necessarily good purposes. Each individual thing has its own
phusis, its own way of growing, behaving, and flourishing according
to what is usual and beneficial for the species of thing it happens to
be. Thus, for example, it is natural for cows to eat grass, but contrary
to the nature of a person to do so. Such specific differences and
variations in the natures of different types of thing is accounted for by
the way in which God, conceived as active matter, blends with the
passive material universe, shaping matter into the diverse forms of
which we are aware. *Phusis* is the supreme organising and creative
principle which brings about the *phusis* possessed by each individual
entity. Stoics hold that the rationality of Zeus/*phusis*/*logos* is manifest
in each human being taken to be (literally) a fragment of God, for
everyone has the capacity to reason, and this being the case, everyone
has the potential to understand in what the good life consists
(*eudaimonia*) and how to attain it. For the Stoics, to acquire
eudaimonia one must 'follow nature', 'live in accordance with
nature', or 'live in harmony with nature' – these are all essentially
synonymous expressions – which mean both (1) accepting our own
fate and the fate of the world, as well as understanding what it means
to be a rational being, and striving for virtue by means of which we
maintain our *prohairesis* in the right condition, and (2) doing what is
appropriate for the type of creature that we happen to be, which for
human beings includes doing what is required with respect to one's
social roles: to live in accordance with nature, a mother for example
must care for her child, and a judge must dispense justice wisely and
impartially. *See* **aretê**, **hêgemonikon**, and **theos**. [See *Discourses* 1.2.6,
1.4.14–15/18/29, 1.6.15/21, 1.9.9, 1.11.5/8, 1.12.19, 1.15.4,
1.16.4, 1.17.18, 1.19.25, 1.20.5, 1.21.2, 1.22.9, 1.26.2, 2.5.24,

2.6.9, 2.11.6, 2.13.11, 2.14.22, 2.20.15, 2.23.42, 2.24.12/19/101–2, 3.1.3/30, 3.4.9, 3.5.3, 3.6.3–4, 3.7.28, 3.9.11/17, 3.10.11, 3.13.20, 3.16.15, 3.23.12, 3.24.1/102, 4.1.121/125, 4.4.14/28/43, 4.5.5–6, 4.8.40, 4.10.8/26, 4.12.2; DL 7.87–9/105/108/147–9/156–7; *Handbook* 1.2–3, 2.4, 6, 13, 26, 27, 30, 48.3, 49; Stob. 2.7.5b3/5b5/5m/6/6e/7a–f/8/8a/10/10a/10e/11i.]

pistos 'trustworthy', of someone possessing *pistis*, trustworthiness; for Epictetus, a key characteristic of the *prokoptôn's prohairesis*. *See also* **aidêmôn**. [See *Discourses* 1.3.4, 2.2.4, 2.4.1–2, 2.14.13, 4.5.14, 4.13.19–20; Stob. 2.7.11m; for *pistos* together with *aidêmôn*, see *Discourses* 1.4.18–20, 1.25.4, 1.28.20–1/23, 2.4.2, 2.8.23, 2.10.22–3/29, 2.22.20/30, 3.3.9–10, 3.7.36, 3.13.3, 3.14.13, 3.17.3, 3.23.18, 4.1.161, 4.3.7, 4.9.17, 4.13.13/15; *Handbook* 24.3–5.]

pleasure *see* **hêdonê**

preferred *see* **proêgmenos**

proêgmenos 'preferred'; used of *adiaphoros* ('indifferent') things, conventionally taken to be good and advantageous, including such things as health and wealth, taking pleasure in the company of others, and so forth. Enjoying any of the preferred indifferents is not in itself constitutive of the *eudaimôn* life sought by the Stoic *prokoptôn*. *See also* **apoproêgmenos**. [See DL 7.102/105–7; LS 58E–F, Stob. 2.7.7b/7f–g.]

progress *see* **prokopê/prokoptô/prokoptôn**

prohairesis 'moral character'; the capacity that rational beings have for making choices and intending the outcomes of their actions, sometimes translated as *will, volition, intention, choice, moral choice, moral purpose*. This faculty is understood by Stoics to be essentially rational. It is the faculty we use to 'attend to impressions' and to give (or withhold) assent to impressions. Those things which are outside the scope of one's *prohairesis* are the *aprohaireta*, which are *aprohairetos* and 'external' (*ektos*), and 'not in our power' (*ouk eph' hêmin*); see *Discourses* 1.30.3, 2.16.1, 3.3.14, 3.8.1–3. *See also* **hêgemonikon, sunkatathesis**. [See *Discourses* 1.1.23, 1.4.18–21, 1.8.16, 1.12.9, 1.17.21/23/26, 1.19.8/16/23, 1.22.10, 1.29.1–3/12/24, 1.30.3, 2.1.4–6/9–10/12/39–40, 2.5.4–5, 2.6.25, 2.10.8/24–9, 2.13.10, 2.15.1, 2.16.1, 2.22.20/26–9, 2.23.5–29, 3.1.40/42, 3.2.13, 3.3.8/14–19, 3.4.9, 3.5.7, 3.7.5, 3.8.1–3, 3.10.18, 3.12.5/8, 3.16.15, 3.19.2, 3.22.13/103, 3.23.5, 3.24.12/56/106/112, 3.26.24, 4.1.84/100, 4.4.18/23/33/39, 4.5.12/23/32, 4.6.9–10, 4.7.8, 4.10.1–2/8, 4.12.7/12/15, 4.13.21; *Handbook* 4, 9, 13, 30.]

prokopê 'progress'; what the Stoic *prokoptôn* tries to maintain by applying the principles of Stoic ethics, by living virtuously and, in particular for Epictetus, by 'following nature', 'following God', and making 'proper use of impressions'. [See *Discourses* 1.4.1–21, 3.2.5, 3.8.4, 3.19.3, 4.2.4–5; DL 7.91; *Ep.* 75.8–18; *Handbook* 12.1, 13.1, 51.2–3; Stob. 2.7.7b.]

prokoptô to make progress.

prokoptôn 'one who is making progress (*prokopê*)' in living as a Stoic, which for Epictetus means above all learning the 'correct use of impressions'. *See phantasia.* [See *Handbook* 48.2, 51.2.]

proper function *see kathêkon*

repulsion *see aphormê*

reservation *see hupexhairesis*

right action *see katorthôma*

Sage *see sophos*

self-respecting *see aidêmôn*

sophos the Stoic 'wise person' or 'Sage', who values only *aretê* and enjoys a *eudaimôn* life. The *sophos* enjoys a way of engaging in life that the *prokoptôn* strives to emulate and attain. The *philosophos* (philosopher), in contrast to the *idiôtês* ('uneducated person'), is someone who has taken up the training that is required to make progress (*prokopê*) towards the condition enjoyed by the *sophos*. Epictetus also refers to such a person as *phronimos*, 'wise' (*Discourses* 2.21.9, 2.22.3, 3.22.37, 4.1.92), as *spoudaios*, 'good' (*Discourses* 1.7.3/29, 3.6.5) and as *kalos kai agathos*, 'fine and good' (*Discourses* 1.7.2, 1.12.7, 1.23.3, 2.10.5, 2.11.25, 2.14.10, 2.21.11, 3.2.1/7, 3.3.1, 3.22.69/87, 3.24.18/50/95/110, 4.5.1, 4.8.24; see also Stob. 2.7.11g/11s). *See also philosophos, philosophia, prokopê, prokoptôn.* [See *Discourses* 3.13.22, 3.22.67, 4.1.6; DL 7.94/117–25; *Handbook* 53.2; Stob. 2.7.5b8/5b10–12/11b/11k/11m–n/11s.]

sunkatathesis 'assent' (noun); a capacity of the *prohairesis* to judge the significance of impressions. It is because we are prone to making incorrect judgements that *eudaimonia* eludes us and we are vulnerable to the *pathê* (passions) under whose influence we lapse into vice. *See also pathos, phantasia.* [See *Discourses* 1.17.22–3, 1.18.1, 1.28.1, 2.17.5, 3.2.2, 3.7.15, 3.12.14/104, 3.22.42–3, 4.1.69, 4.4.13, 4.6.12/26, 4.10.2, 4.11.6; DL 7.91; *Handbook* 45; Stob. 2.7.7b/9b/11m.]

tarachê 'distress', 'disturbance', 'trouble'; what one avoids when one enjoys *ataraxia*. [See *Handbook* 1.3, 3, 5, 12, 28.]

telos 'end' or 'goal'; that which we pursue for its own sake and not for the sake of any other thing. The Stoics accepted the traditional conception of the *telos* being *eudaimonia* ('happiness' or 'flourishing'), but argued that this consists solely in *aretê* (moral excellence); the *telos*, then, can be attained by 'living in accordance with virtue' (Stob. 2.7.6e). Epictetus formulates the end in several different but closely related ways. He says that the end is to maintain one's *prohairesis* in proper order, to follow God, follow nature, live in accordance with nature, or live in harmony with nature – all of which count as maintaining a *eudaimôn* life. The means by which this is to be accomplished is to apply oneself assiduously to the 'three *topoi*'. The earlier Stoics defined the end in a range of related ways: Zeno says it is 'Living in agreement'; Cleanthes added to this, saying it is 'Living in agreement *with nature*'; Chrysippus defined it as 'Living in accord with our experience of what happens naturally' (see LS 63B); Diogenes of Babylon says that the end is 'Being circumspect in selecting and rejecting the things in accordance with nature'; Archedemus says it is 'Living so as to complete everything that is appropriate'; and Antipater says it is 'Living so as always to select what is in accordance with nature whilst rejecting what is contrary to nature' (see Stob. 2.7.6a/6e). [See *Discourses* 1.12.5, 1.20.15, 1.30.4, 4.7.20; DL 7.87–9/96–7; LS 63; Stob. 2.7.5b3/5b5/5k/6a–c/6e.]

theos 'God', who is material, is a sort of fiery breath that blends with undifferentiated matter to create the forms that we find in the world around us. He is supremely rational and, despite our feelings to the contrary, makes the best world that it is possible to make. How we understand and relate to God is of central concern to Epictetus. God is characterised as (a) omniscient (*Discourses* 1.14.9–10); (b) the father of everyone (we all are 'sons of Zeus'; 1.3.1–2, 1.9.6, 1.13.3–4, 1.19.12); (c) who has made everyone to be happy (*eudaimôn*) and to enjoy peace of mind (*eustatheia*; 3.24.2); (d) who (as a matter of fact) protects us and cares for us (1.17.27, 3.24.3); and (e) can be actively *called upon* to protect us (2.18.29); (f) who has given us what we need, including the virtues and the faculty of making proper use of impressions (1.1.12, 1.6.28–9, 1.25.3, 1.29.3–4, 2.16.13–14, 2.23.6–9, 3.24.3, 4.1.100, 4.5.34); and (g) who is wholly providential (1.16, 2.14.11, 2.23.2–4, 3.17). The Stoic's relationship to God is characterised by their (h) regarding God as their benevolent creator and friend (1.16, 3.26.28/37); (i) being a friend to God (4.3.9, 3.24.60); (j) not blaming God for misfortunes or hardships (1.14.16, 3.10.13, 3.22.13/48, 3.24.58, 4.7.9); (k) endeavouring to do God's will, to obey Him and please Him (2.6.9–10, 2.7.13, 2.16.42, 3.1.37, 3.24.110, 4.1.99, 4.3.9, 4.12.11); to 'follow God' and accept the fate that He bestows on them and on the world (1.12.1–7, 1.20.15, 1.30.4, 4.7.20; *Handbook* 53.1–3); (l) showing reverence to and being thankful to God (1.4.32, 2.23.5, 3.7.26, 4.4.18, 4.7.9); (m) understanding that everyone is literally a part (*meros*) or fragment (*apospasma*) of God (1.14.6, 1.17.27, 2.8.10–14, *Ep.* 31.11), that they share His reason (1.9.5) and strive to join His fellowship (*koinônia*) (2.19.27); (n) serving in the post assigned to them by God (1.9.16/24, 1.16.21, 3.22.69, 3.24.99; *Handbook* 22); (o) bearing witness to God's work and their own capacities (1.29.46–9, 3.24.112–13, 3.26.28, 4.8.31); (p) singing praises to God (3.26.29–30); and (q) imitating God (2.14.11–13). God is a frequent topic throughout the *Discourses*; for God as 'the Giver', see 4.1.103–7, 4.4.47, 4.10.14–16, *Handbook* 11; for arguments for the existence of God see 1.6.1–11 and 2.14.25–8. *See also **Zeus***. [See *Discourses* 2.23.42; DL 7.119/124/134–9/147–8; *Handbook* 1.3, 15, 22, 29.2, 31.1/4–5, 32.2, 53.1/3; LS 46/54A–B, Stob. 2.7.5b2/5b12/10c/11g/11k/11s.]

topoi 'topics'. The 'three topics' or 'fields of study' which we find elucidated in the *Discourses* is an original feature of Epictetus' educational programme. The three fields of study are: (1) The Discipline of Desire, concerned with desire and aversion (*orexis* and *ekklisis*), and what is really good and desirable (virtue, using impressions properly, following God, and following nature); (2) The Discipline of Action, concerned with impulse and repulsion (*hormê* and *aphormê*), and our 'appropriate actions' or 'duties' (*see **kathêkon***) with respect to living in our communities in ways that befit a rational being; and (3) The Discipline of Assent (*see **sunkatathesis***), concerned with how we should judge our impressions so as not to be carried away by them into anxiety or disturbing emotions with the likelihood of failing in the first two Disciplines. [See *Discourses* 1.4.11, 1.17.20–6, 1.21.1–2, 2.8.29, 2.17.14–18, 2.24.19–20, 3.2.1–6, 3.12.8–15, 3.26.14, 4.4.13, 4.6.26, 4.10.13, 4.11.6; *Ep.* 89.14–15; MA 7.54, 8.7, 9.6.]

trainining *see **askêsis***

trustworthy *see **pistos***

uneducated *see **apaideutos**, **idiôtês***

vice the opposite of virtue. *See **kakia***.

virtue from the Latin *virtus* which translates the Greek *aretê*, 'excellence'. *See **aretê***.

wish *see **boulêsis***

Zeus the name for God; Epictetus uses the terms 'Zeus', 'God', and 'the gods' interchangeably. The Stoics also identify Zeus with nature, fate, and providence, conceived of as the rational and inevitable coming about of all events that by being located just as they happen to be, within the nexus of causation, constitute the entire history of the universe. *See also **theos**.* [See DL 7.88; *Handbook* 53.1.]

Glossary B
The *Tablet of Cebes*

[References are to the sections of the *Tablet*. Words in **bold** typeface have their own entries in the Glossary. All the personifications in the *Tablet* are female, excepting only the Daimon and Lamentation who are male.]

agnoia see ignorance
Akrasia (Intemperance) *see* **Intemperance**
Alêtheia see **Truth**
Alêthinê Paideia see **True Education**
Andreia see **Courage**
Apatê see **Deceit**
aphobia see fearlessness and **True Education**
aphrosunê see **Folly**
Aplêstia (Insatiability) *see* **Intemperance**
Aretai see **Virtues**
Asôtia (Profligacy) *see* **Intemperance**
Athumia see **Despondency**
beasts (*thêria*) at *Tablet* 22–3 the **Vices** are likened to wild beasts that are tamed and enslaved by those who succeed in their journey to **Happiness**.
Bios see **Life**
Courage (*Andreia*) is one of nine **Virtues** found in **Enclosure D**, sisters whose mother is **Happiness** (20.3). Courage also translates *tharsos*, and is one of **True Education's** gifts to those who arrive at **Enclosure D**, the other being fearlessness (*aphobia*) (18.4). See **True Education**.
Cronus (*Kronos*) the narrative of the *Tablet* is set in the temple (*heiron*) of Cronus, where the narrator and his friends meet an **old man** (2)

who was taught the meaning of the votive tablet they find there by the philosopher who donated it to the temple many years before. Cronus was the youngest of the Titans, the son of Uranus (*Ouranos*), Heaven, and Gaia, Earth. Cronus killed his father, Uranus, to become the ruler of heaven. He married his sister Rhea, and fearing that he would be overthrown by his own children, he devoured them as soon as they were born. But the sixth child, Zeus, was concealed from him by Gaia in the caves of Dicte under Mount Aegeum near Lyctos, on the Island of Crete, where he was brought up by the ash nymphs Adrasteia and Io. He was nursed by the nymph Amaltheia, who fed him goat's milk; in other accounts she was herself a divine goat, from whose horns ambrosia and nectar flowed. Having attained manhood, Zeus was aided by his mother, Rhea, in effecting the overthrow of Cronus who, with all the Titans except Atlas, was banished to the farthest west of the British Isles (as some accounts have it). Zeus now ruled in heaven himself as the 'Father of Men and Gods'. (See, for instance, Hesiod, *Theogony* 116–210, 453–506.)

Daimon (*Daimôn*) is the Deity, the power that controls the destiny of all individuals. He stands outside **Enclosure A** instructing the people who are queuing to enter **Life** as to how they should conduct themselves once they have got inside (1, 4, 24.3, 30–2, 33.2). Specifically, he tells them not to put any trust in **Fortune**, and not to regard as secure anything that they receive from her, and not to regard it as their own property (31.1). Thus he instructs them to be impartial to **Fortune's** gifts (31.2), and not to be surprised at anything she may do (31.3). He urges all those entering into **Life** to flee straightaway to **True Education** who will bestow **knowledge** of what is really advantageous (*sumpherontos*), a gift that is secure, never to be regretted (32.2).

Deceit (*Apatê*) sits outside the **gate** to the **enclosure** of **Life**, giving her draught of **error** and **ignorance** to everyone who enters, which causes them to forget the advice offered by the **Daimon** (5.2, 6.3).

Desires (*Epithumiai*) *see* **Opinions**

Despondency (*Athumia*) is the sister of **Lamentation**, and along with others awaits those who are seduced into **Enclosure B, Luxury**. See **Punishment** (10).

Dikaiosunê see **Justice**

Distress (*Odunê*) awaits, along with others, those who are urged to enter **Enclosure B, Luxury**. See **Punishment** (10).

Doxai see **Opinions**

Education (*Paideia*) *see* **False Education** and **True Education**

Eleutheria see **Freedom**

enclosure (*peribolos*) see Plans One and Two. There are four enclosures in the fable of the *Tablet*. Enclosure A is **Life**, into which the people enter after being directed by the **Daimon** as to how they should conduct themselves (1, 4, 30–2), and after they have drunk **Deceit's** draught of **error** and **ignorance** (5) which makes them forget the **Daimon's** instructions. Enclosure B is **Luxury**, where some people who enter into **Life** are persuaded to stay by **Intemperance**, **Profligacy**, **Insatiability**, and **Flattery** (9–10). Enclosure C is the preserve of **False Education** (12–14), through which travellers have to pass if they are to arrive at Enclosure D, where **True Education**, **Truth**, and **Persuasion** wait to heal and then admit travellers to the abode of **Happiness**, **Knowledge**, and the other **Virtues** (17–21). The enclosures of the *Tablet* do not form a strictly concentric arrangement. Enclosure A, **Life**, encompasses all the other enclosures. Enclosure B, **Luxury**, stands alone, and when someone enters it they cannot progress to any other enclosure without first, with the aid of **Repentance** (10.4–11.1), coming out again. Enclosure D, **True Education**, stands inside Enclosure C, **False Education**, and can be reached only by passing first through Enclosure C (12.3).

Endurance (*Karteria*) along with **Self-Control** waits upon the **great rock** to help up the travellers who come this way, after which is an easier path that leads to **True Education** (15–16).

Enkrateia see **Self-Control**

Epistêmê see **Knowledge**

Epithumiai (Desires) *see* **Opinions**

error (*planos*) one of the two ingredients of the drink that **Deceit** gives to everyone who enters into **Life**. The other ingredient is **ignorance** (5.3).

Eudaimonia see **Happiness**

Eutaxia see **Orderliness**

fable (*muthologia*) the *Tablet* refers to itself as a fable or myth (2.1).

False Education (*Pseudopaideia*), appearing smartly dressed, stands outside **Enclosure C** (via which the path to **True Education** and **Enclosure D** may be found). Within **Enclosure C** are people belonging to all the professions and following all the academic disciplines who are deluded into thinking that they are associating with **True Education** (12–13). With them are **Intemperance** and the others with her whom we have already encountered at *Tablet* 9.1 (see **Intemperance**), along with the **Opinions** (see **Opinions**), who also roam throughout **Enclosure A** (14). Those who renounce **False Education** may enter upon the path to **True Education**.

False Opinion (*Pseudodoxia*) appears only at 11.2. All of those who fail to arrive at **True Education** (**Enclosure D**) wander around, lost under her influence.

fearlessness (*aphobia*) is one of **True Education's** gifts to those who arrive at **Enclosure D**, the other being **courage** (*tharsos*) (18.4). See **True Education**.

Flattery (*Kolakeia*) *see* **intemperance**, **vice**.

Folly (*aphrosunê*) we are told at *Tablet* 14.3 that foolishness, along with **ignorance**, is drunk from **Deceit's** cup by the people who enter into **Life**. Elsewhere, we are told that the draught also contains **error** (5.3). At *Tablet* 3, the **old man** (2) explains that Folly is the **Sphinx** that will bring to ruin all those who do not understand what is good and what is bad.

Fortune (*Tuchê*) is found inside the entrance to **Enclosure A**, **Life**, blind, deaf, mad, and standing on a round stone. She takes from people the things they already have and gives them to other people, only to take them away and pass them to yet other people, all at random. Her round stone symbolises that none of her gifts is safe or certain. Harsh and bitter disappointment await those who put their trust in her (7.3). People who receive the things they want from Fortune call her Good Fortune (*agathê Tuchê*), whilst those from whom she takes such things cause her Bad Fortune (*kakê Tuchê*) (7–8).

Freedom (*Eleutheria*) is one of nine **Virtues** found in **Enclosure D**, sisters whose mother is **Happiness** (20.3).

gate (*pulê*) there are five gates (*pulai*) in the landscape of the *Tablet*. Each of the four **enclosures** has its own gate, and there is also a gate inside **Enclosure C** that leads to the rough and stony path by which the traveller arrives at the high hill surmounted by a **great rock** (15) over which they must climb to continue on to **Enclosure D**, **True Education**.

gerôn see **old man** (1)

Goodness (*Kalokagathia*) is one of nine **Virtues** found in **Enclosure D**, sisters whose mother is **Happiness** (20.3).

great rock (*megalê petra*) the great rock stands atop the high hill in **Enclosure C**, reached via a rough and stony path that few can manage (15). The rock must be surmounted if progress to **True Education** and **Enclosure D** is to be secured, but once the rock has been climbed, the path from that point will become more favourable for the traveller who can endure a little while more. Waiting on the rock are **Self-Control** and **Endurance**, who stretch out their hands to help the traveller climb up (16). Once they have pulled the traveller up, they bid them rest, and give them strength (*ischus*) and **courage** (*tharsos*), and then lead them on to **True Education** via a beautiful meadow bathed in sunlight in the middle of which stands the final **enclosure, D** (17.1–2). **Self-Control** is also one of nine **Virtues** found in **Enclosure D**, sisters whose mother is **Happiness** (20.3).

Greed (*Philarguria*) *see* **vice**.

Grief (*Lupê*) awaits, along with others, those who are enticed into **Enclosure B**, **Luxury**. See **Punishment** (10).

Happiness (*Eudaimonia*) is mother of the **Virtues** (21.1). She sits before the citadel (*akropolis*) in **Enclosure D**, simply dressed and wearing a crown of beautiful flowers (20–1), waiting for her daughters, the **Virtues**, to bring to her the travellers who have successfully completed their journey. Happiness in the allegory of the *Tablet* is thus the end at which progress aims. With the **Virtues**, she crowns the travellers with flowers (22.1), conferring a power (*dunamis*) through which they may now enslave the mightiest of **beasts** (*thêria*; that is, the **Vices**), which previously had enslaved *them* (22.2–23.2). It is through this power that the traveller becomes happy (*eudaimôn*) and blessed (*makarios*) (23.3–4). Once the travellers are crowned, the **Virtues** lead them back to the other **enclosures** so that they can witness the conditions from which they have managed to escape, for now they have a proper understanding of what their plight was, and how they have been saved (24–5); after that they are free to wander wherever they like, because whatever conditions they encounter, they will live nobly and securely, wholly immune to the effects of the **Vices** (26).

Hêdonai (Pleasures) *see* **Opinions**

Hêdupatheia see **Luxury**

ignorance (*agnoia*) one of the two ingredients of the drink that **Deceit** gives to everyone who enters into **Life**. The other ingredient is **error** (5.3, 6.3, 19.5, 25.2).

Insatiability (*Aplêstia*) *see* **intemperance, vice**.

Intemperance, Profligacy, Insatiability, and Flattery (*Akrasia, Asôtia, Aplêstia, Kolakeia*) are dressed as courtesans, and stand at the entrance to **Enclosure B**, **Luxury**, trying to entice in those who have received things from **Fortune**, promising them a pleasant and easy life entirely free from troubles (9). They are also found in **Enclosure C** (14). *See* **vice**.

Justice (*Dikaiosunê*) is one of nine **Virtues** found in **Enclosure D**, sisters whose mother is **Happiness** (20.3).

kakia see **vice**

Kakodaimonia see **Unhappiness**

Kalokagathia see **Goodness**

Karteria see **Endurance**

Kenodoxia (Vanity) *see* **vice**

Kindness (*Praotês*) is one of nine **Virtues** found in **Enclosure D**, sisters whose mother is **Happiness** (20.3).

Knowledge (*Epistêmê*) is one of nine **Virtues** found in **Enclosure D**, sisters whose mother is **Happiness** (20.3).

Kolakeia (Flattery) *see* **Intemperance**

Kronos see **Cronus**

Lamentation (*Odurmos*) is the only male figure within **Life**, and is found with others waiting for those who are lured into **Enclosure B**, **Luxury**. His sister is **Despondency**. See **Punishment** (10).

Life (*Bios*) the name of the outer **enclosure**, **A**, which surrounds all the other **enclosures**.

Lupê see **Grief**

Luxury (*Hêdupatheia*) is one of the two main **enclosures** (designated **Enclosure B** on Plan One) within **Enclosure A**, **Life**; the other is **Enclosure C**, **False Education**. Those who are enticed into Luxury by **Intemperance**, **Profligacy**, **Insatiability**, and **Flattery** (see **Intemperance**) fall prey to **Punishment** and others, where they live out their days in complete misery (9–10), unless they are fortunate enough to be deliberately chosen by **Repentance** who will introduce them to other **Opinions** and **Desires** who lead them to **True Education** or to **False Education** (9–11).

Metanoia see **Repentance**

Moderation (*Sôphrosunê*) is one of nine **Virtues** found in **Enclosure D**, sisters whose mother is **Happiness** (20.3).

muthologia see **fable**

Odunê see **Distress**

Odurmos see **Lamentation**

old man (1) (*geron*) term used to describe the **Daimon** (1.3, 4.3).

old man (2) (*presbutês*) term used of the man who explains the meaning of the *Tablet* to the narrator and his friends in the temple (*heiron*) of **Cronus**.

Opinions, Desires, and Pleasures (*Doxai, Epithumiai, Hêdonai*) await those who enter into **Life**. They lead people to their eventual fates, to their salvation or to their destruction, keeping them within the confines of **Enclosure A**, or taking them to **Enclosure B**, **Luxury**, or to **Enclosure C**, **False Education** (6). The Opinions are also found in **Enclosure C** (14).

Orderliness (*Eutaxia*) is one of nine **Virtues** found in **Enclosure D**, sisters whose mother is **Happiness** (20.3).

Paideia (Education) *see* **False Education** and **True Education**

Peithô see **Persuasion**

Penia see **Poverty**

peribolos see **enclosure**

Persuasion (*Peithô*) is one of **True Education's** daughters, the other being **Truth** (18.2). With her mother and sister, she welcomes travellers to **Enclosure D** (18–19).

petra (rock) *see* **great rock**

Philarguria (Greed) *see* **vice**

planos see **error**

Pleasures (*Hêdonai*) *see* **Opinions**

ploutos see **wealth**

Poverty (*Penia*) at *Tablet* 26.3 is identified as a **Vice**.

Praotês see **Kindness**

presbutês see **old man (2)**

Profligacy (*Asôtia*)*see* **Intemperance, vice**

Pseudodoxia see **False Opinion**

Pseudopaideia see **False Education**

pulê see **gate**

Punishment (*Timôria*) is found behind a small door in a narrow and dark place within **Enclosure B, Luxury**. With her are **Grief** (*Lupê*) and **Distress** (*Odunê*), and also **Lamentation** (*Odurmos*; the only male figure within **Life**), his sister **Despondency** (*Athumia*), and **Unhappiness** (*Kakodaimonia*) (10).

Repentance (*Metanoia*) is found in **Enclosure B, Luxury**. Those whom she deliberately chooses she takes away from **Luxury**, and introduces them to **Opinions** and **Desires** who lead them to either **True Education** or **False Education** (10.4–11.1). Some whom she takes to **False Education** will keep her with them, and she will remind them that, here in **Enclosure C**, they have not yet found **True Education** (35.3).

Self-Control (*Enkrateia*) along with **Endurance** waits upon the **great rock** to help up the travellers who come this way, after which is an easier path that leads to **True Education** (15–16). Self-Control is also one of nine **Virtues** found in **Enclosure D**, sisters whose mother is **Happiness** (20.3).

Sôphrosunê see **Moderation**

Sphinx in mythology is a creature with the body of a lion and the head of a human, familiar to us from the famous monument near to the

Pyramids on the Giza plateau. The *Tablet* is referring to the Sphinx of Boeotian Thebes, who demanded from all who encountered her the answer to the riddle (taught to her by the Muses) as to what is it that has one voice, but in the morning goes on four legs, at noon goes on two legs, and in the evening goes on three legs. The fate of all who answered incorrectly was to be instantly devoured. It was, of course, Oedipus who answered the riddle correctly; it is a person who when an infant crawls on all fours, then when grown walks upright on two legs, but in old age walks with the aid of a stick, which is the third leg specified by the riddle. As soon as Oedipus answered correctly, the enraged Sphinx threw herself down, killing herself, much to the relief of the local people who had been so terrorised by her all this time. In *Tablet* 3, the **old man (2)** points out that people who do not understand the meaning of the *Tablet* (specifically, what is good and what bad) will be destroyed just as the Sphinx destroyed her victims, not by being eaten up all at once, but gradually in the course of life through the ruin wrought by **Folly**.

tharsos see **courage** and **True Education**

Timôria see **Punishment**

True Education (*Alêthinê Paideia*) is also referred to simply as Education (*Paideia*) in the *Tablet*. She wears plain clothes and appears beautiful with a calm expression, standing upon a square stone beside the **gate** (*pulê*) to **Enclosure D** (18.1), and can be approached only via **False Education** and **Enclosure C**. With her are her daughters **Truth** and **Persuasion** (18.2). She stands on a square stone as a sign that the gifts she offers are safe for those who accept them (17.3), and this obviously contrasts with **Fortune**, who stands on a round stone as a sign that *her* gifts are not permanently given, but are insecure and can be snatched back again at any time (7–8). True Education's gifts are **courage** and **fearlessness**, and these constitute **knowledge** (*epistêmê*) that 'in the course of life one need never suffer anything terrible' (18.4). Those who arrive at **True Education** are given by her a drink that has purifying and curative powers (19) that eliminate 'the evils with which they came' (19.4) – these being the **error** and **ignorance** of which they drank from **Deceit** prior to entering into **Life** (5, 19.5). Along with **error** and **ignorance**, **True Education's** draught also eliminates pretentiousness (*alazoneia*), desire (*epithumia*), intemperance (*akrasia*), anger (*thumos*), love of money (*philarguria*), and others (19.5). She then takes them inside the **enclosure** to the **Virtues** (*aretai*), **Knowledge** (*Epistêmê*) and her sisters, **Courage** (*Andreia*), **Justice** (*Dikaiosunê*), **Goodness** (*Kalokagathia*), **Moderation** (*Sôphrosunê*),

Orderliness (*Eutaxia*), Freedom (*Eleutheria*), Self-Control (*Enkrateia*), and Kindness (*Praotês*) (20). The traveller who has been thus received by the Virtues is taken by them to their mother, Happiness (*Eudaimonia*), who sits before 'the citadel [*akropolis*] of all the enclosures' (21.2).

Truth (*Alêtheia*) is one of True Education's daughters, the other being Persuasion (18.2). With her mother and sister, she welcomes travellers to Enclosure D (18–19).

Tuchê see Fortune

Unhappiness (*Kakodaimonia*) waits with others for those encouraged into Enclosure B, Luxury. See Punishment (10).

Vanity (*Kenodoxia*) *see* vice

vice (*kakia*) what one overcomes through the power that Happiness confers (22–3). At *Tablet* 9 we find four key vices inside Enclosure A, Intemperance (*Akrasia*), Profligacy (*Asôtia*), Insatiability (*Aplêstia*), and Flattery (*Kolakeia*), waiting to entice into Enclosure B (Luxury) those who have been favoured by receiving Fortune's unreliable gifts. Their range extends to Enclosure C (14), where they accompany the Opinions (*Doxai*) already encountered in Enclosure A (6). The Pleasures are presumably meant to number among the vices, since it is obvious how they urge the traveller towards Luxury, but it seems that Opinions and Desires may sometimes keep the traveller from making progress to True Education, whilst at other times they may lead them there (11.1, 29.2); one may after all desire happiness, and one may be of the opinion that one outlook or another should be investigated as the possible route to the end that one desires. One's progress begins with such opinions and desires. Ignorance and Error (the components of Deceit's drink) are identified as vices at 23.1, as are Grief, Lamentation, Greed (*Philarguria*), and Intemperance (again) (23.2), where they are said to number among 'every other vice'. Intemperance makes yet another appearance at 24.2, along with Pretentiousness (*Alazoneia*), Greed (*Philarguria*), again, and Vanity (*Kenodoxia*). The vices are likened to wild beasts, and they are all overcome by the power conferred by Happiness (22–3).

Virtues (*Aretai*) the virtues live in Enclosure D, into which True Education, Truth, and Persuasion welcome the traveller who has made it this far. To those thus welcomed, True Education offers a purifying and curative draught to undo the effects of the potion administered by Deceit to everyone who enters into Life. In *Tablet* 20.3, nine Virtues are listed: Knowledge (*Epistêmê*), Courage (*Andreia*), Justice (*Dikaiosunê*), Goodness (*Kalokagathia*),

Moderation   (*Sôphrosunê*),   **Orderliness**   (*Eutaxia*),   **Freedom**
(*Eleutheria*), **Self-Control** (*Enkrateia*), and **Kindness** (*Praotês*) (20).
wealth (*ploutos*) is offered as an example of something indifferent in the
    Stoic scheme (although the term 'indifferent' is not used in the
    Tablet), along with being healthy (*hugiainô*) and being sick (*noseô*)
    (38.4–41.4). What makes someone good (*spoudaios*) is not wealth,
    but **Education** (*Paideia*) (39.3).

Bibliography

[Note: all Loeb Classical Library editions include the original Greek or Latin texts with facing English translations, and all Aris & Phillips editions include the original Latin texts with facing English translations.]

Primary Sources

Aelian

Wilson, N. G. 1997. *Historical Miscellany*. Cambridge, MA: Loeb Classical Library, Harvard University Press.

Athenaeus

Gulick, Charles Burton. 1928. *The Deipnosophists*. Books 3.106e–5. [vol. 2 of Loeb Athenaeus] Cambridge, MA: Loeb Classical Library, Harvard University Press.

Aulus Gellius

Rolfe, John C. 1946, 1948, 1952. *The Attic Nights*. 3 vols. Cambridge, MA: Loeb Classical Library, Harvard University Press.

Marcus Aurelius

Collier, Jeremy. 1887. *The Meditations of Marcus Aurelius*. London: Walter Scott.
Crossley, Hastings. 1882. *The Fourth Book of the Meditations of Marcus Aurelius Antoninus: A Revised Text with Translation and Commentary,*

and an Appendix on the Relations of the Emperor with Cornelius Fronto. London: Macmillan. [English translation faces original Greek text.]

Farquharson, A. S. L. 1989. *The Meditations of Marcus Aurelius Antoninus,* and a *Selection from the Letters of Marcus and Fronto.* trans. with introduction and notes by R. B. Rutherford. Oxford: Oxford University Press.

——. 1992. *Marcus Aurelius: Meditations.* London: Everyman. [Contains the translation and commentary of the original OUP 1944 2-volume edition.]

Grube, G. M. A. 1983. *The Meditations of Marcus Aurelius.* Indianapolis: Hackett.

Haines, C. R. 1930. *Marcus Aurelius.* Cambridge, MA: Loeb Classical Library, Harvard University Press.

Hays, Gregory. 2003. *Marcus Aurelius: Meditations.* London: Weidenfeld & Nicolson.

Hard, Robin. 1997. *Marcus Aurelius: Meditations.* with introduction and notes by Christopher Gill. Ware: Wordsworth.

Hicks, C. Scott and David V. Hicks. 2002. *Marcus Aurelius: The Emperor's Handbook.* New York: Scribner.

Jackson, John. 1948. *The Thoughts of Marcus Aurelius Antoninus.* London: Oxford University Press.

Long, George. 1991. *Meditations: Marcus Aurelius.* Amhurst, NY: Prometheus. [Facsimile reprint of the P. F. Collier & Son edition of 1909. Long's translation was first published in 1862.]

——. 1997. *Meditations: Marcus Aurelius.* Mineola, NY: Dover. [A revised version, modernising the 'archaic language and tangled syntax of Long's Victorian prose'.]

Rendall, Gerald H. 1898. *Marcus Aurelius Antoninus to Himself: An English Translation with Introductory Study on Stoicism and the Last of the Stoics.* London: Macmillan.

Staniforth, Maxwell. 1964. *Marcus Aurelius: Meditations.* London: Penguin.

Cebes

[Items that include illustrations are indicated with an asterisk.]

Banchich, Thomas. 2002. Cebes' *Pinax.* Bryn Mawr, PA: Bryn Mawr Commentaries. [Greek text with grammatical notes, and a short introduction.]

*Fitzgerald, John T. and L. Michael White. 1983. *The Tabula of Cebes.* Chico, CA: Society of Biblical Literature. [English translation with facing Greek text, extensive notes, and comprehensive introduction.]

*Guthrie, Kenneth Sylvan. 1910. *The Greek Pilgrim's Progress: Being a Translation of the Picture, by Kebes.* London: Luzac and Company, and Philadelphia: Monsalvat Press. [English translation.]

Jerram, C. S. 1898. *Cebetis Tabula: with Introduction and Notes.* Oxford: Clarendon Press. [Greek text.]

King, Cynthia. n.d. *The Tablet of Cebes: Selections with Introduction, Facing Vocabulary and Notes.* Amherst, MA: Classical Association of New England (CANE). [Available with a 'translation key' in English.]

*Orgel, Stephen. 1980. *Cebes in England: English Translations of the Tablet of Cebes from Three Centuries, with Related Materials.* New York: Garland. [Includes translations by Francis Poyntz (1557), John Healey (1616), Jeremy Collier (1708), and Anthony Cooper, 3rd Earl of Shaftesbury (1914).]

Parsons, Richard. 1887. *Cebes' Tablet: with Introduction, Notes, Vocabulary, and Grammatical Questions.* Boston: Athenaeum Press. [Greek text.]

Seebohm, Hugh E. 1906. *The Picture of Kebes the Theban.* Chipping Campden, Glos.: Essex House Press. [English translation.]

*Sider, Sandra. 1979. *Cebes' Tablet: Facsimiles of the Greek Text, and of Selected Latin, French, English, Spanish, Italian, German, Dutch, and Polish Translations.* New York: Renaissance Society of America.

Cicero

Falconer, W. A. 1923. *De Senectute, De Amicitia, De Divinatione (Cato the Elder on Old Age, Laelius on Friendship, On Divination).* Cambridge, MA: Loeb Classical Library, Harvard University Press.

Griffin, M. T. and E. M. Atkins. eds. 1991. *Cicero: On Duties*: Cambridge: Cambridge University Press.

Grant, Michael. 1960. *Cicero: Selected Works.* London: Penguin. [Includes 'Against Verres 1', 'Twenty-three Letters', 'The Second Philippic Against Antony', 'On Duties 3', and 'On Old Age'.]

——. 1971. *Cicero: On the Good Life.* London: Penguin. [Includes 'Discussions at Tusculam 5', 'On Duties 2', 'Laelius: On Friendship', 'On the Orator 1', 'The Dream of Scipio' and several useful appendices.]

Graver, Margaret. 2002. *Cicero on the Emotions: Tusculan Disputations 3 and 4.* Chicago: University of Chicago Press. [Translation and commentary.]

King, J. E. 1927. *Tusculan Disputations.* Cambridge, MA: Loeb Classical Library, Harvard University Press.

MacKendrick, Paul. 1989. *The Philosophical Books of Cicero*. London: Duckworth. [Summaries of all Cicero's philosophical works.]

Rackham, H. 1913. *De Officiis*. Cambridge, MA: Loeb Classical Library, Harvard University Press.

——. 1931. *De Finibus*. Cambridge, MA: Loeb Classical Library, Harvard University Press.

——. 1942. *De Oratore (Bk 3), De Fato, Paradoxa Stoicorum, De Partitione Oratoria*. Cambridge, MA: Loeb Classical Library, Harvard University Press.

Walsh, P. G. 1997. *Cicero: The Nature of the Gods*. Oxford: Clarendon Press.

Woolf, Raphael. 2001. *Cicero: On Moral Ends*. edited by Julia Annas. Cambridge: Cambridge University Press.

Wright, M. R. 1991. *Cicero: On Stoic Good and Evil*. Warminster: Aris & Phillips. [Latin with facing English translation, and commentary, of 'De Finibus Bonorum et Malorum 3' and 'Paradoxa Stoicorum'.]

Dio Chrysostom

Cohoon, J. W. 1932. *Discourses 1–11*. [vol. 1 of Loeb Dio Chrysostom] Cambridge, MA: Loeb Classical Library, Harvard University Press.

Diogenes Laertius

Hicks, R. D. 1925, 1931 [1925]. *Lives of Eminent Philosophers*. 2 vols. Cambridge, MA: Loeb Classical Library, Harvard University Press.

Magid, Barry. 1996. *The Life of Zeno: Diogenes Laertius*. Monterey, KY: Larkspur Press. [Selections from Diogenes Laertius' chapter on Zeno]

[*See also* Inwood and Gerson (1997) for another translation of the key section of Book 7 from the *Lives* on Stoic ethics.]

Epictetus

[Note: '*Enchiridion*', '*Encheiridion*', '*Handbook*', and '*Manual*' all refer to the same work.]

Boter, Gerard. 1999. *The* Encheiridion *of Epictetus and its Three Christian Adaptations: Transmission & Critical Editions*. Leiden: Brill.

Bonforte, John. 1974. *Epictetus: A Dialogue in Common Sense*. New York: Philosophical Library. [Well paraphrased selections from the *Discourses*, the *Handbook*, and *Fragments*.]

Carter, Elizabeth. 1910. *The Discourses of Epictetus*. London: Dent &

Sons. [Also includes the *Enchiridion* and *Fragments*; first published in 1758.]

Dobbin, Robert. 1998. *Epictetus: Discourses Book 1*. Oxford: Clarendon Press. [Includes commentary.]

———. forthcoming. *Discourses and Selected Writings*. London: Penguin

Hard, Robin. 1995. *The Discourses of Epictetus*. edited, with introduction and notes, by Christopher Gill. London: Everyman/ Dent. [Includes the complete *Discourses*, the *Handbook*, and *Fragments*.]

Higginson, Thomas Wentworth. 1890. *The Works of Epictetus Consisting of His Discourses, in Four Books, The Enchiridion, and Fragments*. Boston: Little, Brown, & Company.

———. 1944. *Epictetus: Discourses and Enchiridion*. Roslyn, NY: Walter J. Black. [Revised version of the original 1890 edition.]

———. 1948. *The Enchiridion*. Upper Saddle River, NJ: Prentice Hall. [A republishing of the *Enchiridion* from the 1890 edition of the complete works.]

Lebell, Sharon. 1995. *Epictetus: The Art of Living. The Classic Manual on Virtue, Happiness, and Effectiveness: A New Interpretation*. San Francisco: HarperSanFrancisco. [A free paraphrase of the *Handbook*.]

Long, George. 1991. *Enchiridion*. Amherst, NY: Prometheus. [Reprint of the 19th-century text.]

———. 2003. *The Discourses of Epictetus*. 2 vols. Chestnut Hill, MA: Elibron Classics. [Facsimile reprint of the George Bell edition of 1903.]

———. 2004. *The Discourses of Epictetus with the Encheiridion and Fragments*. Whitefish, MT: Kessinger Publishing. [Facsimile reprint of the George Bell edition of 1877. The first edition of this translation was published in 1848.]

Matheson, P. E. 1916. *Epictetus: The Discourses and Manual*. 2 vols. Oxford: Clarendon Press.

———. 2004. *Epictetus: Discourses*. 2 vols. Mineola, NY: Dover.

Matson, Wallace I. 1998. Epictetus: *Encheiridion*. In Louis P. Pojman, ed. 1998. *Classics of Philosophy: Volume 1, Ancient and Medieval*. New York: Oxford University Press.

Oldfather, W. A. 1926, 1928. *Epictetus: The Discourses as Reported by Arrian, The Manual, and Fragments*. 2 vols. Cambridge, MA: Loeb Classical Library, Harvard University Press.

Pierce, Ulysses G. B. 1916. *The Creed of Epictetus*. Boston, MA: Beacon Press.

Rolleston, T. W. 1892. *The Teaching of Epictetus: Being the 'Encheiridion of Epictetus', with Selections from the 'Dissertations' and 'Fragments'*. London: George Routledge.

Schenkl, Heinrich. 1916. *Epicteti Dissertationes ab Arriano Digestae*. 2nd edition. *Leipzig: Teubner*. [Greek text. Includes a very useful *index verborum*.]

Talbot, Thomas. 1881. *The Enchiridion of Epictetus, and the Golden Verses of Pythagoras, translated into English Prose and Verse, with notes and scriptural references, together with some original poems*. London: Sampson Low, Marston, Searle, and Rivington.

Walker, Ellis. 1716. *Epicteti Enchiridion: The Morals of Epictetus Made English in a Poetical Paraphrase*. London: Keble and Gosling.

White, Nicholas. 1983. *Handbook of Epictetus*. Indianapolis: Hackett.

Hesiod and Homeric hymns

Wender, Dorothea. 1973. *Hesiod and Theognis*. London: Penguin. [Includes Hesiod's *Works and Days* and *Theogony*.]

Evelyn-White, Hugh E. 1936 [1914]. *Hesiod, Homeric Hymns, Epic Cycle, Homerica*. Cambridge, MA: Loeb Classical Library, Harvard University Press. [Contains Hesiod's complete corpus including the *Works and Days*, and also the *Homeric Hymns*, the *Epigrams of Homer*, the *Epic Cycle*, and the *Homerica*.]

Hine, Daryl. 2005. *Works of Hesiod and the Homeric Hymns*. Chicago: University of Chicago Press. [Contains Hesiod's *Work and Days* and *Theogony*, the *Homeric Hymns*, and the *Battle of the Frogs and the Mice*.]

Lombardo, Stanley. 1993. *Hesiod: Works and Days* and *Theogony*. introduction and notes by Robert Lamberton. Indianpolis: Hackett.

Tandy, David W. and Walter C. Neale. 1996. *Hesiod's Works and Days*. Berkeley: University of California Press.

West, M. L. 1988. *Hesiod: Theogony and Works and Days*. Oxford: Oxford University Press.

Heraclitus

Kahn, Charles H. 1981. *The Art and Thought of Heraclitus: An edition of the fragments with translation and commentary*. Cambridge: Cambridge University Press.

Robinson, T. M. 1987. Heraclitus *Fragments: A text and translation with a commentary*. Toronto: University of Toronto Press.

Wheelwright, Philip. 1959. *Heraclitus*. Oxford: Oxford University Press

Lucian

Harmon, A. M. 1913. 'Heracles, Slander, Demonax' (with others). [vol. 1 of Loeb Lucian] Cambridge, MA: Loeb Classical Library, Harvard University Press.
——. 1921. 'On Salaried Posts in Great Houses' (with others). [vol. 3 of Loeb Lucian] Cambridge, MA: Loeb Classical Library, Harvard University Press.
——. 1925. 'A Professor of Public Speaking' (with others). [vol. 4 of Loeb Lucian] Cambridge, MA: Loeb Classical Library, Harvard University Press.
——. 1936. 'Toxaris, or Friendship' (with others). [vol. 5 of Loeb Lucian] Cambridge, MA: Loeb Classical Library, Harvard University Press.

Musonius Rufus

Lutz, Cora E. 1947. Musonius Rufus 'The Roman Socrates'. *Yale Classical Studies* 10: 3–147.

Origen

Chadwick, Henry. 2003 [1965]. *Origen: Contra Celsum*. Cambridge: Cambridge University Press.

Plato

Jowett, Benjamin. 1888. *The Republic of Plato: Translated into English with Introduction, Analysis, Marginal Analysis, and Index*. 3rd edition. Oxford: Clarendon Press.

Seneca

Barker, E. Phillips. 1932. *Seneca's Letters to Lucilius*. 2 vols. Oxford: Clarendon Press.
Basore, J. W. 1928, 1932, 1935. *Moral Essays*. 3 vols. Cambridge, MA: Loeb Classical Library, Harvard University Press. [The complete *Moral Essays*.]
Campbell, Robin. 2004 [1969]. *Seneca: Letters from a Stoic*. London: Penguin. [A selection from the *Moral Letters*.]

Cooper, John M. and J. F. Procopé. 1995. *Seneca: Moral and Political Essays*. Cambridge: Cambridge University Press. [Includes 'On Anger', 'On Mercy', 'On the Private Life', and 'On Favours'.]

Costa, C. D. N. 1988. *Seneca: 17 Letters*. Warminster: Aris & Phillips. [A selection from the *Moral Letters*.]

——. 1994. *Seneca: Four Dialogues*. Warminster: Aris & Phillips. [Includes 'The Good Life', 'On Tranquillity of Mind', 'On the Steadfastness of the Wise Man', and 'Consolation to Helvia'.]

——. 1997. *Seneca: Dialogues and Letters*. London: Penguin. [Includes 'Consolation to Helvia', 'On Tranquillity of Mind', 'On Shortness of Life', *Moral Letters* 24, 57, 79 and 110, and three short selections from *Natural Questions*.]

Gummere, Richard M. 1917, 1920, 1925. *Seneca: Epistles*. 3 vols. Cambridge, MA: Loeb Classical Library, Harvard University Press. [The complete *Moral Letters*.]

Hadas, Moses. 1958. *The Stoic Philosophy of Seneca: Essays and Letters of Seneca*. New York: Norton. [Includes 'On Providence', 'On the Shortness of Life', 'On Tranquillity of Mind', 'Consolation to Helvia', 'On Clemency', and a selection from the *Moral Letters*.]

Timothy, H. B. 1973. *The Tenets of Stoicism, Assembled and Systematized, from the Works of L. Annaeus Seneca*. Amsterdam: Adolf M. Hakkert.

Simplicius

Brittain, Charles, and Tad Brennan. 2002a. *Simplicius: On Epictetus Handbook 1–26*. London: Duckworth.

——. 2002b. *Simplicius: On Epictetus Handbook 27–53*. London: Duckworth.

Socrates

Grube, G. M. A. 1981. *Plato: Five Dialogues (Euthyphro, Apology, Crito, Meno, Phaedo)*. Indianapolis: Hackett.

Stobaeus

Pomeroy, Arthur J. 1999. Arius *Didymus, Epitome of Stoic Ethics: Text and Translation*. Atlanta: Society of Biblical Literature. [Contains the text of John Stobaeus' *Anthology* 2.7.5–12, with facing Greek text, extensive notes and a Greek–English glossary.]

[*See also* Inwood and Gerson 1997, below, for another translation.]

Anthologies of Hellenistic Philosophy, including the Stoics

Annas, Julia. ed. 2001. *Voices of Ancient Philosophy: An Introductory Reader*. New York: Oxford University Press. [Readings and commentaries divided into thematic sections covering Plato, Aristotle and the Hellenistic philosophers.]

Hadas, Moses. 1961. *Essential Works of Stoicism*. New York: Bantam Books. [Complete texts of Marcus Aurelius *To Himself*, Epictetus' *Handbook*, Seneca *On Tranquility*, Diogenes Laertius' *Life of Zeno*.]

Holland, Frederic May. 1879. *The Reign of the Stoics: Their History, Religion, Philosophy, Maxims of Self-Control, Self-Culture, Benevolence, and Justice*. New York: Charles P. Somerby.

Inwood, Brad and L. P. Gerson. 1997. *Hellenistic Philosophy: Introductory Readings*. 2nd edition. Indianapolis: Hackett. [Readings from the main schools: Epicureanism, Stoicism and Scepticism.]

Irwin, Terence. 1999. *Classical Philosophy*. Oxford: Oxford University Press. [Readings and commentary. Focuses on mainly the pre-Hellenistic period of Plato and Aristotle, but includes a few useful Stoic texts.]

Long, A. A. and D. N. Sedley. 1987. *The Hellenistic Philosophers*, Volume 1. Cambridge: Cambridge University Press. [Readings from the main schools: Epicureanism, Stoicism, Scepticism, and the Academics. Includes commentaries on the readings. This is the standard primary source text. Volume 2 contains the original Greek and Latin.]

Malherbe, Abraham J. 1986. *Moral Exhortation: A Greco–Roman Sourcebook*. Philadelphia: Westminster Press.

Oates, Whitney J. 1940. *The Stoic and Epicurean Philosophers: The Complete Extant Writings of Epicurus, Epictetus, Lucretius, Marcus Aurelius*. New York: Random House. [Includes the P. E. Matheson translation of the *Discourses* and *Manual* of Epictetus, and the George Long translation of the *Meditations* of Marcus Aurelius.]

Saunders, Jason L. ed. 1996. *Greek and Roman Philosophy after Aristotle*. New York: Free Press. [Readings from Epicureanism, Stoicism, Scepticism, Philo, Plotinus, and early Christian thought. Includes the P. E. Matheson translation of the *Manual* of Epictetus.]

Others

Malherbe, Abraham J. 1977. *The Cynic Epistles: A Study Edition*. Missoula, MT: Scholars Press.

Blakeney, E. H. 1921. *The Hymn of Cleanthes: Greek Text Translated into English, With Brief Introduction and Notes.* London: SPCK.

Secondary Literature

[Items that include illustrations are indicated with an asterisk.]

Adkins, Lesley and Roy A. Adkins. 2004. *Handbook to Life in Ancient Rome.* New York: Facts On File.

Algra, Keimpe, *et al.* eds. 1999. *The Cambridge History of Hellenistic Philosophy.* Cambridge: Cambridge University Press.

———. 2003. Stoic Theology. In Inwood 2003: 153–78.

Annas, Julia. 1992. *Hellenistic Philosophy of Mind.* Berkeley and Los Angeles: University of California Press.

———. 1993a. *The Morality of Happiness.* New York: Oxford University Press.

———. 1993b. Response to Part Five of Bulloch 1993: 354–68.

Anton, John P. and Anthony Preus. eds. 1983. *Essays in Ancient Greek Philosophy: Volume Two.* Albany, NY: State University of New York Press.

Armstrong, A. H. 1989. *Classical Mediterranean Spirituality: Egyptian, Greek, Roman.* New York: Crossroad.

Arnold, E. Vernon. 1911. *Roman Stoicism.* London: Routledge & Kegan Paul.

Art, Brad. 1994. *Ethics and the Good Life: A Text with Readings.* Belmont, CA: Wadsworth.

Balsdon, J. P. V. D. 2002 [1969]. *Life and Leisure in Ancient Rome.* London: Phoenix.

Baltzly, Dirk. 2000. Stoicism. *Stanford Encyclopedia of Philosophy.* [at <http://plato.stanford.edu/archives/fall2000/entries/stoicism/> accessed 15 January 2004]

Barnes, Jonathan. 1999. *The Presocratic Philosophers.* London: Routledge.

Barney, Rachel. 2003. A Puzzle in Stoic Ethics. *Oxford Studies in Ancient Philosophy* 24: 303–40.

Bartsch, Shadi. 1989. *Decoding the Ancient Novel: The Reader and the Role of Description in Heliodorus and Achilles Tatius.* Princeton, NJ: Princeton University Press.

Bauer, Bruno. 1998. *Christ and the Caesars: The Origin of Christianity from Romanized Greek Culture.* trans. Frank E. Schacht. Charleston, SC: Charleston House.

Betegh, Gábor. 2003. Cosmological Ethics in the *Timaeus* and Early Stoicism. *Oxford Studies in Ancient Philosophy* 24: 273–302.

Billerbeck, Margarethe. 1996. The Ideal Cynic from Epictetus to Julian. In Branham and Goulet-Cazé 1996: 205–21.

Becker, Lawrence C. 1998. *A New Stoicism*. Princeton, NJ: Princeton University Press.

———. 2004. Stoic Emotion. In Strange and Zupko 2004: 250–75.

Blakeley, Donald, N. 1994. Stoic Therapy of the Passions. In Boudouris 1994: 30–41.

Bobzien, Susanne. 1997. 'Conceptions of Freedom and their Relations to Ethics'. In Sorabji 1997a: 71–89.

———. 1998. *Determinism and Freedom in Stoic Philosophy*. Oxford: Clarendon Press.

———. 1999. Chrysippus' Theory of Causes. In Ierodiakonou 1999: 196–242.

Bonhöffer, Adolf Friedrich. 1996. *The Ethics of the Stoic Epictetus*. trans. William O. Stephens. New York: Peter Lang.

Bonner, Stanley F. 1977. *Education in Ancient Rome: From the Elder Cato to the Younger Pliny*. Berkeley and Los Angeles: University of California Press.

Boudouris, K. J. ed. 1993. *Hellenistic Philosophy*, Volume 1. Athens: International Center for Greek Philosophy and Culture.

———. 1994. *Hellenistic Philosophy*, Volume 2. Athens: International Center for Greek Philosophy and Culture.

Branham, R. Bracht and Marie-Odile Goulet-Cazé. eds. 1996. *The Cynics: The Cynic Movement in Antiquity and its Legacy*. Berkeley and Los Angeles: University of California Press.

Braund, Susanna Morton and Christopher Gill. eds. 1977. *The Passions in Roman Thought and Literature*. Cambridge: Cambridge University Press.

Brennan, Tad. 1998. The Old Stoic Theory of Emotion. In Sihvola and Engberg-Pedersen 1998: 21–70.

———. 2003. Stoic Moral Psychology. In Inwood 2003: 257–94.

———. 2005. *The Stoic Life: Emotions, Duties, and Fate*. Oxford: Oxford University Press.

Brickhouse, Thomas C. and Nicholas D. Smith. 1989. *Socrates on Trial*. Princeton, NJ: Princeton University Press.

———. 1994. *Plato's Socrates*. New York: Oxford University Press.

———. 2000. *The Philosophy of Socrates*. Boulder, CO: Westview.

———. eds. 2002. *The Trial and Execution of Socrates: Sources and Controversies*. New York: Oxford University Press.

Brittain, Charles. 2002. Non-Rational Perception in the Stoics and Augustine. *Oxford Studies in Ancient Philosophy* 22: 253–308.

Broadie, Sarah. 2001. From Necessity to Fate: A Fallacy? *The Journal of Ethics* 5: 21–37.

Brouwer, René. 2002. Sagehood and the Stoics. *Oxford Studies in Ancient Philosophy* 23: 181–224.

Brunschwig, Jacques and Martha C. Nussbaum. eds. 1993. *Passions and Perceptions: Studies in Hellenistic Philosophy of Mind.* Cambridge, MA: Harvard University Press.

Brunschwig, Jacques and Geoffrey E. R. Lloyd. eds. 2000. *Greek Thought: A Guide to Classical Knowledge.* Cambridge, MA: Harvard University Press.

Brunt, P. A. 1973. Aspects of the Social Thought of Dio Chrysostom and of the Stoics. *Proceedings of the Cambridge Philological Society* 19: 9–34. Also in Brunt 1997: 210–44.

———. 1997. *Studies in Greek History and Thought.* Oxford: Clarendon Press.

Bulloch, Anthony W., *et al.* eds. 1993. *Images and Ideologies: Self-definition in the Hellenistic World.* Berkeley and Los Angeles: University of California Press. [also at <http://ark.cdlib.org/ark:/13030/ft4r29p0kg> accessed 3 August 2004]

Buzaré, Elen. 2002. Stoic Spiritual Exercises. *Stoic Voice Journal* 2–12. [at <http://www.geocities.com/stoicvoice/journal/0102/eb0102e1.htm> accessed 8 July 2002]

Campbell, Keith. 1986. *A Stoic Philosophy of Life.* Lanham, MD: University Press of America.

Carcopino, Jérôme. 2003. *Daily Life in Ancient Rome: The People and the City at the Height of the Empire.* 2nd edition. trans. E. O. Lorimer. edited and annotated Henry T. Rowell. introduction and bibliographic essay Mary Beard. New Haven, CT: Yale University Press. [1st edition 1940]

Casson, Lionel. 1998 [1975]. *Everyday Life in Ancient Rome.* 2nd edition. Baltimore, MD: John Hopkins University Press.

Caizzi, Fernanda Decleva. 1993. The Porch and the Garden: Early Hellenistic Images of the Philosophical Life. In Bulloch 1993: 303–29.

Carone, Gabriela Roxana. 2005. Plato's Stoic View of Motivation. In Salles 2005: 365–81.

Chew, Samuel C. 1962. *The Pilgrimage of Life.* New Haven, CT: Yale University Press.

Christensen, Johnny. 1962. *An Essay on the Unity of Stoic Philosophy.* Copenhagen: Munksgaard.

Clarke, M. L. 1968. *The Roman Mind: Studies in the History of Thought from Cicero to Marcus Aurelius.* New York: Norton.

Colish, Marcia L. 1990. *The Stoic Tradition from Antiquity to the Early Middle Ages*. 2 vols. Leiden: Brill.

Cooper, John M. 1998. Posidonius on Emotions. In Sihvola and Engberg-Pedersen 1998: 71–111.

——. 1999a. *Reason and Emotion: Essays on Ancient Moral Psychology and Ethical Theory*. Princeton, NJ: Princeton University Press.

——. 1999b. Eudaimonism, the Appeal to Nature, and 'Moral Duty' in Stoicism. In Cooper 1999a: 427–48.

——. 1999c. Posidonius on Emotions. In Cooper 1999a: 449–84; and in Sihvola and Engberg-Pedersen 1998: 71–111.

Cowell, F. R. 1980 [1961]. *Life in Ancient Rome*. New York: Perigee Books.

Davidson, William L. 1907. *The Stoic Creed*. Edinburgh: T & T Clark.

DeFilippo, Joseph G. and Philip T. Mitsis. 1994. Socrates and Stoic Natural Law. In Vander Waerdt 1994a: 252–71.

Dillon, John M. 1983. *Metriopatheia* and *Apatheia*: Some Reflections on a Controversy in Later Greek Ethics. In Anton and Preus 1983: 508–17.

Dillon, J. M. and A. A. Long. eds. 1996. *The Question of 'Eclecticism': Studies in Later Greek Philosophy*. Berkeley and Los Angeles: University of California Press.

Dillon, J. T. 2004. *Musonius Rufus and Education in the Good Life: A Model of Teaching and Living Virtue*. Lanham, MD: University Press of America.

Dobbin, Robert. 1991. Προαίρεσις in Epictetus. *Ancient Philosophy* 11–1: 111–35.

Dudley, Donald R. 1998 [1937]. *A History of Cynicism: From Diogenes to the 6th Century AD*, with a foreword and bibliography by Miriam Griffin. London: Bristol Classical Press.

Dupont, Florence. 1992. *Daily Life in Ancient Rome*. trans. Christopher Woodall. Oxford: Blackwell.

Edelstein, Ludwig. 1966. *The Meaning of Stoicism*. Cambridge, MA: Harvard University Press.

Elsner, Jas. 1995. *Art and the Roman Viewer: The Transformation of Art from the Pagan World to Christianity*. Cambridge: Cambridge University Press.

Engberg-Pedersen, Troels. 1986. Discovering the Good: *oikeiôsis* and *kathêkonta* in Stoic Ethics. In Schofield and Striker 1986: 145–83.

——. 1990. *The Stoic Theory of Oikeiosis: Moral Development and Social Interaction in Early Stoic Philosophy*. Aarhus: Aarhus University Press.

——. 1998. Marcus Aurelius on Emotions. In Sihvola and Engberg-Pedersen 1998: 305–37.

——. 2000. *Paul and the Stoics*. Edinburgh: T & T Clark.

Erskine, Andrew. 1990. *The Hellenistic Stoa: Political Thought and Action*. Ithaca, NY: Cornell University Press.

Fagan, Garrett G. 1999. *Bathing in Public in the Roman World*. Ann Arbor, MI: University of Michigan Press.

Fortenbaugh, William W. ed. 2002 [1983]. *On Stoic and Peripatetic Ethics: the Work of Arius Didymus*. New Brunswick, NJ: Transaction Publishers.

Foucault, Michel. 1983a. The Cynic Philosophers and their Techniques. [at <http://foucault.info/documents/parrhesiasts/foucault.diogenes.en.html> accessed 24 August 2003]

——. 1983b. Epictetus and the Control of Representations. [at <http://foucault.info/documents/parrhesia/Lecture-06/04.epictetus.html> accessed 25 August 2003]

——. 1983c. Parrhesia and Public Life: the Cynics. [at <http://foucault.info/documents/parrhesia/Lecture-05/04.publiclife.html> accessed 25 August 2003]

——. 1983d. Parrhesia and Community Life: Epictetus. [at <http://foucault.info/documents/parrhesia/Lecture-05/03.communitylife.html> accessed 25 August 2003]

——. 1983e. Seneca and Evening Examination. [at <http://foucault.info/documents/parrhesia/Lecture-06/02.seneca.html> accessed 25 August 2003]

——. 1986. *The Care of the Self (Volume 3 of the History of Sexuality)*. trans. Robert Hurley. New York: Pantheon Books.

Francis, James A. 1995. *Subversive Virtue: Asceticism and Authority in the Second-Century Pagan World*. University Park, PA: Pennsylvania State University Press.

Frede, Dorothea. 2003. Stoic Determinism. In Inwood 2003: 179–205.

Frede, Michael. 1994 The Stoic Conception of Reason. In Boudouris 1994: 50–63.

——. 1999. On the Stoic Conception of the Good. In Ierodiakonou 1999: 71–94.

——. 1999a. Stoic Epistemology. In Algra 1999. 295–322.

Friedländer, Ludwig. 1907, 1908, 1909, 1913. *Roman Life and Manners Under the Early Empire*. 4 vols. London: George Routledge.

Garnsey, Peter and Richard Saller. 1987. *The Roman Empire: Economy, Society and Culture*. London: Duckworth.

Garrett, Jan Edward. 1999. Is the Sage Free from Pain? *Volga Journal of Philosophy and Social Sciences* 6. [at <http://www.ssu.samara.ru/research/philosophy/frame.asp?journal=6> also at <http://www.wku.edu/~jan.garrett/painst.htm> accessed 8 July 2002]

Gass, Michael. 2000. Eudaimonism, Theology, and Stoicism. *Journal of the History of Ideas* 61–1: 19–37.

Gill, Christopher. 1988. Personhood and Personality: the Four-*personae* Theory in Cicero, *de Officiis* I. *Oxford Studies in Ancient Philosophy* 6: 169–99.

——. 1998. Did Galen Understand Platonic and Stoic Thinking on Emotion? In Sihvola and Engberg-Pedersen 1998: 113–48.

——. 2005. Competing Readings of Stoic Emotions. In Salles 2005: 445–70.

——. 1993. Panaetius on the Virtue of Being Yourself. In Bulloch 1993: 330–53.

——. 2003. The [Stoic] School in the Roman Imperial Period. In Inwood 2003: 33–58.

*Gombrich, E. H. 1952. A Classical 'Rake's Progress'. *Journal of the Warburg and Courtland Institutes* 15: 254–6.

Gould, Josiah B. 1970. *The Philosophy of Chrysippus*. Albany, NY: State University of New York Press.

——. 1983. The Stoic Conception of Fate. In Anton and Preus 1983: 478–94.

Graver, Margaret. 1996. *Therapeutic Reading and Seneca's* Moral Epistles. Ann Arbor, MI:UMI Dissertation Services. [PhD dissertation, Brown University: UMI number 9704034]

——. 1999. Philo of Alexandria and the Origins of the Stoic Προπάθειαι *Phronesis* 44–4: 300–25.

Griffin, Miriam. 1992 [1976]. *Seneca: A Philosopher in Politics*. Oxford: Clarendon Press.

Griffin, Miriam and Jonathan Barnes. eds. 1997 *Philosophia Togata I: Essays on Philosophy and Roman Society*. Oxford: Clarendon Press.

Guhl, E. and W. Koner. 1989. *The Greeks and Romans: Their Life and Customs*. London: Bracken Books. [Facsimile reprint of the Chatto & Windus edition of 1889.]

Gummere, Richard M. 1963. *Seneca the Philosopher and His Modern Message*. New York: Cooper Square.

Hadot, I. 1989. The Spiritual Guide. In Armstrong 1989: 436–59.

Hadot, Pierre. 1995. *Philosophy as a Way of Life*. trans. Michael Chase. Edited with an introduction by Arnold I. Davidson. Oxford: Blackwell.

——. 1998. *The Inner Citadel: The Mediations of Marcus Aurelius*. trans. Michael Chase. Cambridge, MA: Harvard University Press.

——. 2002. *What is Ancient Philosophy?* trans. Michael Chase. Cambridge, MA: Harvard University Press.

Hahm, David E. 1994. Posidonius' Theory of Action. In Boudouris 1994: 76–88.

Hankinson, R. J. 1999. Determinism and Indeterminism. In Algra 1999: 513–41.

Harris, William V. 2001. *Restraining Rage: The Ideology of Anger Control in Classical Antiquity.* Cambridge, MA: Harvard University Press.

Hicks, R. D. 1962. *Stoic and Epicurean.* New York: Russell & Russell.

Hijmans, B. L. 1959. *ΑΣΚΗΣΙΣ: Notes on Epictetus' Educational System.* Assen: Van Gorcum

Hinks, Roger. 1939. *Myth and Allegory in Ancient Art.* London: Warburg Institute.

Hock, Ronald F. 1992. 'By the gods, it's my one desire to see an actual Stoic': Epictetus' Relations with Students and Visitors in His Personal Network. *Semeia* 56: 121–42.

Höistad, Ragnar. 1948. *Cynic Hero and Cynic King: Studies in the Cynic Conception of Man.* Uppsala: University of Uppsala.

Holowchak, M. Andrew. 2004. *Happiness and Greek Ethical Thought.* London: Continuum.

Hornblower, Simon and Antony Spawforth. 1996. *The Oxford Classical Dictionary.* 3rd edition. Oxford: Oxford University Press.

Huskinson, Janet. ed. 2000. *Experiencing Rome: Culture, Identity and Power in the Roman Empire.* London: Routledge.

Ierodiakonou, Katerina. ed. 1999. *Topics in Stoic Philosophy.* Oxford: Clarendon Press.

Inwood, Brad. 1985. *Ethics and Human Action in Early Stoicism.* Oxford: Clarendon Press.

——. 1997. 'Why do fools fall in love?' In Sorabji 1997a: 57–69.

——. 1999. Rules and Reasoning in Stoic Ethics. In Ierodiakonou 1999: 95–127.

——. ed. 2003. *The Cambridge Companion to the Stoics.* Cambridge: Cambridge University Press.

Inwood, Brad and Pierluigi Donini. 1999. Stoic Ethics. In Algra 1999: 675–738.

Irwin, Terence. 1986. Stoic and Aristotelian Conceptions of Happiness. In Schofield and Striker 1986: 205–44.

——. 1989. *Classical Thought.* Oxford: Oxford University Press. [A basic introduction to ancient Greek philosophy as a whole, including the Hellenistic schools.]

——. 1990 Virtue, Praise and Success: Stoic Responses to Aristotle. *The Monist* 73–1: 59–79.

——. ed. 1995. *Classical Philosophy: Collected Papers Volume 8, Hellenistic Philosophy.* New York and London: Garland.

———. 1998. Stoic Inhumanity. In Sihvola and Engberg-Pedersen 1998: 219–41.

Johnston, Harold Whetstone. 2002. *The Private Life of the Romans*. Honolulu: University Press of the Pacific. [Facsimile reprint of the Scott, Foresman & Company 1903 edition.]

Kahn, Charles H. 1996. Discovering the Will: From Aristotle to Augustine. In Dillon and Long 1996: 234–59.

———. 2001. *Pythagoras and the Pythagoreans: A Brief History*. Indianapolis: Hackett.

Kalouche, Fouad. 2003. The Cynic Way of Living. *Ancient Philosophy* 23: 181–94.

Kamtekar, Rachana. 1998. ΑΙΔΩΣ in Epictetus. *Classical Philology* 93–2: 136–60.

Kerford, G. B. 1978. What Does the Wise Man Know? In Rist 1978a: 125–36.

Kidd, I. G. 1978. Moral Actions and Rules in Stoic Ethics. In Rist 1978a: 247–58.

———. 1996. Stoic Intermediates and the End for Man. in Long 1996a: 150–72.

Kimpel, Ben. 1985. *Stoic Moral Philosophies: Their Counsel for Today*. New York: Philosophical Library.

Kirk, G. S., J. E. Raven and M. Schofield. 1983. *The Presocratic Philosophers*. 2nd edition. Cambridge: Cambridge University Press.

Knuuttila, Simo. 2004. *Emotions in Ancient and Medieval Philosophy*. Oxford: Clarendon Press.

Knuuttila, Simo and Juha Sihvola. 1998. How the Philosophical Analysis of the Emotions was Introduced. In Sihvola and Engberg-Pedersen 1998: 1–19.

Kraiker, Christoph. 2000. Modifying what you say to yourself: The therapeutic philosophy of Epictetus. [at <http://www.paed.uni-muenchen.de/~kraiker/EPIKTET.HTM> accessed 26 December 2003]

Kristeller, Paul Oskar. 1993. *Greek Philosophers of the Hellenistic Age*. trans. Gregory Woods. New York: Columbia University Press.

Laks, André and Malcolm Schofield. eds. 1995. *Justice and Generosity: Studies in Hellenistic Social and Political Philosophy (Proceedings of the Sixth Symposium Hellenisticum)*. Cambridge: Cambridge University Press.

Ledbetter, Grace. 1994. The Propositional Content of Stoic Emotions. In Boudouris 1994: 107–13.

Lesses, Glen. 1989. Virtue and the Goods of Fortune in Stoic Moral Theory. *Oxford Studies in Ancient Philosophy* 7: 95–127.

——.1993a. Austere Friends: The Stoics and Friendship. *Apeiron* 26: 57–75.

——. 1993b. Austere Friends: The Stoics on the Impartiality of Friendship. In Boudouris 1993: 84–92. [An abbreviated version of 1993a.]

Lloyd, A. C. 1978. Emotion and Decision in Stoic Psychology. In Rist 1978a: 233–46.

Long, A. A. 1967. Carneades and the Stoic Telos. *Phronesis* 12:59–90. Also in Irwin 1995: 377–408.

——. 1968. The Stoic Concept of Evil. *The Philosophical Quarterly* 18–4: 329–43.

——. 1978. Dialectic and the Stoic Sage. In Rist 1978a: 101–24.

——. 1982. Soul and Body in Stoicism. *Phronesis* 27: 34–57. Also in Irwin 1995: 154–77.

——. 1986. *Hellenistic Philosophy: Stoics, Epicureans, Sceptics*. 2nd edition. Berkeley and Los Angeles: University of California Press.

——. 1989. Epicureans and Stoics. In Armstrong 1989: 135–53.

——. 1993. Introduction to Part Five of Bulloch 1993: 299–302.

——. ed. 1996a. *Problems in Stoicism*. London: Athlone.

——. 1996b. *Stoic Studies*. Cambridge: Cambridge University Press.

——. 1996c. Greek Ethics After MacIntyre. In Long 1996b: 156–78.

——. 1996d. Freedom and Determinism in the Stoic Theory of Human Action. In Long 1996a: 173–99.

——. 1996e. The Harmonics of Stoic Virtue. In Long 1996b: 202–23.

——. 1996f. Heraclitus and Stoicism. In Long 1996b: 35–7.

——. 1996g. Representation and the Self in Stoicism. In Long 1996b: 264–85.

——. 1996h. Socrates in Hellenistic Philosophy. In Long 1996b: 1–34.

——. 1996i. The Socratic Tradition: Diogenes, Crates, and Hellenistic Ethics. In Branham and Goulet-Cazé 1996: 28–46.

——. 1996j. Stoic Eudaimonism. In Long 1996b: 179–201.

——. 1997. Stoic Philosophers on Persons, Property-ownership and Community. In Sorabji 1997a: 13–31.

——. 1999. Stoic Psychology. In Algra 1999: 560–84.

——. 2001. Ancient Philosophy's Hardest Question: What to Make of Oneself? *Representations* 74: 19–36.

——. 2002. *Epictetus: A Stoic and Socratic Guide to Life*. Oxford: Oxford University Press.

——. 2004. The Socratic Imprint on Epictetus' Philosophy. In Strange and Zupko 2004: 10–31.

Lutz, Cora. 1975 *Essays on Manuscripts and Rare Books*. Hamden, CT: Archon Books.

McCabe, Mary Margaret. 2005. Extend or Identify: Two Stoic Accounts of Altruism. In Salles 2005: 413–43.

Mansfeld, Jaap. 1999. Theology. In Algra 1999: 452–78.

Menn, Stephen. 1995. Physics as a Virtue. *Proceedings of the Boston Area Colloquium in Ancient Philosophy* 11: 1–34.

Mitsis, Phillip, 1999. The Stoic Origin of Natural Rights. in Ierodiakonou 1999: 153–77. [also at <http://www.nyu.edu/gsas/dept/philo/faculty/mitsis/papers/stoic.pdf> accessed 28 April 2003]

Moes, Mark. 2000. *Plato's Dialogue Form and the Care of the Soul*. New York: Peter Lang.

More, Paul Elmer. 1923. *Hellenistic Philosophies*. Princeton, NJ: Princeton University Press.

Morris, Tom. 2001. The Stoic Art of Living: Seneca, Epictetus and Marcus Aurelius on Life Achievement. [at <http://www.morrisinstitute.com/os_04.html> accessed 2 February 2003]

——. 2004. *The Stoic Art of Living: Inner Resilience and Outer Results*. Chicago and La Salle: Open Court.

Motto, Anna Lydia. 1970. *Seneca Sourcebook: Guide to the Thought of Lucius Annaeus Seneca*. Amsterdam: Hakkert. [A book-length index of topics and names referencing Seneca's entire philosophical corpus.]

——. 1973. *Seneca*. New York: Twayne.

——. 2001. *Further Essays on Seneca*. Frankfurt: Peter Lang.

Motto, Anna Lydia and John R. Clark. 1993. *Essays on Seneca*. Frankfurt: Peter Lang.

——. 1993a. The Development of the Classical Tradition of Exile to Seneca. In Motto and Clark 1993: 189–96.

Murphy, Peter. 1999. The Existential Stoic. *Thesis Eleven* 59: 87–94. [at: <http://www.sagepub.co.uk/PDF/JOURNALS/FULLTEXT/a010162.pdf> accessed 24 November 2003]

Navia, Luis E. 1996. *Classical Cynicism: A Critical Study*. Westport, CT: Greenwood Press.

——. 1998. *Diogenes of Sinope: The Man in the Tub*. Westport, CT: Greenwood Press.

Nock, A. D. 1933. *Conversion: The Old and the New in Religion from Alexander the Great to Augustine of Hippo*. Oxford: Clarendon Press.

Nussbaum, Martha C. 1986. Therapeutic Arguments: Epicurus and Aristotle. In Schofield and Striker 1986: 31–74.

——. 1994. *The Therapy of Desire: Theory and Practice in Hellenistic Ethics*. Princeton, NJ: Princeton University Press.

——. 1995. Commentary on Menn. *Proceedings of the Boston Area Colloquium in Ancient Philosophy* 11: 35–45.

Obbink, Dirk. 1999. The Stoic Sage in the Cosmic City. In Ierodiakonou 1999: 178–95.

Ogilvie, R. M. 1986. *The Romans and Their Gods*. London: Hogarth Press.

Osler, Margaret J. ed. 1991. *Atoms, Pneuma, and Tranquillity: Epicurean and Stoic Themes in European Thought*. Cambridge: Cambridge University Press.

Pépin, Jean. 1989. Cosmic Piety. In Armstrong 1989: 408–35.

Powell, J. G. F. 1995. *Cicero the Philosopher: Twelve Papers*. Oxford: Clarendon Press.

Price, A. W. 2005. Were Zeno and Chrysippus at Odds in Analyzing Emotion? In Salles 2005: 471–88.

Reale, Giovanni. 1985. *A History of Ancient Philosophy: 3. The Systems of the Hellenistic Age*. ed. & trans. John R. Catan. Albany, NY: State University of New York Press.

———. 1990. *A History of Ancient Philosophy: 4. The Schools of the Imperial Age*. ed. & trans. John R. Catan. Albany, NY: State University of New York Press.

Reedy, Jeremiah. 1994. Stoic Attitudes Towards the Contemplative Life. In Boudouris 1994: 187–92.

Reesor, Margaret E. 1965. Fate and Possibility in Early Stoic Philosophy. *Phoenix* 19: 285–97.

———. 1978. Necessity and Fate in Stoic Philosophy. In Rist 1978a: 187–202.

———. 1989. *The Nature of Man in Early Stoic Philosophy*. London: Duckworth.

Reeve. C. D. C. 1989. *Socrates in the Apology: An Essay on Plato's Apology of Socrates*. Indianapolis: Hackett.

Reydams-Schils, Gretchen. 2002. Human Bonding and *Oikeiôsis* in Roman Stoicism. *Oxford Studies in Ancient Philosophy* 22: 221–51.

Rist, John M. 1969. *Stoic Philosophy*. Cambridge: Cambridge University Press.

———. ed. 1978a. *The Stoics*. Berkeley and Los Angeles: University of California Press.

———. 1978b. The Stoic Concept of Detachment. In Rist 1978a: 259–72; also in Rist 1996.

———. 1982. Are You a Stoic? The Case of Marcus Aurelius. In Ben F. Meyer and E. P. Sanders. 1982. *Jewish and Christian Self-Definition*. London: SCM Press: 23–45. Also in Rist 1996.

———. 1983. Zeno and Stoic Consistency. In Anton and Preus 1983: 465–77.

———. 1985. Epictetus: Ex-Slave. *Dialectic* 24: 3–22. Also in Rist 1996.

——. 1996. *Man, Soul and Body: Essays in Ancient Thought from Plato to Dionysius*. Aldershot: Variorum.

Rowe, Christopher and Malcolm Schofield. eds. 2000. *The Cambridge History of Greek and Roman Political Thought*. Cambridge: Cambridge University Press.

Rubarth, Scott. 2002. Stoic Philosophy of Mind. *Internet Encyclopedia of Philosophy*. [at <http://www.utm.edu/research/iep/s/stoicmind1.htm> accessed 4 April 2003]

Rutherford, R. B. 1989. *The Meditations of Marcus Aurelius: A Study*. Oxford: Clarendon Press.

Salles, Ricardo. ed. 2005. *Metaphysics, Soul, and Ethics in Ancient Thought: Themes from the Work of Richard Sorabji*. Oxford: Clarendon Press.

Sambursky, S. 1959. *Physics of the Stoics*. London: Routledge and Kegan Paul.

Sandbach, F. H. 1985. *Aristotle and the Stoics*. Cambridge: Cambridge Philological Society.

——. 1989. *The Stoics*. London: Duckworth, and Indianapolis: Hackett.

——. 1996. Phantasia Katalêptikê. In Long 1996a: 9–21.

Sayre, Farrand. 1948. *The Greek Cynics*. Baltimore: J. H. Furst.

Schofield, Malcolm and Gisela Striker. eds. 1986. *The Norms of Nature: Studies in Hellenistic Ethics*. Cambridge: Cambridge University Press.

Schofield, Malcolm. 1999 [1991]. *The Stoic Idea of the City*. with a new foreword by Martha C. Nussbaum. Chicago: University of Chicago Press.

——. 2003. Stoic Ethics. In Inwood 2003: 233–56.

Seddon, Keith. 1987. *Time: A Philosophical Treatment*. Beckenham: Croom Helm.

——. 1999. Do the Stoics Succeed in Showing How People Can be Morally Responsible for Some of Their Actions Within the Framework of Causal Determinism? *Volga Journal of Philosophy and Social Sciences* 6. [at <http://www.ssu.samara.ru/research/philosophy/frame.asp?journal=6 < also at <http://www.wku.edu/~jan.garrett/seddon1.htm> accessed 8 July 2002]

——. 2000. The Stoics on Why We Should Strive to Be Free of The Passions. *Practical Philosophy* 3–3: 6–11. [also at <http://www.wku.edu/~jan.garrett/seddon2.htm> accessed 8 July 2002]

——. 2001. Epictetus. *Internet Encyclopedia of Philosophy*. [at <http://www.utm.edu/research/iep/e/epictetu.htm> accessed 8 July 2002]

——. 2005. Epictetus. In Patricia O'Grady. ed. 2005. *Meet the Philosophers of Ancient Greece: Everything You Always Wanted to Know*

About Ancient Greek Philosophy but Didn't Know Who to Ask. Aldershot: Ashgate.

Sedley, David. 1999a. Hellenistic Physics and Metaphysics. In Algra 1999: 355–411.

———. 1999b. The Stoic–Platonist Debate on *kathêkonta.* In Ierodiakonou 1999: 128–52.

Sellars, John. 2003. *The Art of Living: The Stoics on the Nature and Function of Philosophy.* Aldershot: Ashgate.

Sharp, Nicholas S. 1914. *Epictetus and the New Testament.* London: Charles H. Kelly.

Sharples, R. W. 1981. Necessity in the Stoic Doctrine of Fate. *Symbolae Osloenses* 56: 81–97.

———. 1996. *Stoics, Epicureans, and Sceptics: An Introduction to Hellenistic Philosophy.* London: Routledge.

Scheid, John. 2003. *An Introduction to Roman Religion.* trans. Janet Lloyd. Bloomington and Indianapolis: Indiana University Press.

Sheldon, Jo-Ann. 1998. *As the Romans Did: A Sourcebook in Roman Social History.* 2nd edition. New York: Oxford University Press.

Sherman, Nancy. 2002. Educating the Stoic Warrior. In William Damon. ed. 2002. *Bringing in a New Era in Character Education.* Stanford, CA: Hoover Institution Press: 85–111. [also at <http://www-hoover.stanford.edu/publications/books/fulltext/character/85.pdf> accessed 8 July 2002]

Sihvola, Juha and Troels Engberg-Pedersen. eds. 1998. *The Emotions in Hellenistic Philosophy.* Dordrecht: Kluwer.

Smith, R. R. R. 1993. Kings and Philosophers. In Bulloch 1993: 202–11.

Sorabji, Richard. ed. 1997a. *Aristotle and After.* London: Institute of Classical Studies.

———. 1997b. Is Stoic Philosophy Helpful as Psychotherapy? In Sorabji 1997a: 197–209.

———. 1998. Chrysippus – Posidonius – Seneca: A High-Level Debate on Emotion. In Sihvola and Engberg-Pedersen 1998: 149–69.

———. 2000. *Emotion and Peace of Mind: From Stoic Agitation to Christian Temptation.* Oxford: Oxford University Press.

Starr, Chester G. 1949. Epictetus and the Tyrant. *Classical Philology* 44: 20–9.

Stephens, William O. 1990. *Stoic Strength: An Examination of the Ethics of Epictetus.* [PhD dissertation, University of Pennsylvania: UMI number 9026654]

———. 1994. Stoic Love in Epictetus. In Boudouris 1994: 216–24.

———. 1996. Epictetus on How the Stoic Sage Loves. *Oxford Studies in Ancient Philosophy* 14: 193–210.

———. 2003. Stoic Ethics. *Internet Encyclopedia of Philosophy.* [at <http://www.iep.utm.edu/s/StoicEth.htm> accessed 13 January 2004]

Stock, St. George. n.d. *A Guide to Stoicism* (Little Blue Book No. 347). Girard, KS: Haldeman–Julius.

Stockdale, James B. 1993. *Courage Under Fire: Testing Epictetus's Doctrines in a Laboratory of Human Behavior.* Stanford, CA: Hoover Institution/Stanford University. Also in Stockdale 1995a: 185–201.

———. 1995a. *Thoughts of a Philosophical Fighter Pilot.* Stanford, CA: Hoover Institution/Stanford University.

———. 1995b. Arrian's *Enchiridion* and *The Discourses* of Epictetus. In Stockdale 1995a: 222–37.

———. 1995c. The Tough Mind of Epictetus. In Stockdale 1995a: 177–84.

———. 2001. *Stockdale on Stoicism I: The Stoic Warrior's Triad.* Annapolis, MD: Center for the Study of Professional Military Ethics [also at <http://www.usna.edu/Ethics/stoicism1.pdf> accessed 17 January 2003]

———. 2001. *Stockdale on Stoicism II: Master of My Fate.* Annapolis, MD: Center for the Study of Professional Military Ethics [also at <http://www.usna.edu/Ethics/stoicism2.pdf> accessed 17 January 2003]

Stough, Charlotte. 1978. Stoic Determinism and Moral Responsibility. In Rist 1978a: 203–31.

Stowell, Melanie Celine. 1999. *Stoic Therapy of Grief: A Prolegomenon to Seneca's 'Ad Marciam, de Consolatore'.* Ann Arbor, MI:UMI Dissertation Services. [PhD dissertation, Cornell University: UMI number 9941194]

Strange, Steven K. 2004. The Stoics on the Voluntariness of the Passions. In Strange and Zupko 2004: 32–51.

Strange, Steven K. and Jack Zupko. eds. 2004. *Stoicism: Traditions and Transformations.* Cambridge: Cambridge University Press.

Striker, Gisela. 1983. *The Role of* Oikeiôsis *in Stoic Ethics. Oxford Studies in Ancient Philosophy* 1: 145–67. Also in Irwin 1995: 353–75, and in Striker 1996: 281–97.

———. 1986. Antipater, or the Art of Living. In Schofield and Striker 1986: 185–204. Also in Striker 1996a: 298–315.

———. 1990. *Ataraxia*: Happiness as Tranquillity. *The Monist* 73–1: 97–110. Also in Striker 1996a: 183–95.

———. 1991. Following Nature: A Study in Stoic Ethics. *Oxford Studies in Ancient Philosophy* 9: 1–73. Also in Striker 1996a: 221–80.

——. 1994. Plato's Socrates and the Stoics. In Vander Waerdt 1994a: 241–51. Also in Striker 1996a: 316–24.

——. 1996a. *Essays on Hellenistic Epistemology and Ethics*. Cambridge: Cambridge University Press.

——. 1996b. Greek Ethics and Moral Theory. In Striker 1996a: 169–82.

——. 1996c. Κριτήριον τῆς ἀληθείας. In Striker 1996a: 22–76.

——. 1996d. Origins of the Concept of Natural Law. In Striker 1996a: 209–20.

——. 1996e. The Problem of the Criterion. In Striker 1996a: 150–65.

Taylor, Richard. 1992. *Metaphysics*. 4th ed. Englewood Cliffs, NJ: Prentice Hall.

——. 2002. *An Introduction to Virtue Ethics*. Amherst, NY: Prometheus.

Trapp, M. B. 1997. On the *Tablet* of Cebes. In Sorabji 1997a: 159–80.

Vander Waerdt, Paul A. ed. 1994a. *The Socratic Movement*. Ithaca, NY: Cornell University Press.

——. 1994b. Zeno's *Republic* and the Origins of Natural Law. In Vander Waerdt 1994a: 272–308.

Veyne, Paul. 2003. *Seneca: the Life of a Stoic*. trans. David Sullivan. New York & London: Routledge.

Watson, Gerard. 1966. *The Stoic Theory of Knowledge*. Belfast: The Queen's University.

Wenley, R. M. 1924. *Stoicism and its Influence*. Boston, MA: Marshall Jones.

White, Nicholas P. 1979. The Basis of Stoic Ethics. *Harvard Studies in Classical Philology* 83: 143–78. Also in Irwin 1995: 317–52.

——. 1990. Stoic Values. *The Monist* 73–1: 42–58.

Williams, Bernard. 1997. Stoic Philosophy and the Emotions: reply to Richard Sorabji. In Sorabji 1997a: 211–13.

Xenakis, Jason. 1969. *Epictetus: Philosopher-Therapist*. The Hague: Martinus Nijhoff.

Zanker, Paul. 1995. *The Mask of Socrates: The Image of the Intellectual in Antiquity*, trans. Alan Shapiro. Berkeley and Los Angeles: University of California Press.

Zeyl, Donald. ed. 1997. *Encyclopedia of Classical Philosophy*. London: Fitzroy Dearborn.

Index of key terms in the *Handbook* of Epictetus

[References are to Chapters and Sections in the *Handbook*.]

English–Greek

abject (*tapeinos*), 21
abuse (noun) (*loidoria*), 10; (verb) (*hubrizô*), 20
accuse (*enkaleô*), 48.2
actions (*erga*), 46.2, 49; *see also* task, undertaking, work
actor (*hupokritês*), 17
admire (*thaumazô*), 22
adult (*anêr*, man), 51.1
advantageous (*sumpheron*), 31.4
agitate, disturb, or trouble the mind (*tarassô*), 5
angry (*epachthês*), 33.8
Apollo, *see* Pythian Apollo
appear, *see* falsely appear
appropriate (*kathêkon*), 42
appropriate actions (duties) (*ta kathêkonta*), 30
assent (verb) (*sunkatatithemai*), 45
assign (*tassô*), 22
at hand (*procheiros*), 53.1
attention, *see* pay attention
aversion (*ekklisis*), 1.1, 2.1, 2.2, 31.4, 32.2, 48.3

bad (*kakos*), 12.1, 16, 24.1, 25.1, 29.7, 30, 31.2, 32.1, 33.9, 42, 53.1; *see also* evil
badly (*kakôs*), 42, 45
badness (*kakia*), 14.1
banquet (*hestiasis*), 24.1, 25.1, 25.4, 33.6, 36; (*sumposion*), 15, 46.1
become accustomed or habituated to something (*ethizô*), 10
belonging to another (*allotrios*), 1.2, 1.3
beneficial (*ôphelimos*), 31.3
benefit (noun) (*ôpheleia*), 48.1
benefit (verb) (*ôpheleô*), 18
best (*beltistos*), 22, 51.1, 51.2
better (*kreissôn*), 44
blame (verbs) (*aitiaomai*), 5; (*memphomai*), 31.1, 31.2; (*psegô*), 33.2, 48.2; *see also* find fault with
body (*to sôma*), 1.1, 9, 18, 28, 33.7, 41, 47

capacities (*phusis*, nature), 29.5
capacity (*dunamis*), 10, 37
captain (*kubernêtês*), 7

character (*charaktêr*), 33.1, 48.1
child (*meirakion,* boy), 51.1;
   (*paidion*), 3, 7, 11; (*teknon*), 14.1,
   15, 16, 18, 26, 31.4
Chrysippus (*Chrusippos*), 49
commit sacrilege (*asebeô*), 50
compare (*sunkrinô*), 33.2
condition (*stasis*), 48.1
contrary to nature (*para phusin*), 2.1
control (verb) (*krateô*), 20
convincing, or cognitive, impression
   (*phantasia katalêptikê*), 45
critical (*elenktikos*), 33.8

death (*thanatos*), 2.1, 5, 21
deceive (*exapataô*), 42
delay (noun) (*diatribê*), 20
desire (noun) (*orexis*), 1.1, 2.1, 2.2,
   31.4, 32.2, 48.3
desire (verb) (*oregô*), 2.1, 2.2, 14.1
Destiny (*Peprômenê*), 53.1
destiny (*anankê*), 53.2
devotion (to the gods) (*eusebeia*),
   31.4
dignity (*semnos*), 33.11
disapprove (*epiplêssô*), 35
disposition (*tupos*), 33.1
distress (noun) (*tarachê*), 3
distress, trouble, or agitate the mind
   (*tarassô*), 1.3; *see also* agitate,
   perturb
distressed, to be (*lupeô*), 5; (*thlibô*),
   16
divination (*mantikê*), 32.1, 32.3
diviner (*mantis*), 32.1, 32.2, 32.3

earthenware pot (*chutra*), 3
endurance (*karteria*), 10
enemy (*ho echthros*), 1.3, 48.3
envy (noun) (*phthonos*), 19.2
equanimity (*eustathês*), 33.11
essence of good (*ousia tou agathou*),
   19.2
evil (*to kakon*), 27
examine (*exetazô*), 1.5

excellence (*proterêma*), 6
exercise (verb) (*askeô*) 14.1
exile (noun) (*phugê*), 21
external (*ektos*), 16
external things (*ta ektos*), 13, 23,
   29.7, 33.13, 48.1

falsely appear (*kakôs phainomai*) ['if
   someone has a false opinion...' '*ei
   kakôs phainetai...*'], 42
fate (*anankê*), 53.2
find fault with (*memphomai*), 1.3,
   48.2; *see also* blame
flow well (*euroeô*), 8
follow (*hepomai*), 49, 53.1
fondness for something, to have
   (*stergô*), 3
foolish (*abelteros*), 25.4; (*anous*), 13;
   (*hêlithios*), 14.1, 48.3; *see also*
   stupid
foolishness (*aphuia*), 41
free (adjective) (*eleutheros*), 1.2, 1.3,
   14.2, 19.2
free from distress (*alupos*), 12
free from fear (*aphobos*), 12
freedom (*eleutheria*), 1.4, 29.7
freedom from passion, *see* peace of
   mind
freedom from troubles, serenity
   (*ataraxia*), 12; *see also* serenity
friend (*philos*), 14.1, 32.3

gentle (*praôs*), 42
give back (*apodidômi*), 11
Giver, the (*ho dotêr*), 11
God (*theos*), 22
gods (*theoi*), 1.3, 31.1, 32.2
good (adjective) (*agathos*), 6, 24.3,
   25.1, 29.7, 30, 31.2, 31.4, 32.1;
   see also essence of good
guard against (*phulassô*), 34; *see also*
   keep guard over

handle (noun) (*labê*), 43
happiness (*eudaimonia*), 1.4

happy (*makarios*), 19.2
hardship (*ponos*), 10, 47
harm (noun) (*blabê*), 31.3, 48.1
harm (verb) (*blaptô*), 1.3, 30, 31.3, 42
harmful (*blaberos*), 31.3
have sex with someone
(*sunkoimaomai*), 40; *see also* sex
having value (*axios*), 40; *see also* value
hinder (*empodizô*), 1.3, 5; (*kôluô*),
1.3, 48.2; *see also* impede
hit (*tuptô*), 20
hold to (*echô*), 22
hold fast to (*emmenô*), 50
human being (*anthrôpos*), 3

ignorant (*amathês*), 48.3
impede (*empodizô*), 48.2; *see also*
hinder
impression (*phantasia*), 1.5, 10, 16,
18, 19, 20, 34
improvement (*epanorthôsis*), 33.10,
51.1
impulse (*hormê*), 1.1, 2.2
in accordance with nature (*kata
phusin*), 4, 6, 13, 30
in our power (*eph' hêmin*), 1.1, 1.2,
1.5, 2.2, 19.2, 24.1, 24.2, 31.2
indifferent (*adiaphoros*), 32.2
inn (*pandokeion*), 11
insult (noun) (*loidoria*), 20
invalid (adjective) (*asunaktos*), 44
invincible (*anikêtos*), 19.1
irritated, to feel (*aganakteô*), 4

jealousy (*zêlotupia*), 19.2
jeer (*katamôkaomai*), 22
judgement (*dogma*, plural *dogmata*),
5, 16, 20

keep guard over (*paraphulassô*), 48.3
keep silent (*aposiôpaô*), 33.16;
(*siôpaô*), 33.2, 33.3

lacking value or honour (*atimos*),
24.1

law (*nomos*) 51.2
laws (*nomoi*), 50

'madam' (*kuria*), 40
magnanimous (*megalophrôn*), 24.3
make progress (*prokoptô*), 48.2, 51.1,
51.2; *see also* progress
master (*kurios*), 14.2
measure or standard (*to metron*), 39
mind (*hê gnômê*), 28, 41
miserable (*dustuchês*), 2.1
miserable, to be (*dustucheô*), 2.1;
(*pentheô*, lament), 1.3
misfortune, to suffer (*atucheô*), 2.2
moral character (*prohairesis*), 4, 9,
13, 30

nature (*phusis*), 30, 49; *see also* will of
nature
necessity (*anankê*), 53.2
not in our power (*ouk eph' hêmin*),
1.1, 1.5, 2.2, 19.1, 19.2, 25.1,
31.2, 32.1

oath (*horkos*), 33
obol (*obolos*, a coin of low value),
25.3
offence, *see* without offence
offended (*daknô*), 46.2
Olympic Games (*ta Olumpia*), 29.2,
51.2: *see also* public games
opinion (*hupolêpsis*), 1.1, 20
ostentatious (*epideiktikos*), 46.1

part, role (*prosôpon*), 17
patience (*anexikakia*), 10
pay attention (*epistrephô*), 50;
(*prosechô*), 51.3
pay/pay the price (*antikatallassomai*,
exchange one thing for another),
29.7; (*pôleô*, exchange or barter
goods), 12; (*proïemai*, pay), 25.2,
25.3, 25.4; (*didômi*, give), 25.3,
25.4; ('*dos to diaphoron*', 'give the
balance'), 25.4

peace of mind (*apatheia*, without passion, freedom from passion), 12.2, 29.7

persist (*emmenô*), 22

perturb the mind (*tarassô*), 12.1, 12.2

philologist or grammarian or critic (*grammatikos*), 49

philosopher (*philosophos*), 22, 23, 29.3, 29.4, 29.7, 32.1, 46.1, 48.1, 49

philosophical principles (*theôrêmata*), 46.1, 46.2, 51.1

philosophy (*philosophia*), 22

plain simple living (*euteleia*), 47

plan of life (*enstasis*), 23

play (noun) (*drama*), 17

playwright (*didaskalos*), 17

please (*areskô*), 23

pleasure (*hêdonê*), 34

plenty (*aphthonos*), 12

portent (*sêmeion*), 18

possession (*ktêseidion*, diminutive of *ktêsis*), 18; (*ktêsis*), 1.1; *see also* property

poverty (*penia*), 2.1

praise (verb) (*epaineô*), 25.2, 25.5, 33.2, 48.2

preference (*hormê*), 48.3

principles (*dogmata*), 52.1

progress (noun) (*prokopê*), 12, 13; *see also* make progress

property/possessions (*ktêsis*), 39, 44; *see also* possession

propose (*protithêmi*), 50

provoke (*erethizô*), 20

public games (*to theatron*), 33.10; *see also* Olympic Games

Pythian Apollo (*Puthios*), 32.3

raven or crow (*korax*), 18

rebuke (verb) (*epiplêssô*), 33.16

regret (verb) (*metanoeô*), 34

relationship (*schesis*), 30

reproach (verbs) (*enkaleô*), 1.3; (*loidoreô*), 31.4, 34

repulsion (*aphormê*), 2.2

reputation (*doxa*), 1.1; (*doxarion*, diminutive of *doxa*), 18

reservation (*hupexhairesis*), 2.2

respect (noun) (*aidôs*), 33.15

restrain (*anaireô*), 2.2

ridicule (noun) (*katagelôs*), 22

right (adjective) (*orthos*), 35

right opinions (*orthai hupolêpseis*), 31.1

role, part (*prosôpon*), 17, 37

rule (noun) (*kanôn*), 1.5

ruling principle (*to hêgemonikon*), 29.7, 38

sacrilege, *see* commit sacrilege

self-control (*enkrateia*), 10

self-respecting (*aidêmôn*), 24.3, 24.4, 24.5, 40

sell (*pôleô*), 25.4

serenity (*ataraxia*, without trouble), 29.7; *see also* freedom from troubles

sex (*aphrodisia*), 33.8; *see also* have sex with

show off, make a display (*kallôpizô*), 47

sick (*arrôstos*), 48.2

sickness (*nosos*), 2.1

silent, *see* keep silent

slave (*doulos*), 14.2

slave-boy (*paidarion*, diminutive of *pais*), 26, 29.6; (*pais*), 12.1, 12.2, 14.1

social feeling (*koinônikos*), 36

Socrates (*Sôkratês*), 5, 32.3, 33.12, 46.1, 51.3; quoted in, 53.3, 53.4

status (*archê*, the office that one holds), 1.1, 15, 24.1, 29.6

status (*archô*, to hold office), 1.4

stupid (*hêlithios*), 13

submit (*eikô*), 31.1

Greek–English

phulassô (guard against), 34

phusis (capacities), 29.5; (nature), 30, 49

pistos (trustworthy), 24.3, 24.4, 24.5

plouteô (to be wealthy), 1.4

ploutos (wealth), 15

pôleô (pay/pay the price; literally, exchange or barter goods), 12; (sell), 25.4

ponos (hardship), 10, 47

praôs (gentle), 42

procheiros (at hand), 53.1

prohairesis (moral character), 4, 9, 13, 30

proïemai (pay/pay the price), 25.2, 25.3, 25.4

prokopê (progress) (noun), 12, 13

prokoptô (make progress), 48.2, 51.1, 51.2

prosechô (pay attention), 51.3

prosôpon (part, role), 17, 37

proterêma (excellence), 6

protithêmi (propose), 50

psegô (blame) (verb), 33.2, 48.2

Puthios (Pythian Apollo), 32.3

schesis (relationship), 30

sêmeion (portent), 18

semnos (dignity), 33.11

siôpaô (keep silent), 33.2, 33.3

skopos (target) (noun), 27

Sôkratês (Socrates), 5, 32.3, 33.12, 46.1, 51.3; quoted in, 53.3, 53.4

sôma, to (body), 1.1, 9, 18, 28, 33.7, 41, 47

stasis (condition), 48.1

stenazô (weep), 16

stergô (to have a fondness for something), 3

sumpheron (advantageous), 31.4

symposion (banquet), 15, 46.1

sunkatatithemai (assent) (verb), 45

sunkoimaomai (have sex with someone), 40

sunkrinô (compare), 33.2

tapeinos (abject), 21

tarachê (distress) (noun), 3

tarassô (agitate, distress, disturb, perturb, or trouble the mind), 1.3, 5, 12.1, 12.2

tassô (assign), 22

teknon (child), 14.1, 15, 16, 18, 26, 31.4

thanatos (death), 2.1, 5, 21

thaumazô (admire), 22

theatron, to (public games), 33.10

theia, ta (things divine, the acts of the gods, the course of providence), 53.2

thelô (wish) (verb), 8, 14.1

theoi (gods), 1.3, 31.1, 32.2

theôrêmata (philosophical principles), 46.1, 46.2, 51.1

theos (God), 22

thlibô (to be distressed), 16

tupos (disposition), 33.1

tuptô (hit), 20

zêlotupia (jealousy), 19.2

Zênôn (Zeno), 33.12

Zeus (Zeus), 53.1

Index